WOMEN, PEACE AND SECURITY IN NORTHEAST INDIA

Women, Peace and Security in Northeast India

Edited by
ÅSHILD KOLÅS

zubaan

ZUBAAN
128 B Shahpur Jat, 1st Floor
New Delhi 110049
Email: contact@zubaanbooks.com
Website: www.zubaanbooks.com

First published by Zubaan Publishers Pvt. Ltd 2017

10 9 8 7 6 5 4 3 2 1

ISBN 978 93 85932 30 4

Zubaan is an independent, feminist publishing house based in New Delhi with a strong academic and general list. It was set up as an imprint of India's first feminist publishing house, Kali for Women, and carries forward Kali's tradition of publishing world quality books to high editorial and production standards. *Zubaan* means tongue, voice, language, speech in Hindustani. Zubaan publishes in the areas of the humanities and social sciences, as well as in fiction, general non-fiction and books for children and Young Adults under its Young Zubaan imprint.

Printed and bound at Gopsons Papers Ltd

Contents

Abbreviations

AASU	All Assam Students' Union
AFSPA	Armed Forces (Special Powers) Act
AGP	Asom Gana Parishad
AMKIL	All Manipur Kanba Ima Lup
AMADA	All Manipur Anti-Drug Association
APMS	Assam Pradeshik Mahila Samiti
AMUCO	All Manipur United Club Organisation
BWJF	Bodo Women's Justice Forum
CEDAW	Convention on the Elimination of All Forms of Discrimination against Women
CRPF	Central Reserve Police Force
CSWI	Committee on the Status of Women in India
GEDI	Global Entrepreneurship and Development Index
ENPO	Eastern Naga People's Organization
FNR	Forum for Naga Reconciliation
INC	Indian National Congress
INGO	International Non-governmental Organization
KLO	Kamatapur Liberation Organization
LPCs	Local Peace Committees
MSS	Mahila Shanti Sena
MMR	Maternal mortality ratio
NCRB	National Crime Research Bureau
NCW	National Commission for Women
NDFB	National Democratic Front of Bodoland
NMA	Naga Mothers' Association
NMEW	National Mission for Empowerment of Women
NPMHR	Naga People's Movement for Human Rights
NREGA	National Rural Employment Guarantee Act
NSCN	National Socialist Council of Nagaland
NTC	Nagaland Tribes Council

NWC	Naga Women's Union
PCG	People's Consultative Group
PLA	People's Liberation Army
PLMPAM	Poirei Leimarol Meira Paibi Apunba Manipur
PMSA	Panchayat Mahila Shakti Abhiyan
PREPAK	People's Revolutionary Party of Kangleipak
PRIs	Panchayati Raj Institutions
PSK	Poorna Shakti Kendra
RGSY	Rashtriya Gram Swaraj Yojana
RJD	Rashtriya Janata Dal
SP	Samajwadi Party
SJA	Sanmilita Jatiya Abhivartan
STH	Sümi Totomi Hoho
ULFA	United Liberation Front of Assam
UNC	United Naga Council
UNDP	United Nations Development Programme
UNESCO	United Nations Educational, Scientific and Cultural Organization
UNFPA	United Nations Population Fund
UNIFEM	United Nations Development Fund for Women
VDBs	Village Development Boards
WIA	Women's Indian Association
WRB	Women's Reservation Bill

Introduction: Women, Peace and Security in Northeast India

Åshild Kolås

Though well documented, the history of women's movements in northeast India is usually interpreted within the context of the region's larger self-determination struggles, rather than as movements with significance and agendas of their own. Despite the complexities of the region's conflicts, the focus remains on the granting of statehood and territorial autonomy, political settlements and 'homeland' politics (Baruah 2003, 2005; Samaddar 2004). Women are still viewed primarily as victims, or as helpless bystanders caught between 'two armed patriarchies' (Banerjee 2001). By focusing heavily on the signing of ceasefires and provision of surrender packages, the Indian government and security establishment continue to give importance to the male-dominated militant groups in the 'underground' while ignoring the role of women in conflict as well as peacebuilding. The situation is quite similar in Jammu and Kashmir (see Akhtar 2006; Shekhawat 2014; Suri 2006).

In many parts of the Northeast, women's organizations are vocal in civil society's attempts to engage in conflict resolution and peacebuilding, despite only sporadic responses from the government's mediators and interlocutors (Banerjee and Dey 2012; Laimayum 2012; Manchanda 2005). Security analysts remain absorbed with the fault lines between armed groups and security forces, and between 'sons of the soil' and settlers. In its negotiations with 'underground' groups, the Ministry of Home Affairs (MHA) keeps a focus on the same fault lines. While 'ethnic conflict' continues to be the key conceptual framework of the security establishment, civil society involvement in conflict resolution remains unacknowledged or underestimated. This applies particularly to the contributions of women.

The aim of this volume is to generate awareness about women's contributions as promoters of peace and equality in northeast India, and as political actors and stakeholders in their own right. By critically investigating so-called 'women's empowerment' during conflict and peacebuilding, new light can also be shed on the gendered disempowerment that inevitably accompanies political violence.

Formally recognized 'post-conflict' settings have received a lot of attention among researchers of women, peace and security. The focus has primarily been on the implementation of the United Nations Security Council Resolution 1325 (2000) (henceforth UNSCR 1325), and measures for gender equality as prescribed by the international community. This has had little bearing on conflict-affected regions of India. Gender perspectives are still missing in formal Indian peace processes and conflict management efforts. In northeast India, peace talks are carried out behind closed doors, isolated from both civil society participation and the international organizations and multilateral agencies that are so prevalent in 'post-conflict' settings such as Nepal. In India, conventional security studies continue to dominate research on conflict. Gender is often seen as a marginal issue, and there is a reluctance to acknowledge the importance of women, whether as peace activists or stakeholders in conflict. There is also a lack of resonance between Indian conflict studies and the global discourse on women, peace and security. We want to bridge these disconnects.

The research presented in this volume highlights women's political agency and activism, for political change as well as conflict resolution. Women have a long history of engagement in peacebuilding and mediation, and have mobilized effectively for community survival and mitigation of violence. As stakeholders in conflict, women have also played a significant role as supporters of armed groups, and, in some cases, armed fighters. Women cadres in the United Liberation Front of Assam (ULFA) are a case in point.

Contrary to idealistic assertions, women are not inherently peaceful. While there are good reasons for women to participate in peace processes, we cannot take their positive contributions for granted, despite the claims of the international community of multilateral agencies and international non-governmental organizations (INGOs). We should also ask whether peace negotiations really are the best window of opportunity for promoting gender equality and women's empowerment. And, if so, can women's independent agency really be achieved through the top-down interventions of multilateral agencies and INGOs? In Nepal, such methods are frequently accused of being culturally inappropriate and insensitive to local contexts. The dilemmas are obvious.

GENDER, CONFLICT AND PEACE STUDIES

Conflict can be understood as a consciously constructed effort to employ violence to reconfigure the social landscape and relations of power (Keen 2008; Wilmer 2002; Wood 2008). Political violence not only tears societies apart, it reconstructs them, whether temporarily or in the longer term (Duffield 1994). Gendered power relations and identity are equally recast or reconfigured in the course of conflict, and should be seen as mutually constructed in the process.

The gendered nature of war and conflict has been widely researched and debated (Afshar 2003; Cooke and Woollacott 2003;

Enloe 1989, 1993, 2000, 2007; Jacobs, Jacobson and Marchbank 2000; Jordan 2003; Pankhurst 2003). Much of the early literature in this field was preoccupied with issues such as gender and militarism, women and security, wartime violence against women, and women's victimhood. The increased vulnerability of women during conflict is well documented (see, for example, Anderlini 2007; Tripp 2005; Zarkov 2008).

There is still considerable attention given to women as victims of conflict, including the use of rape and sexual assault as weapons of war. However, recent studies have also directed attention to the potential of new opportunities for women arising during and after conflict (Cohn 2012; Eliatamby 2011; Haynes, Aolain and Cahn 2011; Kaufman and Williams 2013; Porter and Mundkur 2012). Assuming that conflict entails a disturbance of established norms, researchers argue that conflict might have unintended positive effects on the status and role of women within their societies by affecting the gendered division of labour and allowing women to perform jobs previously held by men (Rana-Deuba 2005; USAID 2007; Waylen 2007).

The promotion of women's rights and equal political participation are among the key objectives of multilateral interventions to end conflict. Reflective of this, a substantive scholarly effort has gone into the study of women's empowerment in peacebuilding (for example, Beckwith 2005; Porter 2003; Waylen 2007). Much of this work has been carried out in 'post-war' countries such as Nepal, where multilateral and international organizations have played a major role in peacemaking and post-conflict interventions for women's rights and gender equality. Such interventions have often been a key topic of study (Black 2009; Falch 2010; Kuehnast, Oudraat and Hernes 2011; Mazurana, Raven-Roberts and Parpart 2005; Tryggestad 2009). Multilateral agencies such as the United Nations Development Fund for Women (UNIFEM), United Nations Entity for Gender Equality and the Empowerment of Women (UN Women), United Nations Educational, Scientific and Cultural Organization (UNESCO), United Nations Development

Programme (UNDP) and United Nations Population Fund (UNFPA) have also contributed extensively to the literature on women's post-conflict empowerment, in support of their work to promote women's political participation (see, for example, Burke, Klot and Bunting 2001; Chinkin 2003; Klot 2007; Mayanja 2010; UNDP 2010b; UNESCO 2006; UNFPA 2007; UNIFEM 2006; UNSC 2009). Seeking to advance the implementation of UNSCR 1325 and promote the active participation of women in peace processes, aid and advocacy organizations have espoused a similar agenda, arguing that women must be empowered both politically and economically, and adequately represented at all levels of democratic decision making (Acharya 2003; CARE 2010; GAPS 2009; USAID 2007).

A related strand of research focuses on the contributions of women peacebuilders towards the establishment of a more egalitarian post-conflict gender order. Following the lead of UNSCR 1325, conflict resolution is viewed as an opportunity for addressing gender inequality, women's equal rights and political participation, especially by way of constitutional revisions. Beginning with the negotiations for a settlement, peacebuilding is understood as a site where women can contribute to and benefit from a lasting, just and inclusive peace (Banaszak et al. 2005).

While post-conflict Nepal figures prominently in the 'women, peace and security' research, India is almost completely absent from the scene. This arguably reflects the Indian government's resistance to international interference in its internal conflicts. It also reflects the government's related efforts to deny the existence of such conflicts and block foreign researchers from accessing conflict-affected areas. A further obstacle is the guarded and sensitive nature of peace talks, in which secretive negotiations with militants are interspersed with equally opaque military operations. In short, Indian conflict management is heavily securitized, creating serious obstacles to research. However, Indian case studies can offer vital insights into women's empowerment in peacebuilding. This makes it all the more critical to bring Indian cases into the 'women, peace and security' framework, not only to fill knowledge gaps, but also to shed new light on the dilemmas of interventionism, and reflect on the cultural and political premises underpinning the liberal peacebuilding paradigm.

The international community has long prescribed women's equal representation and political participation. Nevertheless, women's participation in politics and policymaking remains weak, even in highly developed countries. On a global scale, female heads of state make up only 5 per cent of the total in Arab states, 16 per cent in Asia, 19 per cent in sub-Saharan Africa, 23 per cent in the Americas, and 42 per cent in Europe (Kabeer 2005). Within Asia and the Pacific, India is at the top of the charts when it comes to women's participation at the subnational government level (37 per cent), though the share of women at the national level is much lower (10.8 per cent) (UNDP 2010a). As feminist studies amply illustrate, discriminatory practices against women are historically evident across the world. Highly skewed gender relations, deeply embedded in social, family and community institutions, have obstructed women's development in education as well as employment opportunities and political representation (Duflo 2005).

For decades, women leaders and activists have called for stronger participation of women in political processes and structures to advance gender equality. Against this backdrop, UNSCR 1325 called for increased representation of women in decision making and in mechanisms for conflict prevention, management and resolution. The idea was that peace processes in which women were included would bring more lasting peace, in addition to strengthening political participation of women and women's rights in post-conflict societies. Backed by UNSCR 1325 (2000) and subsequent UNSC Resolutions 1674 (2006), 1820 (2008), 1882 (2009), 1888 (2009) and 1889 (2009), multilateral agencies and INGOs promote gender equality and women's political participation in numerous countries emerging from civil war. With the same objectives in mind, the United Nations (UN) has also enhanced its 'women, peace and security' architecture, appointing Special Representatives and Special Envoys and establishing the UN Women. However, the question remains: Are these efforts actually creating more lasting peace and more empowered women?

STORIES OF WOMEN'S EMPOWERMENT

As early as 1992, India enacted constitutional reforms to increase women's participation in governance. The 73rd Amendment to the Constitution stipulates that one-third of seats in the Panchayati Raj Institutions (PRIs) are to be reserved for women, with recent proposals to increase the share to 50 per cent. However, the situation is far less promising in India's conflict-affected regions. In northeast India, the 73rd Amendment has been blocked in the states of Nagaland, Meghalaya and Mizoram, and is also exempt in hill areas of Manipur and Assam under the Sixth Schedule of the Constitution. Because of their status as tribal, these areas are left out of the panchayati system and exempt from the requirement to reserve seats for women in local assemblies. The same areas are also among the most severely affected by conflict. In addition, the state of Assam was exceedingly slow to act on the 73rd Amendment, postponing its implementation for a decade.

In contrast, post-war Nepal experienced a huge leap in women's representation in the 2008 election to the Constituent Assembly. Thanks partly to reservations stipulated by the Interim Constitution, 197 women were elected to the Constituent Assembly, comprising one-third of the members. Often portrayed as a landmark victory for women's empowerment in South Asia, this allowed Nepali women to play an important role in post-war amendments of discriminatory legal provisions related to property ownership, citizenship, mobility, marriage, abortion, sexual minorities, domestic violence and marital rape (Aguirre and Pietropaoli 2008; Ariño 2008). Meanwhile, INGOs competed to provide opportunities to marginalized lower-caste people, youth and women, in the name of grass-roots empowerment (Miklian, Lidén and Kolås 2011). District-level Local Peace Committees (LPCs) were also set up, in which women also comprise a mandatory one-third of representatives.

On the surface, post-conflict Nepal may seem to be a success story. However, the majority of Nepali women leaders remain involved with informal sectors of civil society, as members of NGOs and peace activists, whereas those wielding formal, decision-making power remain almost exclusively male, whether it be as military leaders, politicians, government ministers or diplomats. Researchers have questioned the effects of globalization (or 'NGOization') on Nepali political life, in which women's empowerment runs the risk of being seen as an alibi, as 'gender-sensitivity' in international development schemes legitimizes the presence of INGOs and their interventions into Nepali society. Encouraged by INGOs, women's rights agendas may in fact have been pursued by female politicians to the detriment of other policymaking work (Falch 2010). Finally, researchers have questioned what reservations actually do for women's empowerment. Similar concerns have been raised with regard to reservations for Indian women in the panchayati structure. Are women necessarily more empowered due to reservations, and, contrarily, does the absence of reservations for women in tribal areas of northeast India mean that women in these areas are less empowered? These are some of the dilemmas that need to be brought up for debate.

What can northeast Indian women tell us about their own concerns? During fieldwork in Assam, I noticed that members of the local women's groups had a very pragmatic way of thinking about women's empowerment. Greater opportunities for girls' education, women's self-employment and better job opportunities for women were regarded as key issues. For women to be able to support themselves and their family independently, the main obstacle was employment and other opportunities for income generation. Women leaders of the local mother's association also asserted that 'their women' were already empowered, and that, in fact, the women of their tribe were 'almost equal' to the men. However, contrary to the claims of their own leaders, other members of the association described the situation in very different terms. As expressed by one interviewee: 'Women are not empowered. Wherever they go, whatever they do depends on their husband' (Kolås 2014: 46). Tribal identity and political competition appears to have been of greater concern to the leaders of the association, compared to women's political agency as experienced by their own members. This highlights the tension between women leaders and rank and file members, even within the same organization. It also highlights the difference between 'motherhood' in its ethnically prefixed form, as a device to propagate one's own tribal identity, and 'motherhood' without the prefix, as an appeal to a common female identity with an implicit peacebuilding potential. There is a similar tension between the contribution of the 'mothers' to tribal and factional 'homeland politics' and conflict on the one hand, and their interest and involvement in peacebuilding on the other.

Regardless of the divisions and differences among them, women activists are a force to be reckoned with, whether in conflict or peacebuilding. Through alliances and interactions with other conflict stakeholders, they are steadily building power and relevance on the political stage. Women are just as motivated as their male counterparts when they engage in political competitions, whether for the sake of personal gains or social capital. This counters the 'conventional wisdom' that expects women to always stand united, be 'natural mediators' between conflict actors, or act as 'anchors of peace' (ibid.: 46). In short, women's political inclusion does not guarantee a more enduring peace. Women are as divided as men, and should not be expected to offer shortcuts to peace.

Women's participation in conflict resolution is not a panacea against all post-conflict evils. Nor can women's empowerment be achieved through 'one-size-fits-all' peacebuilding templates, as can be seen in Nepal. Nevertheless, we insist on the significance of women's agency in both conflict and peacebuilding in northeast

India and elsewhere in the world. It is important to study the successes and failures of women's movements and women's contributions to both war and peace. It is also important to engage critically with the 'women, peace and security' literature and its interventionist biases and assumptions. In this volume we try to counter these biases by highlighting both local perspectives on the meaning of gender (in)equality and experiences from conflicts without multilateral intervention. Contributing new knowledge on women's disempowerment and empowerment in conflict as well as peacebuilding, we question the argument that conflict resolution necessarily serves as a window of opportunity for women's empowerment.

Attempting to understand the politics of the Northeast through the lens of gender, this volume highlights the complexity and multifaceted dynamics of women's agency, as it is played out in everyday negotiations of power. In order to better understand and be able to evaluate the successes and failures of women's movements and women's contributions to peacebuilding, we investigate and critically analyse the goals and activities of women's organizations and the agency, challenges and aspirations of women responding to conflict.

AN OVERVIEW OF THE VOLUME

This volume presents findings from a project entitled 'Making Women Count for Peace: Gender, Empowerment and Conflict in South Asia'. The project investigated women's participation in local governance and politics in northeast India and Nepal, focusing on women's participation in peacebuilding and the conditions for greater post-conflict gender equality. Throughout the project, the researchers attempted to capture a diverse range of local perspectives on gender equality, empowerment and political participation, and explore emic understandings of women's empowerment in a variety of culturally and historically unique settings. While the project as a whole covered both Nepal and northeast India, the relative lack of primary research in the Northeast made the work presented in this volume stand out as all the more important.

The chapters of this volume are organized as follows. The first chapter by Priyankar Upadhyaya provides an overview of the formal structures that are meant to promote women's political participation and agency in India. For historical context, this chapter deals with the Indian women's movement and the post-Independence legislation in support of women's empowerment. In the second chapter, Arunima Deka investigates the 73rd Amendment to the Constitution, and discusses what it has meant for women's political participation in Assam. The next chapter, by Dolly Phukon, provides a critical account of women's unrecognized contributions to peacebuilding and political change. This, again, is set in the context of Assam. Following this, a study by Rakhee Kalita Moral uncovers women's active participation in conflict, as expressed in the narratives of female ex-combatants of ULFA. The next chapter, by Anungla Aier, offers a rich analysis of gendered citizenship and representation in Naga society.

The final chapters of this volume provide further accounts of women's activism for peace. The first, by Rita Manchanda and Seema Kakran, presents an in-depth analysis of Naga women's struggle for a voice in peacemaking and reconciliation. Following this, a study by L. Basanti Devi describes the Meira Paibi 'torchbearers' and their activism for social change and peace in Manipur. Last but not least, Roma Dey reimagines the 'mother' as she deconstructs the nude protest of the Meira Paibis, thereby highlighting the power of this protest as a challenge to the Indian imagination of womanhood. Roma Dey's chapter makes an excellent conclusion to the volume, in its approach to women's empowerment. While acknowledging women's victimhood and rights, it goes beyond concerns about security to focus squarely on women's political agency and activism for social change and justice.

REFERENCES

Acharya, Meena. 2003. *Efforts at Promoting Women in Nepal.* Kathmandu: Tanka Prasad Memorial Foundation, Friedrich Stiftung.

Afshar, Halerh. 2003. 'Women and Wars: Some Trajectories towards a Feminist Peace', *Development in Practice*, 13(2/3): 178–88.

Aguirre, Daniel and Irene Pietropaoli. 2008. 'Gender Equality, Development, and Transitional Justice: The Case of Nepal', *The International Journal of Transitional Justice*, 2: 256–377.

Akhtar, Shaheen. 2006. 'Women and Peacebuilding in Azad Jammu and Kashmir', in Waheguru Pal Singh Sidhu, Bushra Asif and Cyrus Samii (eds), *Kashmir: New Voices, New Approaches*, pp. 97–116. Boulder, CO: Lynne Rienner Publishers.

Anderlini, Sanam Naraghi. 2007. *Women Building Peace: What They Do, Why It Matters.* Boulder, CO: Lynne Rienner Publishers.

Ariño, María Villellas. 2008. *Nepal: A Gender View of the Armed Conflict and the Peace Process.* Quaderns de Constucció de Pau. Barcelona: Escola de cultura de pau.

Banaszak, Klara, Camille Pampell Conaway, Anne Marie Goetz, Aina Iiyambo and Maha Muna. eds. 2005. *Securing the Peace: Guiding the International Community Towards Women's Effective Participation Throughout Peace Processes.* United Nations Development Fund for Women UNIFEM).

Banerjee, Paula. 2001. 'Between Two Armed Patriarchies: Women in Assam and Nagaland', in Rita Manchanda (ed.), *Women, War and Peace in South Asia: Beyond Victimhood to Agency*, pp. 131–76. New Delhi: Sage Publications.

Banerjee, Paula and Ishita Dey. 2012. 'Women, Conflict, and Governance in Nagaland', *Policies and Practices* 51. Kolkata: Mahanirban Calcutta Research Group.

Baruah, Sanjib. 2003. 'Citizens and Denizens: Ethnicity, Homelands, and the Crisis of Displacement in Northeast India', *Journal of Refugee Studies*, 16(1): 44–66.

———. 2005. *Durable Disorder. Understanding the Politics of Northeast India.* New Delhi: Oxford University Press.

Beckwith, Karen. 2005. 'The Comparative Politics of Women's Movements', *Perspectives on Politics*, 3(3): 583–96.

Black, Renee. 2009. 'Mainstreaming Resolution 1325? Evaluating the Impact on Security Council Resolution 1325 on Country-Specific UN Resolutions', *Journal of Military and Strategic Studies*, 11(4): 1–30.

Burke, Enid de Silva, Jenifer Klot and Ikaweba Bunting. 2001. *Engendering Peace: Reflections on the Burundi Peace Process.* Nairobi: UNIFEM.

CARE. 2010. *From Resolution to Reality: Lessons Learned from Afghanistan, Nepal and Uganda on Women's Participation in Peacebuilding and*

Post-conflict Governance, CARE International. http://www.carefrance.org/images/CARE-FROM_RESOLUTION_TO_REALITY1.pdf (accessed 21 February 2017).

Chinkin, Christine. 2003. 'Peace Agreements as a Means for Promoting Gender Equality and Ensuring Participation of Women'. Paper prepared for the UN Division for the Advancement of Women, Expert Group Meeting, 10–13 November, Ottawa.

Cohn, Carol. 2012. *Women and Wars: Contested Histories, Uncertain Futures.* New York: Polity Press.

Cooke, Miriam and Angela Woollacott. eds. 2003. *Gendering War Talk.* Princeton: Princeton University Press.

Duffield, Mark. 1994. 'The Political Economy of Internal War: Asset Transfer, Complex Emergencies and International Aid', in J. Macrae and A. Zwi (eds), *War and Hunger: Rethinking International Responses to Complex Emergencies*, pp. 50–69. London: Zed Books.

Duflo, E. 2005. *Gender Equality in Development.* Cambridge, MA: Department of Economics, MIT.

Eliatamby, Maneshka. 2011. *Women Waging War and Peace: International Perspectives of Women's Roles in Conflict and Post-Conflict Reconstruction.* New York: Bloomsbury Publishing.

Enloe, Cynthia. 1989. *Bananas, Bases and Beaches, Making Feminist Sense of International Politics.* Berkeley: University of California Press.

———. 1993. *The Morning After: Sexual Politics at the End of the Cold War.* Berkeley: University of California Press.

———. 2000. *Maneuvers: The International Politics of Militarizing Women's Lives.* Berkeley: University of California Press.

———. 2007. *Globalization and Militarism: Feminists Make the Link.* Plymouth: Rowman and Littlefield Publishers.

Falch, Åshild. 2010. 'Women's Political Participation and Influence in Post-Conflict Burundi and Nepal'. PRIO Paper, Peace Research Institute, Oslo. http://www.peacewomen.org/assets/file/Resources/Academic/partpol_postconburundinepal_falch_2010.pdf (accessed 28 November 2016).

GAPS (Gender Action for Peace and Security). 2009. Global Monitoring Checklist on Women, Peace and Security. http://www.peacewomen.org/assets/file/Resources/NGO/WPS_ChecklistWPS_GAPS_2009.pdf (accessed 21 February 2017).

Haynes, Dina F., Fionnuala Ni Aolain and Naomi R. Cahn. 2011. *On the Frontlines: Gender, War, and the Post-Conflict Process.* Oxford: Oxford University Press.

Jacobs, Susie, Ruth Jacobson and Jennifer Marchbank. eds. 2000. *States of Conflict: Gender, Violence and Resistance.* London: Zed Books.

Jordan, Ann. 2003. 'Women and Conflict Transformation: Influences, Roles, and Experiences', *Development in Practice* 13(2–3): 239–52.

Kabeer, Naila. 2005. 'Gender Equality and Women's Empowerment: A Critical Analysis of the Third Millennium Development Goal 1', *Gender & Development*, 13(1): 13–24.

Kaufman, Joyce P. and Kristen P. Williams. 2013. *Women at War, Women Building Peace*. Boulder, CO: Lynne Rienner Publishers.

Keen, David. 2008. *Complex Emergencies*. Cambridge: Polity Press.

Klot, Jennifer F. 2007. 'Women and Peacebuilding'. Independent expert paper commissioned by UNIFEM and UN Peacebuilding Support Office, Social Science Research Council, 29 January.

Kolås, Åshild. 2014. 'Mothers and Activists in the Hills of Assam', *Economic and Political Weekly*, 49(43): 41–48.

Kuehnast, Kathleen, Chantal de Jonge Oudraat and Helga Hernes. eds. 2011. *Women and War: Power and Protection in the 21st Century*. Washington, D.C.: United States Institute of Peace Press.

Laimayum, Basanti Devi. 2012. 'Women's Protest Movement and Ideology of Motherhood in Manipur', Ph.D. thesis, Centre for the Study of Social Systems, School of Social Sciences, Jawaharlal Nehru University, New Delhi.

Manchanda, Rita. 2005. *Naga Women Making a Difference: Peace Building in Northeastern India*. Women Waging Peace Policy Commission. Sanam Naraghi Anderlini, Series editor, January 2005. http://www.inclusivesecurity.org/wp-content/uploads/2012/08/13_naga_women_making_a_difference_peace_building_in_northeastern_india.pdf (accessed 21 February 2017).

Mayanja, Rachel. 2010. 'Armed Conflict and Women: 10 Years of Security Council Resolution 1325', *UN Chronicle*, XLVII(1).

Mazurana, Dyan, Angela Raven-Roberts and Jane Parpart. eds. 2005. *Gender, Conflict and Peacekeeping*. New York: Rowman and Littlefield.

Miklian, Jason, Kristoffer Lidén and Åshild Kolås. 2011. 'The Perils of 'Going Local': Liberal Peace-building Agendas in Nepal', *Conflict, Security & Development*, 11(3): 285–308.

Pankhurst, Donna. 2003. 'The "Sex War" and Other Wars: Towards a Feminist Approach to Peace Building', *Development in Practice*, 13(2–3): 154–77.

Porter, Elisabeth. 2003. 'Women, Political Decision-Making, and Peace-Building', *Global Change, Peace & Security*, 15(3): 245–62.

Porter, Elisabeth and Anuradha Mundkur. 2012. *Peace and Security: Implications for Women*. Brisbane: University of Queensland Press.

Rana-Deuba, Arzu. 2005. *A National Study on Changing Roles of Nepali Women Due to Ongoing Conflict and its Impact*, Samanata Studies No. 6. Kathmandu: Samanata Institute for Social and Gender Equality.

Samaddar, Ranabir. 2004. *The Politics of Autonomy: Indian Experiences*. New Delhi: Sage Publications.

Shekhawat, Seema. 2014. *Gender, Conflict and Peace in Kashmir: Invisible Stakeholders*. New Delhi: Cambridge University Press.

Suri, Kavita. 2006. 'Women in the Valley: From Victims to Agents of Change', in Waheguru Pal Singh Sidhu, Bushra Asif and Cyrus Samii (eds), *Kashmir:*

New Voices, New Approaches, pp. 81–96. Boulder, CO: Lynne Rienner Publishers.

Tripp, Aili Mari. 2005. 'Empowering Women in the Great Lakes Region: Violence, Peace and Women's Leadership', Social and Human Science Papers in Women's Studies/Gender Research, No. 3, UNESCO, Paris.

Tryggestad, Torunn L. 2009. 'Trick or Treat? The UN and Implementation of Security Council Resolution 1325 on Women, Peace, and Security', *Global Governance*, 15: 539–57.

UNDP (United Nations Development Programme). 2010a. *Women's Representation in Local Government in Asia-Pacific. Status Report 2010: Going beyond National Targets in Monitoring Status for MDG 3 on Women's Political Empowerment*, UNDP.

———. 2010b. *Power, Voice and Rights: A Turning Point for Gender Equality in Asia and the Pacific, Asia-Pacific Human Development Report*, Colombo: UNDP.

UNESCO (United Nations Educational, Scientific and Cultural Organization). 2006. 'Forms and Patterns of Social Discrimination in Nepal', UNESCO Kathmandu Series of Monographs and Working Papers, No. 8, UNESCO, Paris.

UNFPA (United Nations Population Fund). 2007. 'Gender Equality and Empowerment of Women in Nepal', UNFPA. http://un.org.np/sites/default/files/report/tid_67/2009-03-17-Gender-equality.pdf (accessed on 21 February 2017).

UNIFEM (United Nations Development Fund for Women) 2006. *A Rapid Scan: Organizations Working on Women and Peace in Nepal*, Kathmandu: UNIFEM Programme Office, Nepal.

UNSC (United Nations Security Council). 2009. *Women and Peace and Security*, Report of the Secretary-General, 16 September, New York: United Nations Security Council.

USAID. 2007. *Women and Conflict. An Introductory Guide for Programming*, Washington, DC: USAID.

Waylen, Georgina. 2007. *Engendering Transitions: Women's Mobilization, Institutions, and Gender Outcomes*. New York: Oxford University Press.

Wilmer, Franke. 2002. *The Social Construction of Man, the State, and War*. London: Routledge.

Wood, Elisabeth J. 2008. 'The Social Processes of Civil War: The Wartime Transformation of Social Networks', *Annual Review of Political Science*, 11:539–61.

Zarkov, Dubravka. ed. 2008. *Gender, Violent Conflict and Development*. New Delhi: Zubaan.

CHAPTER 1

Women's Rights and Empowerment: The Indian Context

Priyankar Upadhyaya

Women's involvement in policymaking is vital for transforming social, political, legal, cultural and economic structures that traditionally serve as sites of both direct and indirect violence. As such, it creates opportunities for their emancipation from existing structural and cultural violence while setting new standards for the future. According to a UNIFEM-sponsored study: 'Gender equality brings to peacebuilding new degrees of democratic inclusiveness, faster and more durable economic growth and human and social capital recovery' (Klot 2007: 2). Indeed, there are a myriad of visible and invisible ways in which empowered women can engender sustainable peace within and across their communities.

Women partaking in peace work evidently depend on their capability to participate and influence socio-economic and political activities. The problematic of women's empowerment is thus central to their quest for peacebuilding. Hence, this chapter provides some inputs through a broad-brush evaluation of contemporary laws, legislations and acts in India, and how they engender women's empowerment amidst the much-highlighted crisis of governance. This critical template of contemporary visions and policies on women's empowerment would also highlight their significance for peacebuilding. Of course it is not easy to draw specific inferences applicable to Indian womanhood across India's vast timeline or geography. One is also constrained by the contrary streams of feminist discourses, which interrogate the legal campaign per se as a transformative strategy for women's emancipation.

While the World Bank describes 'empowerment' as a 'process of increasing the capacity of individuals or groups to make choices and to transform those choices into desired actions and outcomes' (cited in Heinsohn 2004: 126), the Country Report of the Government of India describes 'empowerment' as moving from a position of enforced powerlessness to one of power (GOI 1995). In India, the discourse of empowerment has mostly resonated around Amartya Sen's (1999) 'development as freedom' approach, wherein development is seen as the expansion of freedom of choice and action to shape one's life, as also the expansion of capabilities as opposed to achieving a certain set of indicators. However, some sceptics find the emphasis on choice as linked with liberal arguments that suggest people should be 'looking after themselves' rather than relying on state provision (Jeffrey and Harriss 2014: 61). There are others who call for a more nuanced and contextual understanding of political and economic structures, cultural assumptions, and laws and practices to give true meaning to women's empowerment.

Although 'women's empowerment' has multifaceted ramifications, it is generally seen as a critical objective, in the absence of which women could neither realize their rights, nor participate effectively in social and political processes. In the Indian context, the idea of 'women's empowerment' has caught popular imagination in recent decades as a process through which women gain greater control over resources, and thus assume greater say in decision making at home and in the community, society and nation. This is vitally important in India's patriarchal society, wherein women are born into gendered inequality. Along with widespread gender discrimination, marginalized women also experience hardship from poverty, caste and ethnic discrimination. Evidently, the 'empowered' women, among other competences, promise household and community well being through family planning, higher child survival rate, and healthier and better-fed children (Kandpal, Baylis and Arends-Kuenning 2013).

REALITY CHECK OF WOMEN'S EMPOWERMENT

The imperative of women's empowerment, long recognized in India, is well enshrined in its constitutional and legal processes, as also in its international obligations.[1] However, these norms hardly correspond with the reality. After six decades of democratic experience, India scores rather poorly in global ranking on the status of women. The Global Gender Gap Index (2013) ranked India 101 among 136 countries based on how opportunities and resources are divided between men and women in four main areas: health, education, politics, and the economic position on gender parity (WEF 2013: 12–13). Though India was ranked 9th with regard to political empowerment, the inequality in health and survival (at 135th), participation and opportunity (124th), and education (120th) reduced its overall position. The Global Entrepreneurship and Development Index (GEDI) measured female entrepreneurs in 30 countries. Here India joins ranks with 3rd Tier Low Performers, while ranking 26th on the list (GEDI 2014). The *Human Development Report 2014* (UNDP 2014) assigns India the 132nd position among 148 countries.[2]

A World Bank study has discovered that more Indian women between the ages of 15 and 44 are killed or seriously injured due to gender-based violence compared to conflicts, malaria or cancer (Roychowdhury 2013). And, worse still, a recent global perceptions survey ranked India as the fourth most dangerous country for women (after Afghanistan, Congo and Pakistan), and the worst among the G20 countries in this regard.[3] The situation is still worse for women from disadvantaged groups such as Scheduled

Tribes (STs) and Scheduled Castes (SCs), who face exploitation, discrimination and limited opportunities for employment and education (UNDP 2014).

Such a dismal portrayal is rather shocking for a country that prides itself on endowing a high position to women for several millennia, and one which recognized the prerequisite of gender equality and equal opportunities as it attained independence. How to account for such a paradox? How could the Indian state fulfil its constitutional promise of 'equality' in all spheres for women?

There is indeed no dearth of credulous visions and studies on women's position in India, many still rivet to the historically circulated stereotypes of their glorious status in ancient India and how it declined amidst foreign invasions. There are also culture-specific streams of thought distinguishing Indian women for their traditional role as family maker and their community-based values, different from Western notions of individualistic women's liberation. The constitutional, legal and official provisions on women's empowerment are amplified without evaluating their implementation and actual impact (Kumar 2005; Nayak 2005; Padia 2011). Drawing rather selectively on past and present narratives, these studies tend to obfuscate the real picture of women's empowerment in India, as well as the diversity of women's interests and concerns, and their multifaceted expressions throughout the Indian subcontinent.

AN HISTORICAL OVERVIEW

India's long history is embedded within varied and often contrary perspectives on women. Historians have pointed out that the ancient Hindu scriptures like the Vedas and Upanishads of the early Vedic period (1500–1000 bce) refer to the high status of women reflecting eminent women sages like Gargi and Maitreyi. However, the Manu Smriti (1 bce), the first Hindu legal scripture, carries a skewed description of women. It says that in the abode where women are provided honour, the Gods happily reside,[4] yet it denies women autonomy by insisting that she better be in the protective custody of her menfolk in all stages of her life, and not work independently even at her place of residence. A girl is supposed to be in the custody of her father when young, a woman must be under the custody of her husband when married and under the custody of her son as a widow. In no circumstances is she allowed to assert herself independently (Dave 1990: 5/150 and 5/151).

The popular Hindu narratives attribute the declining status of women to the Mughal invasion. The medieval era saw several heinous rituals and practices being imposed on women, ostensibly to save them from invaders. These practices included sati (a widow burning to death on her husband's funeral pyre), child marriage and the devadasi system among others.[5] Women sacrificing their lives were hailed as icons of true devotion and virtue. There were sporadic social protests and movements such as the Bhakti cult of the medieval era, which opposed such dehumanization and sought women's liberation. Spurred by these protests, the British government eventually banned these practices lawfully, though it took quite a while. The situation of women did not improve much in colonial times, yet one begins to discern increasingly greater assertions of women in the public arena during the period.

Mahatma Gandhi's clarion call to women to join the independence struggle unshackled women across urban and rural India. A long chain of women freedom fighters and social reformers subsequently defied social taboos and restrictions, challenging the hitherto dominant male hegemony.[6] As early as 1917, Sarojini Naidu, Annie Besant, Dorothy Jinarajadasa, Malathi Patvardhan, Ammu Swaminathan, Margaret Cousins and others founded the Women's Indian Association (WIA), seeking political suffrage for women (Basu 2008). Sarojini Naidu later became the president of the Indian National Congress (INC).

In 1928, Jawaharlal Nehru exhorted Indian women to fight for their rights, as Indians and as women, stating that: 'Women of India will not attain their full rights by the mere generosity of the men of India. They will have to fight for them and force their will on the menfolk before they can succeed' (cited in Deo 2012: 52). Leaders from the oppressed castes, like B.R. Ambedkar and Periyar, also called for women's emancipation as part of their struggle. Ambedakar famously remarked: 'I measure the progress of community by the degree of progress which women had achieved' (cited in Katulkar 2008). Ambedkar located the linkages between caste and gender, and found that the superimposition of endogamy on exogamy engenders the caste system, which thrives on the subjugation of women. He seemingly resigned from Nehru's cabinet when a bill of reforms integral to promoting equal rights for women moved sluggishly through Parliament. Ambedkar also raised the issues of legal rights for women of depressed classes and Muslim communities.

Many Indian women, particularly Dr Annie Besant, played a pivotal role in instilling gender sensitivity in the freedom struggle. During the Karachi Congress (1931), the INC proclaimed formal equality between the sexes. Amid the strident demand of women's suffrage, the British government in 1919 authorized the provincial legislatures to grant such rights albeit based on property rights. The gradual acceptance of women's electorate rights in different legislative assemblies emboldened women to include nation building as one of their objectives. However, while pleading for political modernization, the women leaders were conscious not to denigrate the traditional gender roles. It was argued that both traditions could coexist in the pursuit of nation building (Southard 1993). This was quite characteristic of cultural fault lines which were to impinge on the role of Indian women in times to come.

CONSTITUTIONAL PROVISIONS ON GENDER EQUALITY

The importance of women as valuable human resources was duly recognized by the Constitution of India, which accorded equality to women and empowered the states to adopt measures of positive discrimination. The makers of the Constitution were committed to the socio-economic development of women and upholding their political rights. The codification of the Common Civil Code for Hindu law in respect of marriage, divorce and succession ensured the equality and dignity of women and provided norms and principles extendable to other religious communities as well.

The principle of gender equality is well enshrined in the Indian Constitution in its Preamble, Fundamental Rights, Fundamental Duties and Directive Principles. The guarantee of social, economic and political justice mandates the state to adopt proactive actions to affect gender justice. The equality of women and children is firmly spelled out in Article 14 as well as Article 15(1) of the Constitution, which refer to Fundamental rights. Article 15(3) enables the state to take necessary measures in this regard. Article 16 ensures equal opportunities for women in public employment. Article 21A guarantees the right to education for 'all children', irrespective of gender. Article 23 prohibits traffic in human beings and forced labour. Article 42 relates to human conditions of work and maternity relief, while Article 46 ordains the state to promote, with special care, the educational and economic interests of weaker sections of people and to protect them from social injustice and all forms of exploitation. Similarly, Article 47 mandates the state to raise the level of nutrition and standard of living of its people and improve public health and so on. Article 51A(e) provides that it shall be the duty of every citizen of India to renounce practices derogatory to the dignity of women.

The right to be protected from sexual harassment and sexual assault is, therefore, guaranteed by the Constitution, and serves as one of the foundations on which the very construct of gender justice stands.[7] The entitlements of women are further supplemented by the Directive Principles of State Policy contained in Articles 38, 39 and 39(a), which are to be construed harmoniously with the Fundamental Rights in Part III of the Constitution. While Article 39 (a) ensures that the citizens, men and women equally, have the right to an adequate means of livelihood, Article 39 (d) stipulates equal pay for equal work for both men and women. In fact, the promulgation of the Equal Remuneration Ordinance issued on 26 September 1975 reflected the said Article. Article 39 (e) refers to the health and strength of workers, men and women, and that citizens are not forced by economic necessity to enter avocations unsuited to their age or strength. Article 42 makes provisions for securing just and humane working conditions for women along with the special treatment that a woman must get during the maternity period.

ACTS AND LEGISLATION

The issue of women's empowerment became the focus of much debate in the 1970s, in response to the poor assessment of Indian women's status by an international comparative report entitled *Towards Equality: Report of the Committee on the Status of Women in India* (GOI 1974). This report fostered debates about the constitutional rights of women, and the need to reform earlier legislation such as the Hindu Marriage Act (1955), Hindu Succession Act (1956), and Prohibition Act (1961). Several significant laws were enacted during this phase, including the Equal Remuneration Act (1976), Child Marriage Restraint Amendment Act (1976), Immoral Trafficking (Prevention) Act (1986), and the Pre-natal Diagnostic Technique (Regulation and Prevention of Misuse Act (1994). The Hindu law of inheritance was amended in 2005 to provide equal rights to women in ancestral land and property, negating patriarchal norms that deprived women of such rights.

In the 1990s, the government set up the National Commission for Women (NCW) as an autonomous organization mandated to advise the government on all policy measures affecting women, and to review, recommend and influence national and state-level legal and social policies, laws, programmes and budgets to ensure full benefits to women. The NCW has set up grievance investigation cells at the state level to receive complaints of gender-based violence, to investigate, provide referrals and counselling, and, ultimately, report on such cases.[8] However, the role of the

NCW so far has been limited to reactive interventions, and its membership is mainly decided by political consideration, not always in keeping with professional capability.[9]

The 1990s also saw the launch of several schemes to uplift the position of women, including the Mahila Samriddhi Yojana (MSY) (1993), Rashtriya Mahila Kosh (RMK) (1993), Indira Mahila Yojana (IMY) (1995), Development of Women and Children in Rural Areas (DWCRA) (1997), and Balika Samriddhi Yojana (BSY) (1997). In 2001, the MSY and IMY were merged into the integrated self-help group (SHG) programme known as Swayamsiddha. The National Policy for the Empowerment of Women was another government initiative to ensure women's empowerment through positive economic and social policies. Swayamsiddha has since become an integrated project for the development of women through SHGs, with emphasis on services, developing access to microcredit and promoting microenterprises. The Swadhar scheme was launched as a central sector scheme to provide holistic and integrated services to women in difficult circumstances. The package of services made available under this scheme includes provisions of food, clothing and shelter; health-care counselling; legal support; and social and economic rehabilitation. Swadhar also supports a helpline for women in distress.

In 2010, the government launched the National Mission for Empowerment of Women (NMEW) to achieve gender equality, gender justice and holistic development of women through inter-sectoral convergence of programmes relating to women, with an aim to forge synergy between various stakeholders and create enabling environments conducive to social change. NMEW plans to facilitate the economic empowerment of girls and women through skills development, microcredit, vocational training and entrepreneurship. The Poorna Shakti Kendra (PSK) is a focal point of action through which services to grass-roots women would be facilitated. Village coordinators at the PSK would reach out to the women with the motto '*Hum sunenge naari ki baat*!' ('We will listen to women's voices!').[10] The PSK aims to facilitate the availability and access to government schemes, services and programmes across health, education and livelihood sectors, and help in training and capacity building on various issues like leadership and legal rights. Since its inception, NMEW has held consultative meetings across the country and has commissioned several instructive studies and reports. It has also signed a Charter of Collaboration with UNESCO, which will provide technical support in facilitating a 'Gender Equality Observatory', allow them to undertake joint projects, research and evaluation studies, and create a '360-degree approach' in media and communications on issues related to gender equality in the areas of UNESCO's competence (UNESCO 2012).

In more recent times, several new acts have addressed long-drawn imperatives of Indian women, both directly and indirectly. The National Food Security Act, 2013 ensures food and nutritional security to identified eligible households, and contains specific provisions for women and children. Other legislation has addressed the protection of children from sexual offences, and sexual harassment of women in the workplace. The Gender Budget Statement, a part of the Union Budget, emerged as an important tool for reporting allocations for women. According to the 2013 statement, 30 ministries were involved in schemes and programmes for women, while the gender budget had reached 5.83 per cent.

POLITICAL REPRESENTATION

The history of political empowerment of women in India is replete with paradoxes. Indian women were accorded suffrage soon after Independence, even ahead of some Western democracies. Many distinguished women made notable contributions to the Indian freedom movement. The list includes Vijay Lakshmi Pandit, Sarojini Naidu, Padmaja Naidu and Sucheta Kripalani. In more recent times, Indira Gandhi served as prime minister of India, and Mira Kumar as the speaker of the Lok Sabha. Women like Sonia

Gandhi, Sushma Swaraj, Brinda Karat and Mayavati also lead major political parties. However, these politically elevated women hardly reflect the overall situation of women's empowerment.

The first Indian parliament (Lok Sabha) had only 4.4 per cent female members. In the parliamentary elections held between 1952 and 1996, the share of women contestants to the Lok Sabha remained virtually stagnant at 3.2 per cent.[11] Although the number of female Members of Parliament (MPs) increased to 61 during later Lok Sabha elections, this made up only 11.23 per cent of the total 543 parliamentary seats. This remains far below the global average of 21.3 per cent. In fact, in a recent study by the Inter-Parliamentary Union (IPU), India ranks 111th among 189 countries in terms of its female presence in Parliament.[12]

Noting the chronic marginalization of women in Parliament, in 1974 the Committee on the Status of Women in India (CSWI) famously remarked that 'the rights guaranteed by the Constitution have helped to build an illusion of equality and power which is frequently used as an argument to resist protective and accelerating measures to enable women to achieve their just and equal position in society' (Mohan et al. 2005: 6). After four decades, these remarks hold good. The truth is that there has been very little space and opportunity for the political empowerment of women, and their presence in political processes and decision-making bodies even now is largely symbolic. Their entry into public spaces is persistently disabled by prevailing historical constructions of gender, created and perpetuated within the family, in religious and educational institutions, and other dominant state institutions (CLRA 2008: 2). Their disempowerment is accentuated by unresponsive political, social and legal systems along with weak public constituencies.

Women continue to lack awareness of their rights and responsibilities as elected members in the absence of training and information dissemination on governance processes. The gender sensitization of male elected members is also remiss. Due to the near absence of women in decision-making positions within political parties and in governance, women's agendas are not reflected or addressed in policies and programmes. As elected representatives, women are often prevented from getting key portfolios and they have to be content with relatively less important ones. Even within political parties, women are rarely found in leadership positions.

In a few of the tribal communities of northeast India, women have customary rights to land. The argument has been set forth that, particularly in the case of matrilineal tribal societies, women have traditionally been endowed with a higher social status along with the inheritance of property. However, there is an ongoing debate over the historical evidence as well as the implications of the alleged higher status of women, both historically and in a contemporary context. For instance, it is argued that Garo, bride burning, female feticide, dowry, or stigmatization of widowhood does not afflict Khasi and Jaintia women of Meghalaya, and that remarriage is prevalent. However, there is also evidence that their situation is no better than their counterparts in the rest of India in terms of social problems like illiteracy, incomplete schooling, unemployment, early marriage and divorce. Moreover, women are still not accepted as equal participants in the traditional decision-making bodies and forums such as the village councils and durbars. Therefore, tribal women should not be forgotten in schemes to support 'empowerment' of women, even in matrilineal societies (Pisharoty 2013).

PANCHAYATI RAJ INSTITUTIONS

The Indian Constitution (Articles 243D and 243T) stipulates reservation of seats for women from SCs and STs in the Panchayati Raj system and municipalities respectively. In 1992, the 73rd and 74th constitutional amendments were enacted to ensure effective participation of women at the grass-roots level of governance.[13] These amendments provide for at least one-third reservation of seats for women in the local bodies of the panchayat (village council) and municipalities. The 73rd Amendment thus promotes the participation of women in the political institutions at the village, block (*taluka*) and district level.

With the passing of the 73rd and 74th amendments, India now has more than 597 district panchayats, over 6,344 block panchayats, and about 250,000 village panchayats; over 100 municipal corporations, 1,800 municipal councils, and 20,000 nagar panchayats.[14] Schemes like the Rashtriya Gram Swaraj Yojana (RGSY) and Panchayat Mahila Shakti Abhiyan (PMSA) have helped facilitate the political participation of women in panchayats. Over one million women have served as elected representatives in these local governmental bodies so far.

Mandatory female participation in local governance has provided opportunities, as women have gradually learned to use their authority to address issues such as alcohol abuse, education of the girl child, health care for women, and domestic violence. However, their efficacy in raising and implementing women's issues is often in doubt due to the continued sway of patriarchy. Many elected women serve as proxies for their male family members or a male leader of their political party due to lack of political experience and limitations imposed by male relatives and local leaders. Thus, when Prime Minister Narendra Modi was welcomed to his adopted village Jayapur by the female chief (*pradhan*) of the village council, she announced rather proudly before the media that her office is run entirely by her brother-in-law.[15] Despite the undeniable numerical increase in female political participation (Rathod 2014), rural women continue to struggle against patriarchal social barriers.

THE WOMEN'S RESERVATION BILL

The Women's Reservation Bill (WRB) has the potential to significantly alter Indian politics by facilitating women's full and equal participation. The Bill was first introduced as the Constitution Amendment (81st) Bill on 12 September 1996, in the aftermath of the effective passing into law of the 73rd and 74th amendments. The WRB envisaged one-third of all seats in the Lok Sabha and state legislative assemblies to be reserved for women. Reservations shall also apply in the case of seats reserved for SCs and STs. Seats would be reserved in rotation, determined by the drawing of lots in such a way that a seat would be reserved only once in three consecutive general elections.

The passage of this crucial Bill would have necessitated broad support from across political opinions. However, many political parties have questioned its intent and content. Amid acrimonies, the Bill has now been pending for over 18 years. It still awaits approval in the Lok Sabha, despite being passed by the Rajya Sabha in 2010. Even political parties that claim to favour women's reservation do not wish to assign more than 10 to 15 per cent of seats to women. Parties like the Samajwadi Party (SP) and Rashtriya Janata Dal (RJD) have made unrealistic demands to have a quota within the quota. The delay in the passage of the Bill is rather frustrating if one looks at its potential for increasing the share of female parliamentarians. For instance, there would have been 179 female MPs in the present Lok Sabha instead of the current 48. In Kerala, there would have been 47 women legislators instead of the current eight women members of a total of 140. In West Bengal, there would have been 98 women instead of the current 36 women out of a House of 294. In Haryana, the 90-member assembly would have had 30 women legislators instead of only 11 at present. Clearly, the delay in the passage of the WRB is symptomatic of the cavalier fashion in which the question of women's empowerment is being dealt with in India. However, the WRB has created a country-wide desire to ensure greater participation of women in politics, challenging male domination of society and government.

Today, more and more women are contesting for office. However, the current democratic frailty, deficits in democratic institutions and widespread corruption does not easily allow women to access the dividends of their increased political participation. The introduction of quotas alone is not enough to realize the goal of empowerment. In order to foster women's political agency, it is important to employ additional strategies that will promote the self-reliance of women and remove obstacles. Furthermore, it is unrealistic to expect that female politicians will represent women's interests alone. It is therefore important to encourage strong women's movements that can pressure all elected representatives.

VIOLENCE AGAINST WOMEN

Violence against women has pervaded widely the structures and cultures of Indian society, while being wrapped in silence. Such insidious violence deeply diminishes the possibilities of women's empowerment. In addition to many direct instances of violence, Indian women also encounter multiple forms of indirect violence rooted in poverty, illiteracy and patriarchal structures. Devoid of basic health and safety, Indian women cannot be empowered.

The cycle of violence begins with the high mortality rates of women in pregnancy and childbirth. Nearly a quarter of all maternal deaths in the world take place in India.[16] Due to their low status in a patriarchal society, women are married at an early age (nearly 40 per cent before the age of 18 in rural areas), and have no control over their sexuality or family planning. Other factors contributing to women's vulnerability include poverty, illiteracy, poor nutrition and inadequate health services. According to some estimates, over 10 million female foetuses have been aborted illegitimately in India (Morrall 2006: 56). Allied to this is the phenomenon of bride burning, which has claimed several thousand lives in recent years. Both types of violence are linked to the dowry custom, which continues unabated despite several laws.[17] Dowry is not only given before the wedding, the husband's family also expects to receive gifts and/or cash after the wedding. Discontentment with the dowry often entails violence towards the bride, sometimes causing her death. The Dowry Prohibition Act (1961) was amended by Act 63 (1984) with growing numbers of dowry deaths. The offence was hence made cognizable so that the police was given power to register a case under the Act to take up an investigation. The Act also made it clear that the demand for dowry itself was an offence, and made it punishable with imprisonment of no less than six months. The enforcement of this Act has been an entirely different matter.

The 1970s is often seen as a turning point in terms of women's political consciousness and activism. The concept of gender-based violence became the umbrella term to denote a range of violence: female infanticide, rape and bride burning, among others. In India, gender-based violence caught the nation's attention with the custodial rape of a young tribal girl, Mathura, on 26 March 1972, and the Supreme Court judgement that followed which declared that due to the fact that the victim was known to have a previous sexual history, she could not have been raped. This judicial inference galvanized an unprecedented response from the fledgling women's movement across the country, which led to the review of the case. In 1978, the Supreme Court had to make a fundamental change to the law on rape, shifting the onus of an investigation from the victim to the rapist. Thus, the rape of Mathura by two policemen in a police station compelled the government to amend the Indian Evidence Act, 1872, the Code of Criminal Procedure Act, 1973 and the Indian Penal Code, to introduce the category of custodial rape.

Close on the heels of the Mathura judgement came the gruesome case of Tarvinder Kaur, who was burnt alive for not meeting the dowry demands of her in-laws. A nationwide campaign led the government to pass a more comprehensive legislation against dowry, mandating investigations of the deaths of recently married women. Another significant case was that of Roop Kanwar, who was burnt to death in 1987 on her husband's funeral pyre. Known as 'Deorala sati', the case became rather contentious with women's protest groups being branded as a Western and neo-colonial ploy to destroy Hindu culture and traditions. In 1991, the case of Bhanwari Devi, a gang rape victim, unravelled the distortions in India's social and legal system. The trial court initially acquitted the accused, observing that the rapists were middle-aged and respectable persons of a higher caste who could not have raped a lower-caste woman. Amidst nationwide fury against the skewed judgement, the Supreme Court of India, in a landmark judgement, reversed the earlier verdict.

The Vishakha judgement laid down the guidelines for judging and preventing sexual harassment at the workplace. Subsequently, the NCW elaborated these guidelines into a Code of Conduct for employers. However, as the Varma Committee observed recently, justice continues to elude victims of sexual harassment and sexual assault even two decades after the Vishakha judgement. It also flagged the issue of the dismal sex ratios in several states, and the existence of chauvinistic institutions like 'khap-panchayats',[18] using extra-legal, oppressive methods of punishment (Verma, Seth and Subramanium 2013: 23).

The rising scale of atrocities against women has increasingly led to concerted protests from both women and men activists. Becoming more visible in the 1980s, the women's movement in its varied incarnations launched incessant campaigns to demand legislative changes to pre-empt violence against women. This led to the passing of various acts and legislations including the Criminal Law Amendment Act, 1983, Dowry Prohibition (Amendment) Act, 1984, Indecent Representation of Women (Prohibition) Act, 1986, and Commission of Sati (Prevention) Act, 1987.

While government agencies have dithered on how to prevent gender-based violence, civil society, led by women's groups and youth, has campaigned vigorously on this count. Most significant was the unprecedented protest after the gruesome gang rape of a young medico in Delhi on 16 December 2012, known as the 'Nirbhaya case'. The nationwide campaign in this case succeeded in transforming national consciousness and securitized the issue for emergency measures. The unprecedented protests in the wake of the brutal Delhi rape case almost forced the enactment of the Criminal Law Amendment Act, 2013, which widened the definition of rape to include non-penetrative sex and included offences such as acid attacks and sexual harassment. Provisions for aggravated rape had been widened to include rape committed by a person in a position of dominance, a member of the armed forces, rape committed during communal or sectarian violence, or on a woman incapable of giving consent. Increased penalty, including capital punishment, had been provided for gang rape and for causing serious injury to the victim (Ministry of Law and Justice 2013). However, as laws have become more stringent, there have been fewer convictions than before (Menon 2004: 5). The enforcement of the new legislation thus remains flawed, and has been aptly critiqued.

EMPOWERMENT MEETS WOMEN, PEACE AND SECURITY

In a presentation before the Committee on the Elimination of Discrimination against Women (CEDAW) on 14 July 2014, the Indian government highlighted the 2013 amendments to criminal law, legislation relating to food security, manual scavenging, protection of children from sexual offences, and sexual harassment of women in the workplace. However, the CEDAW committee raised doubts about the status of the convention in domestic legislation, budgetary allocations for women, and special measures to improve representation of women in political life. Violence against women in conflict situations was cited as an issue of great concern, and, related to this, the Armed Forces (Special Powers) Act or AFSPA and the impunity it offers to members of the armed forces. Experts were also concerned about violence against women of disadvantaged backgrounds, such as Adivasis, and asked what was being done to address this violence and ensure access to justice for victims (OHCHR 2014).

A Shadow Report to CEDAW, authored by non-governmental organizations (NGOs), is highly critical of the Indian government (ISAWN, IWFNEI and AIPP 2014). The Shadow Report explicates on the discriminatory attitudes and practices against Adivasi and tribal women in the Indian judicial system, maintaining that there is little understanding of the customary practices, history, concerns, perspectives and aspirations of Adivasi and tribal peoples. Despite being criminalized, trafficking remains another significant problem, with 90 per cent of cases involving trafficking of women within India. As the Shadow Report warns, women and girls continue to be trafficked for forced labour and forced marriage, organ harvesting and commercial sexual exploitation.

On 23 December 2012, a three-member committee led by Justice J.S. Verma, former Chief Justice of the Supreme Court, was constituted to recommend amendments to the criminal law so as to provide for quicker trial and enhanced punishment for criminals accused of committing sexual assault against women. The Verma Committee identified the failure of governance as the root cause of sexual violence and recommended drastic changes (Verma, Seth and Subramanium 2013). The report maintains that women in India have suffered in various spheres of life—physical health and mental well-being; bodily integrity and safety; social relations; political empowerment; access to education and knowledge; domestic work burden, lack of paid work; access to shelter; mobility; time autonomy; and respect. The Verma Committee report also brings up the brutalities of the armed forces faced by residents in the border areas and warned that the serious allegations of persistent sexual assault on women in conflict areas are causing more alienation (ibid.).

The Indian Parliament, in 2013, criminalized sexual harassment and enforced the death penalty on repeat offenders, and in cases of rape leading to the death of the victim. However, there has been criticism that the new legislation is more of a quick fix and reflects a knee-jerk reaction to international and national pressure. The high-profile rape cases in recent times have caught the attention of the international media making it difficult for the Indian government to evade the issue of gender-based violence. It is clear that the threats to women's safety and their continued disempowerment is not so much due to the want of needed legislation, but more because of weak rule of law and failure of good governance. It is also evident that law and legislation per se cannot usher in desirable changes in cultural practices and societal mind-set. It is equally vital to challenge the arcane superstition and the misogynist traditions and practices that hamper the quest for equality and empowerment. Equally critical is to bring about attitudinal changes to rectify the scourge of patriarchy wherein the discrimination between sexes is an acceptable norm in the family as well as the community at large. An overall holistic change of consciousness is imperative to ensure that women feel and perceive equality, whether in their quotidian life or at the workplace. A key challenge is how to raise awareness among women about their rights and rectify male stereotypes of women.

CONCLUDING REMARKS

Women cannot challenge gender biases within institutions of governance and their work culture unless they are amply represented therein and have the ability to equally access authority. This requires much greater attention to the provision of education, training and advocacy to women at all levels, so that they can lead development and governance processes in gender-sensitive ways. This is obviously an enormous task, which the state must perform in tandem with civil society.

It is not simply enough that women occupy a few symbolic political positions to ensure the true empowerment of women. Indeed, there is a world of difference between educated and aware Indian women from well-to-do families and rural illiterate women from poor backgrounds. The Justice Verma Committee raised this paradox rather succinctly:

> Does the Indian State live at two levels? One, which comprises those who are affluent and who have access to the Constitution and its machinery, and the other comprising those who live in the silent domination of the superior, will of tradition, customs and practices, which are derogatory to women? (ibid.: 12)

Any understanding of women's empowerment in India must relate to the larger social context wherein a substantial section of the population, whether male or female, adult or child, suffer from disabilities and inequalities due to systemic oppression and exploitation. Any remedial legislation must draw on a crosscutting approach to realize the diversity of social structures that govern women's lives. As Veena Mazumdar observes:

> Any policy or movement for the emancipation and development of women has to form a part of a total movement for removal of inequalities and oppressive social institutions, if the benefits and privileges won by such action are to be shared by the entire women population and not be monopolized by a small minority. (Mazumdar 1998: 258)

There is no doubt that legislation and governmental measures have left their imprint on the process of transforming the position of women considerably, but as such their systemic impact has been scant on women from less privileged classes, castes and regions. It is therefore vital to promote constitutional promises of a rights-based approach to women's empowerment; cutting across community, caste, class and urban/rural divides. Further, there is a need to establish effective monitoring mechanisms on how these agencies are functioning in addressing the rights, welfare and needs of poor and underprivileged women. The government's accountability to marginalized women needs to be strengthened. While there is a credible current of social movements in India struggling to ensure the representation of traditionally marginalized communities such as Dalit and tribal communities into the mainstream, women's rights within these movements are often side-lined. It is important, therefore, to recognize the lived realities of multiple layers of discrimination that hinder women's empowerment in our society.

Finally, it is vital to reckon with the criticism and scepticism surrounding the limits of legal campaigns as transformative strategy. As aptly suggested by Nivedita Menon: 'At most, women's groups see legal campaigns as a broad strategy to achieve legitimacy, to create public awareness on specific issues and to secure some short-term legal redress. The struggle to transform the patriarchal nature of existing laws can only be part of a wider struggle' (2004: 4).

NOTES

1. India has signed the Convention on the Elimination of All Forms of Discrimination against Women (CEDAW) in 1979, which legally binds it to adopt measures to combat gender-based violence.
2. India had a maternal mortality ratio (MMR) of 200 (per 100,000) in 2010; 10.9 per cent females in Parliament in 2012; 26.6 per cent females over 25 years with secondary and above education (2006–10); and a 29 per cent female workforce in 2011. See Human Development Report 2013 available at http://hdr.undp.org/en/composite/GII (accessed on 5 December 2016).
3. Trustlaw, a legal news service run by Thomson Reuters Foundation (London), asked 213 gender experts from five continents to rank countries by overall perceptions of danger and six risks: health threats, sexual violence, non-sexual violence, cultural/religious factors, access to resources, and trafficking (see: www.trust.org/trustlaw).
4. *'Yatra naryastu pujyante ramante tatra Devata, yatraitaastu na pujyante sarvaastatrafalaah kriyaah'*. Dave (1990: 3/56).
5. Devadasi system is a religious practice in parts of southern India whereby parents marry a daughter to a deity or a temple.The marriage usually occurs before the girl reaches puberty and requires her to become a prostitute for upper-caste community members. 'The Devadasi System: Genesis & Growth'. Available at iml.jou.ufl.edu/projects/Spring02/Chattaraj/genesis.html (accessed on 6 December 2016).
6. Among the freedom fighters were Bhikaji Cama, Annie Besant, Pritilata Waddedar, Vijayalakshmi Pandit, Rajkumari Amrit Kaur, Aruna Asaf Ali, Sucheta Kriplani, Kasturba Gandhi, Sarala Devi Chaudhrani, Rustomji Faridoonji, Durgabai Deshmukh, Kamala Devi Chattopadhya, Begum Sharifa, Hamid Ali and Fatima Jinnah.
7. See the Supreme Court of India observation in *Vishakha vs. State of Rajasthan*, AIR 1997 SC 3011. http://www.iiap.res.in/files/VisakaVsRajasthan_1997.pdf (accessed on 3 November 2016).
8. NCW Complaint & Investigation Cell, http://ncw.nic.in/frmComplaintUnit.aspx (accessed on 3 November 2016).
9. The Varma Committee has lamented the poor performance of the NCW and has recommended an institutionalized and transparent process to select its members.
10. Convergence through Poorna Shakti Kendras, http://www.nmew.gov.in/searchdetails.php?lang=1&lid=28&skey=psk (accessed on 3 November 2016).
11. The exception was in 1957, the second general election, where the share of women representatives was 4.4.
12. Data on women in national parliaments, 2014, http://www.ipu.org/wmn-e/world.htm (accessed on 3 November 2016).

13. Prior to this, only the state of Karnataka offered reservations for women in institutions of local self-governance.
14. A nagar palika or nagar panchayat is a form of an urban political unit in India comparable to a municipality. An urban centre with more than 30,000 and less than 100,000 inhabitants is classified as a nagar panchayat. Figures provided by Ministry of Panchayati Raj, Government of India. http://lgdirectory.gov.in/rptConsolidateforRuralLB.do, http://www.panchayat.gov.in/background-and-objective (accessed on 3 November 2016).
15. Reported by *Hindustan* (Hindi, Varanasi edition), 9 November 2014.
16. Each year, nearly 117,000 Indian women die due to childbirth complications.
17. In 1961, the government passed a Dowry Prohibition Act, which was amended in the early 1980s to correct inherent flaws and loopholes. Its provisions can now be evoked within the first seven years of marriage.
18. A Khap Panchyat is an informal justice system of various clans in the Jat-dominated areas of north-western India.

REFERENCES

Basu, Aparna. 2008. 'Women's Struggle for the Vote: 1917–1937', *Indian Historical Review*, 35(1): 128–43.

Centre for Legislative Research and Advocacy (CLRA). 2008. 'Women's Reservation: A Long Delayed and a Much Needed Step', Policy Brief Series 3, July.

Dave, J.H. 1990. Manu-Smriti with Nine Commentaries. Volumes II and III. Mumbai: Bharatiya Vidya Bhavan.

Deo, Nandini. 2012. 'Running From Elections: Indian Feminism and Electoral Politics', *India Review*, 11(1): 46–64.

Global Entrepreneurship and Development Institute (GEDI). 2014. *The Gender Global Entrepreneurship and Development Index (GEDI).* Produced by Global Entrepreneurship and Development Institute with the generous support of The Dell Women's Entrepreneur Network, Washington. http://www.womenable.com/content/userfiles/Gender_GEDI_Executive_Report-2014-final.pdf (accessed on 3 November 2016).

Government of India (GOI). 1974. *Towards Equality: Report of the Committee on the Status of Women in India.* New Delhi: Department of Social Welfare, Ministry of Education and Social Welfare.

Government of India (GOI). (1995). *Country Report: Fourth World Conference on Women, Beijing,* Department of Women and Child Development, Ministry of Human Resource Development..

Heinsohn, Nina. 2004. 'Working Meeting on Power, Rights, and Poverty Reduction: A Summary', in Ruth Alsop (ed.), *Power, Rights, and Poverty: Concepts and Connections*, pp. 126–36. Washington, D.C.: The World Bank.

Inter State Adivasi Women's Network (ISAWN) of Mainland India, Indigenous Women's Forum of North East India (IWFNEI) and Asia Indigenous Peoples Pact (AIPP), Chian Mai, Thailand. 2014. *India NGO Cedaw Shadow Report and Status of Adivasi/Tribal Women in India.* For the 58th Session of the Committee on the Elimination of All Forms of Discrimination against Women (4th and 5th Periodic Review), June, Geneva, Switzerland. Submitted by ISAWN, IWFNIE and AIPP.

Jeffrey, Craig and John Harriss. 2014. *Keywords for Modern India.* New York: Oxford University Press.

Kandpal, Eeshani, Kathy Baylis and Mary Arends-Kuenning. 2013. 'Measuring the Effect of a Community-Level Program on Women's Empowerment Outcomes: Evidence from India', Policy Research Working Paper Series 6399, The World Bank, Washington, D.C.

Katulkar, Ratnesh. 2008. 'Dr. Ambedkar on Women Liberation'. http://www.countercurrents.org/katulkar310808.htm (accessed on 28 November 2016).

Klot, Jennifer F. 2007. 'Women and Peacebuilding'. Independent Expert Paper, commissioned by UNIFEM and PBSO, Social Science Research Council, New York. http://www.un.org/en/peacebuilding/pdf/doc_wgll/wgll_backgroundpaper_29_01_08.pdf (accessed on 3 November 2016).

Kumar, Hajira. 2005. *Women's Empowerment: Issues, Challenges and Strategies. A Source Book.* New Delhi: Daya Publishing House.

Mazumdar, Veena. 1998. 'Women: From Equality to Empowerment', in Hiranmay Karlekar (ed.), *Independent India: The First Fifty Years*, pp. 255–79. New Delhi: Oxford University Press.

Menon, Nivedita. 2004. *Recovering Subversion: Feminist Politics beyond the Law.* Chicago: University of Illinois Press.

Ministry of Law and Justice. 2013. The Criminal Law Amendment Act 2013: No. 13 of 2013. New Delhi: The Gazette of India, Extraordinary Part II, 2 April. http://indiacode.nic.in/acts-in-pdf/132013.pdf.

Mohan, N.S. et al. 2005. *Baseline Report Women and Political Participation in India.* Bangalore: National Institute of Advanced Studies (NIAS), Gender Studies Unit.

Morrall, Peter. 2006. *Murder and Society.* University of Leeds: John Wiley & Sons.

Nayak, Sarojini. 2005. *Women's Empowerment in India.* Jaipur: Pointer Publisher.

Office of the United Nations High Commissioner for Human Rights (OHCHR). 2014. 'Committee on the Elimination of Discrimination Against Women (CEDAW) Considers Report of India', 2 July, United Nations Office, Geneva.

Padia, Chandrakala. 2011. *Theorizing Feminism.* Jaipur: Rawat Publications.

Pisharoty, Sangeeta Barooah. 2013. 'Faced with Changing Times', *The Hindu*, 19 February. http://www.thehindu.com/todays-paper/tp-features/faced-with-changing- times/article4429715.ece (accessed on 1 December 2016).

Rathod, Apoorva. 2014. 'Women's Political Participation and Representation in India', *Issue Brief*, April, Delhi Policy Group, New Delhi. http://www.delhipolicygroup.com/uploads/publication_file/1066_Women_in_Politics_final.pdf (accessed on 12 March 2015).

Roychowdhury, Poulami. 2013. 'Focus on Rape in India Ignores Gender Violence as a Global Tragedy', *CNBC*, 9 January. http://www.cnbc.com/id/100368113 (accessed on 5 December 2016).

Sen, Amartya. 1999. *Development as Freedom*. New York: Oxford University Press.

Southard, Barbara. 1993. 'Colonial Politics and Women's Rights: Woman Suffrage Campaigns in Bengal, British India in the 1920s', *Modern Asian Studies*, 27: 397–439.

United Nations Educational, Scientific and Cultural Organization (UNESCO). 2012. 'UNESCO New Delhi and the Indian National Mission for Empowerment of Women Sign a Charter of Collaboration', UNESCO, New Delhi Office, 3 December. http://www.unesco.org/new/en/newdelhi/about-this-office/single-view/news/unesco_new_delhi_and_the_indian_national_mission_for_empowerment_of_women_sign_a_charter_of_collaboration-1/#.VIheoa0cRMs (accessed on 3 March 2014).

United Nations Development Programme (UNDP). 2014. *Sustaining Human Progress: Reducing Vulnerabilities and Building Resilience, Human Development Report 2014*. New York: UNDP. http://hdr.undp.org/sites/default/files/hdr14-report-en-1.pdf (accessed on 28 November 2016).

Verma, J.S., L. Seth and G. Subramanium. 2013. *Report of the Committee on Amendments to Criminal Law*. http://www.thehindu.com/multimedia/archive/01340/Justice_Verma_Comm_1340438a.pdf (accessed on 1 December 2016).

World Economic Forum (WEF). 2013. *The Global Gender Gap Report 2013*. New York: WEF. http://www.weforum.org/reports/global-gender-gap-report-2013 (accessed on 1 December 2016).

CHAPTER 2

Debating Empowerment: The 73rd Amendment in Assam

Arunima Deka

Reiterating its commitment to democratic decentralization, gender equality and inclusion, the Indian state mandated reservation for women in local governance bodies. In the process, a debate on women's empowerment has come up as an important corollary. The notion of empowerment has stirred debate not only regarding its reach and goals, but also the methods to be employed, the expected outcomes, and the understanding of gender, equality and social relationships. The notion of empowerment has been integrally linked with that of power, and with efforts to bring people within the ambit of decision making.

In this context, the 73rd Constitutional Amendment can be viewed as a considerable step towards women's empowerment and the inclusion of women in political power structures from which they were hitherto excluded. However, it has also been found that panchayats as bodies of local governance are steeped in unequal power relations and patriarchal norms. Therefore, we need to ask whether the state is able to pave the way for women's empowerment by merely providing formal representation in local governance without addressing key issues of disempowerment in the community and family, and within the governance bodies where women are now supposed to participate. The political and social space of women is essentially linked to overall power dynamics, and, therefore, formal inclusion of women through reservation often proves to be insufficient.

Within the larger debate of empowerment and democratic decentralization, this chapter argues that grass-roots democratization has been a process of both exclusion and inclusion. While the state takes formal steps for inclusion of women in decision making, the prevalence of patriarchal norms exclude women from equal participation. This chapter essentially addresses the following questions: (a) Does empowerment only mean sharing of the formal space of politics, leaving out the informal or private sphere of domestic life? (b) Does the numerical strength of elected women representatives sufficiently lead to their empowerment? (c) Does women's participation in the formal structure of politics efface unequal power structures and male hegemony? These questions are corroborated with qualitative findings from empirical research, and a critical examination of women's empowerment and the reservation policies of the state of Assam.

In the process it also attempts, at first, to analyse the interrelationship between politics and gender (or womanhood) as a category. Second, it looks into the question of how institutions and structures of power influence this category. In this regard, I revisit the construction of the category of womanhood in the day-to-day experiences of women, drawing on Joan W. Scott's analysis of gender as 'a primary way of signifying relationships of power' (Scott 1986: 1067), but not the only axis of oppression which is worked upon by patriarchy. I investigate ways in which women engage with the state, the construction of gender identities and representation, and how this is ultimately linked with the question of empowerment. The chapter is divided into three main parts. The first part elaborates on panchayat politics and women in India, while the second offers a brief history of Panchayati Raj in Assam. The third part seeks to analyse empowerment and women's political participation in Assam, corroborated with insights from the field.

POLITICS, POWER, PANCHAYAT AND WOMEN

The question of women's political reservation and participation in Panchayati Raj Institutions (PRIs) needs academic re-engagement even after two decades of institutionalization as an important tier of the democratic structure. Feminists around the world have emphasized the need for access to institutional power, especially through the process of suffrage. The liberal democratic affinity for political and legal rights ensures that such rights are not only widely recognized, but deeply institutionalized. Internationally, these rights still form part of a dominant discourse around which policies are formulated, because of which there are international conventions for the equal status of women and their ability to exercise their political rights. The Convention on the Political Rights of Women, of which India too is a signatory, was adopted by the United Nations (UN) in 1952 and has been ratified by 122 countries. However, speaking of political rights without addressing other sociocultural impediments does not provide a viable solution to the class, racial, ethnic and other oppression faced by women in a developing country like India. For this we need to recognize that, as Rai points out, 'institutional processes themselves are embedded in structures of social power, which limit the effectiveness of the outcomes of deliberation' (Rai 2007: 65). By guaranteeing constitutional rights, the state, therefore, paves the way for formal inclusion of women into the power ambit, but does not extend its transformative control to question the prevalent gender oppression in the private sphere or society at large.

India has made various international commitments on gender equality over the past decades. The 1974 report *Towards Equality* launched the idea of reservation for women at the grass-roots level of governance and eventually the 73rd Constitutional

Amendment Act was passed in 1993. This Act provided a 'much-needed opportunity for women to actively participate in the decision-making processes of their locality through the political right that was conferred on them' (Mathew 2003: 159). This Act ensured reservation of one-third of the seats in panchayats for women. It brings into debate the individualistic identity of women as opposed to the community identity with which she was hitherto identified. The post-Independence democratic experience reasonably made way for political participation of both men and women, unlike countries like Switzerland which did not grant women suffrage until fairly recently. In India, as in many other countries, womanhood was always subsumed under competing facets of identity, especially class, caste and religion. Yet, reservation of seats for women in the panchayat 'signalled some acceptance of the category of "women" as a legitimate target of such public policies' (Jenkins 2003: 166).

The 73rd Constitutional Amendment opened the political space to women, paving a way for their huge participation in the decision-making process, and also charting a change in the political discourse of the country. Preceding this important piece of legislature, there were many deliberations for providing adequate representation to the weaker sections of society, basically the Scheduled Castes (SCs) and the Scheduled Tribes (STs). Nevertheless, 'women's representation continued to be only token, even in the legal stipulations developed in the first four decades of independence', with some exception provided by Karnataka and Andhra Pradesh introducing some reservation for women (Buch 2000: 6).

The panchayat quota strategy was adopted as a means to compensate women for their 'historically and culturally bounded exclusion from public political life' (Rai 2007: 76). However, many studies have actually proved that the benefit of reservation did not reach women. Rather, power was accrued on their behalf by powerful male members of the community. In the study of the Gangoh Kshetra Panchayat in Uttar Pradesh, Mahi Pal found that the role of the female representative was actually performed either by her husband or any male member of the family. She also found widespread discrimination of women both inside and outside the household, and most often these women representatives had very little awareness about their powers and authority (Pal 1998: 152). In the context of Assam, Sujata Dutta Hazarika notes that the implementation of the 73rd Amendment led to 'increase participation of women in politics only numerically, without really contributing in changing governance qualitatively' (Dutta Hazarika 2005: 18).

Essentially, scholarly literature over the past decades has both eulogized and critiqued the process of democratic decentralization and women's participation, providing a variety of analytical positions. A study conducted in Kathua and Jammu districts of Jammu and Kashmir revealed that neither reservation nor women's presence in the panchayats made any significant change in attitude towards women. Women representatives were not treated with respect in panchayat meetings and their views were often ignored. According to this study, very few women representatives were allowed to express their views in the panchayat and often women chose to abstain from further meetings (Kaul and Sahni 2009: 29–38). Likewise, Nanivadekar carried out fieldwork in Maharashtra and identified counterproductive trends following the reservation for women. She particularly focused on the role of 'proxies' and found that more often the role of an elected representative was merely 'an extension of their role as a housewife' (Nanivadekar 1998: 1815). Contrarily, another study in Karnataka discovered that wherever women held positions in local bodies, there was greater efficiency and transparency in the running of public affairs, better water supply facilities and more emphasis on promoting education of girls (Vyasulu and Vyasulu 1999: 3677). In her study of the impact of PRI reservation for women in the three northern states of Madhya Pradesh, Rajasthan and Uttar Pradesh, Buch points out to the beginning of an emerging women's leadership in rural India, despite all the challenges and difficulties facing them (Buch 2000). A similar conclusion was also drawn in the case of Manipur where women were effectively playing their role (Brara 2009: 290).

Continued discussions around the gender sensitiveness of grass-roots institutions have built arguments for institutional reforms and a review of the outcomes of such involvement of women. Rai suggests a model of deliberative politics that focuses on 'process, outcome and context' to enhance efficiency and to bring about a 'gender-sensitive political equality agenda' (Rai 2007: 64–80). The gendered nature of the state and the panchayat bodies is further reflected in the move to regulate reproduction through this institution. In their study, Chattopadhyay and Duflo criticize the policies by which states like Haryana, Rajasthan, Andhra Pradesh, Odisha, Madhya Pradesh and Himachal Pradesh have laws restricting panchayat members from having more than two children, adversely affecting women who do not necessarily control their procreation choices and are 'unlikely to find it worthwhile to fight their family' for contesting elections (Chattopadhyay and Duflo 2004: 985). Positively, many studies on the other hand have also pointed to the tremendous potential of 'social transformation' through the 73rd Constitutional Amendment, though slow in pace, yet 'will lead to active participation in the decision making process' (Baviskar and Mathew 2009: 16).

The transformation towards women's participation requires some closer attention, especially regarding the rising centrality of the category of 'women' in the changing political discourse of the country. The nationalist discourse of the colonial period in India, as Chatterjee points out, has in its typical way answered the 'women's question' using the analogous dichotomy of 'home/world'. Nationalist leaders refused to make the 'women's question an issue of political negotiation with the colonial state', but after Independence this question again acquired significance and became a 'political issue in the life of the nation state' (Chatterjee 1989: 622–33). The universalization of the notion of rights, equality and freedom were extended to women at the dawn of the new nation state, although this can be regarded as a paternalistic granting of supposedly equal rights with very little consideration to how these rights would actually be exercised.

Interestingly, a recent report prepared by the Inter-Parliamentary Union (IPU) ranked India at the 111th position out of 189 countries in terms of women Members of Parliament (MPs), with 11.97 per cent in the Lok Sabha and 12.76 per cent in the Rajya Sabha.[1] The lower visibility of Indian women in the sphere of active politics has been a concern for Western and Indian academicians alike. However, does addressing this numerical concern adequately provide an answer to the gender divide that operates in Indian society? Does the institutional intervention aimed through reservation policies sufficiently address the gender question or even lead to women's empowerment?

The discourse of empowerment has garnered special attention of the Government of India, under whose auspices a Committee on Empowerment of Women (2009–10), submitted its third report titled *Empowerment of Women through Panchayati Raj Institutions* (CEW: 2010). Special emphasis is laid on building 'substantial representation of women in Panchayats', to facilitate 'women to use their collective strength more effectively' through schemes like Panchayat Mahila Sakti Abhiyan (PMSA) (ibid.: 14). With greater stress on participatory politics, the discourse on empowerment is only a resonance of the state's overemphasis on ensuring participation as a tangible end rather than empowering women to challenge any status quo. It is an agreeable point, where Rai succinctly points that empowerment 'addresses audiences as if they were all potential converts to 'the cause', and often leaves one to ask 'empowerment of whom, by whom, through what and for what' (Rai 2002: 135).

Within the present neo-liberal regime, empowerment is seen as a prerequisite for the attainment of social, cultural and political emancipation and the issue of women's control over her own self, essentially shifting the responsibility to the individual. It has been powerfully linked with the prospect of improving women's condition in developing countries. It has specially garnered the attention of donor agencies and international organizations as a means to improve the lives of these women, most importantly through efforts involving sustained education, reproductive choices, self-help groups etc. But it also raises certain questions: Whose empowerment is sought? Whose choices are we talking about? What dimension would it assume being intertwined with the struggle around identities like gender, class, caste and other social attributes? Central to my discussion on the empowerment debate, I would argue that this notion is built on an essentialist understanding of 'powerful' and 'powerless'. Such binaries reflect the traditional male/female dichotomies, translating them into gendered hierarchies in relations of power. Empowerment would rather entail not only creating but also enabling women to engage and rework relations of entrenched gender subordination in both the public and private domains.

PANCHAYATI RAJ IN ASSAM

Assam was a pioneer state in India in the enactment and establishment of PRIs. In the post-Independence period, its first experiment with local governance started in 1948 with the passing of the Assam Rural Panchayat Act, providing for a two-tier system: a primary panchayat at the village level and a secondary panchayat at the *mouza* (cluster of revenue villages) level. Under this Act, 422 Mouza Panchayats and 2,656 Village Panchayats were created (Sarmah 2006; SIRD 2005). However, the Act could not function in an effective manner mainly due to paucity of funds, leading to its reappraisal in 1953 (Sarmah 2006). Meanwhile, the Government of India constituted a committee to study local self-government nationwide, and eventually the Mehta Committee so constituted submitted its report.

In tune with the Mehta Committee report, Assam enacted the Assam Panchayat Act, 1959. This provided for a three-tier system and accordingly the Gaon Panchayat was set up at the village level, the Anchalik Panchayat at the intermediate level and the Mahkuma Panchayat at the sub-divisional level. At this time there were 2,574 Gaon Panchayats, 121 Anchalik Panchayats and 20 Mahkuma Panchayats in Assam. Importantly, this Act also made a provision for the inclusion of two women representatives, in addition to the two each from both SC and ST communities. This Act was further amended in 1964 to enable the panchayats to function more effectively, empowering these bodies to implement village-level schemes. Frequently amended panchayat acts point at the state's continued effort in institutionalizing an effective form of local government and legitimate structure of power at the grass roots. However, the process has shifted the onus of local governance to the people without adequate financial devolution.

The next significant change in the Panchayati Raj Act took place in 1972, where the Government of Assam abolished the intermediate level or the Anchalik Panchayat and reverted to a two-tier system (SIRD 2005). The 1972 Act was replaced by the Assam Panchayati Raj Act of 1986, again introducing the three-tier system, along with a reservation of 33 per cent of total seats in each tier for women candidates. The Act of 1986 also made provisions for SCs and STs to elect the Gaon Panchayat president and Anchalik Panchayat member if they accounted for more than one-third of the total population.

Finally, in 1992, the 73rd Constitutional Amendment Act was passed, institutionalizing panchayats with constitutionally guaranteed powers and making mandatory the reservation of seats for women, SCs and STs. Subsequently, the Assam Panchayati Raj Act, 1994 incorporated these provisions. While other states of India implemented women's participation in PRIs from 1994, Assam had its first experience in December 2001, when 9,889 women representatives were elected to the PRIs (Sarmah 2006: 235). The interim period saw the process of democratic decentralization stalled by political instability. In 1996, the Asom Gana Parishad (AGP) came into power and dissolved all local governance bodies. Though the subsequent elections should have been held within six months, they were deferred on the pretext of issues like insurgency and problems of law and order (ibid.: 165). Elections were eventually held in 2001 when the Congress party came back to power a year earlier. The Congress party made a victorious gain in the elections to the PRI by winning 311 seats out of the total 390 Zilla Parishad seats (*EPW* 2002: 87). The party's sweeping victory in the panchayat polls reflected the tenacity of the rural masses in securing the return of democratic politics. Nevertheless, evaluations of the functioning of local government often find the autonomy of panchayat bodies being heavily influenced by party and state politics, making such bodies vulnerable and sometimes virtually redundant.

The most recent elected panchayat bodies in Assam were constituted in 2013. As of that year, there were a total of 2,206 Village Panchayats, 191 Intermediate Panchayats and 21 District Panchayats. The state has a total of 24,222 elected representatives in the village panchayat, 2,202 in the intermediate panchayat, and 420 in the district panchayat. Of the total 26,844 panchayat members in Assam, 1,344 (5 per cent) are SCs, 886 (3.3 per cent) are STs and 9,903 (36.9 per cent) are women.[2] In a recent move to make panchayats even more inclusive, many states, including Assam, have adopted 50 per cent reservation for women. The average share of women in panchayats in India has thus reached 46.7 per cent. Though, superficially, apprehension about gender inequality and women's political marginalization can be addressed by greater numerical inclusion of women in the panchayats, questions regarding the effectiveness of such participation still hold ground.

IS THE 'PERSONAL' ALSO 'POLITICAL'? WOMEN AND GRASS-ROOTS EMPOWERMENT

To focus on the relationship between women's engagement with active politics and the state, fieldwork was carried out in Sontipur and Dibrugarh districts, and women members of all three tiers of the Panchayati Raj system, i.e. at the Gaon Panchayat (GP), Anchalik Panchayat (AP) and Zilla Panchayat (ZP) levels were interviewed. After positing the experiences of several women representatives of Sontipur, most of whom were very new entrants in the field of politics, this section then focuses on a woman representative of the tea tribe,[3] long associated with panchayat politics in Assam, and her political trajectory.[4] Through the case studies and various discussions with people in the GP investigated in this section, an effort has been made to reflect on entrenched gender ideology and functioning of the local self-government in Assam, especially in reference to the 73rd Constitutional Amendment.

After the 73rd Constitutional Amendment, the panchayats have become sites of both democratic devolution and power concentration. As a unit of decentralized democracy, the panchayat system is caught in various forms of power play, where issues of caste, class and gender come to the forefront. Caste is a sociopolitical reality of Indian society, and has manifested even at the local level of governance in Assam. While this kind of power hierarchy and hegemony is more visible in other parts of India, the caste-based disparities in Assam are more subtle in nature. Caste identity has become more of a political identity for women representatives, empowering them to acquire an official position. One of the members of the ZP, Sumati Das,[5] noted that 'without reservation it would have been very difficult for women to find representation in such official bodies'. But reservation, according to her, has only provided a 'political platform to women who have a supporting husband and family', and not much social change has been achieved in the socio-economic condition of the people from the lower castes.

Sumati, 42 years old, became a member of the Parbatia ZP for the first time. She has no previous political experience, though she always took part in various sociocultural and political activities in her village. Not having much formal schooling, she feels constrained to approach the higher officials and functionaries for any official matters, for which she always prefers to be accompanied by her husband. Further, Sumati feels that by being in a position of power she has to always be conscious of her actions and cannot depend on others for assistance in her official duties. Therefore, in such cases it is usually the husband or a close relative who helps the women perform their official work. Though they cannot be labelled as 'proxy' representatives, as studies from other states of India suggest, these elected women representatives often require their family member and/or husband to aid and advise them.

Despite being politically empowered, women like Sumati do not enjoy the capacity to manage official problems with ease. Many of these women also showed great hesitation while answering questions pertaining to financial issues of the panchayat, or even of their personal expenditure. Even in domestic matters, women respondents feel that they are not experts in managing their personal finances and usually depend on a male member to take care of these issues. However, as a ZP member Sumati is under constant stress to be present at the district office in order to avail various schemes for her area. According to her, without constant pestering of the district officials, representatives will fail to get any schemes allotted to them.

Financial devolution is an important feature of the functioning of the PRIs. A host of centrally sponsored schemes are undertaken through the panchayat, and therefore having the necessary acumen would have greatly benefited women. But women have traditionally been trained only for managing the 'private' affairs of a family, taking care of the household and performing domestic chores, leaving issues of 'public' politics and finance to male counterparts. Despite spending a huge amount of money on the election campaign, Sumati was not comfortable disclosing the amount and time and again glanced at her husband to provide the appropriate answer. She even remarked that since she was not an expert in financial matters, the expenditures were handled by her husband, and she didn't know exactly how much was spent on the election. However, women's active engagement in politics often extends as a source of political resource for the family and also allows them to come into the limelight, like Sumati's husband did. Sadly these women representatives, apart from serving their familial interests, do not create a kind of individual leadership that would be significant while contesting for a position of power in subsequent elections. For many of these women, being in formal positions of power burdens them with the expectations of people, which if not fulfilled maligns their career and future prospects. So, while challenges related to financial issues and inability to ensure benefits for their areas are faced by both male and female representatives, for the female representatives this becomes a far greater hurdle. Not only does she have to face the questions of the '*raiz*' (common people/voters of the constituency), but she also sees this as a test of her ability as a 'woman', an apprehension that she is unable to disregard easily.

Starting with 2001, the Panchayati Raj experience in Assam and women's role therein has not been widely debated. This kind of paucity of research seems to stem from the widely held opinion that reservation for women has, to a large extent, solved the problem of missing women in the public sphere. Since it is now mandatory on the part of the state to make provisions for women's participation in these local bodies, the issue does not evoke critical engagement. Such laxity is also observed on the ground, where making way for political representation seems to be a solution to all the common problems facing women. Once in the seat of power, these women representatives often face high expectations and people often approach them with various needs, like speeding up the process of receiving old age remuneration paid by the state, housing benefits, and getting themselves registered in the list of beneficiaries for various state-sponsored schemes, among others. People often approach them with problems regarding 'schemes and accruing their benefits' feels Minoti Bania, a member of the Parbatia GP. According to her, what people fail to understand is that very limited resources or power is available to them, and that they are mere agents of the state government without much say in the higher echelons where plans are set. Minoti further elaborated with instances from her own experience, where she found that for the state-sponsored schemes like Indira Awas Yojana (IAY), members like her have very little say and benefits are usually siphoned off by people who are close to the power circle at the block level. Poor women like Minoti, with no formal education or support from others, despite being elected as a people's representative, cannot function efficiently. Despite these impediments, the women representatives were regular in their attendance in meetings and were never barred from expressing their opinion, nor in taking part in the deliberation process of such meetings.

Minoti's personal life has been a major motivating factor for her to join politics. She has always been active in the village-level Mahila Samitis (women's collectives), for which people of the locality pressurized her to contest the election. Mahila Samitis existed as important spaces of collective gathering for women, yet research shows that they were purely apolitical in nature and never intended to question the power and gender hierarchy existing in society (Deka 2013). At around the same time, the local Congress body extended their support to her and even paid the nominal deposit fee required to contest elections. The seat she contested from was not reserved for women, yet she won with a considerable margin defeating her rival, a male candidate. But, for Minoti, working for the Mahila Samiti and amongst women is quite different from working in a politically charged environment, which is always a full-time engagement, with people coming to her with problems every day. She often feels frustrated because of the expectations of the poor people, which she is not often able to meet immediately. Being from an SC background she feels that the backwardness of her community is a historical wrong that is not possible to change overnight, as an attitude of 'helplessness' has seeped into the minds of the people in her community. Though she acknowledged very candidly that there was no visible caste-based discrimination against the SCs in her village, the poverty of these people is stark. Though she has utter faith in the political franchise for the deprived, Minoti feels that members of her community would take decades to reach the minimum standard socio-economic conditions, and that political rights for them do not have much appeal without corresponding improvements in other spheres.

Her personal life is fraught with similar struggles too, where just prior to the election in 2013, she, at the age of 57, divorced her husband. Her marriage was often a source of ridicule for others in the locality, as her husband was already living with another woman belonging to a nearby village. Her four children are all grown up now, because of which she could muster the courage to do away with a bad marriage. However, she felt that taking such a decision would not be easy for women of a lot younger age, as people always construct women's behaviour as 'good or bad' based on her 'personal conduct and family life'. But to her favour, her homestead land is owned by her, as she inherited it from her maternal side by dint of being from a family with no sons. Ownership of property can be a source of her strength to fight the oppressive patriarchal structure and even provide her with the much required economic sustenance. Minoti provided validation for this.

Rupa Bora, 37 years old, member of the AP, came from a well-to-do family. She was not keen to join politics, being happily settled in her family life, a husband with a successful business and two children to take care of. But the seat for the AP was reserved for women, for which her family along with people from the locality insisted she contest the election. The GP office is very close to her residence, and therefore she visits it every day after carrying out all the household chores. She, however, pointed out that she was enjoying her new role outside the family and feeling confident about herself and about performing a better role in the years to come. Though she had completed only a few months of office when this interview was conducted, she finds people approaching her for various official favours and treating her with some kind of respect for being their elected representative. On the personal front, Rupa feels this job has added to her domestic burden. However, in order to lessen their domestic workload, many women like Rupa are now hiring maids to help them.

Here, another issue that evolved was the insufficient remuneration for their work and time spent in the panchayat. Without a fixed salary, these members of the panchayat, and especially women representatives, face a very difficult situation at home, spending considerable hours of the day in *somaj kolyan* (social work).

Sadly, however, joining active politics and the panchayat is viewed as a lucrative option by many of these representatives. So, even if there is no fixed salary, many are hopeful of recovering their election expenditures by siphoning some money off the development fund of the panchayat, if necessary.

The various schemes implemented under the panchayat also suffice the gendered nature of the development project of the state. Development schemes usually allotted to these bodies mainly pertain to, for example, construction of roads and digging of wells, and such activities only provide indirect benefits to the women along with others in the village. Little scope is available for women representatives to act for women's issues or economic empowerment at the grass-roots level. It is often with the schemes conceived at the Centre that they have to prove their efficacy of leadership. Even in matters of accruing schemes, these women representatives have to be very tactful and continuously bargain with officials in order to avail benefits for the development of their areas by demanding any particular scheme (scheme *dhora*) and making sure it reaches the people. Representatives are continuously judged in this way for their performance, how efficiently they are able to accrue these schemes for their areas and also by the number of beneficiaries they are able to reach.

While the political institution of local democracy has elevated the formal participation of women in the 'public' arena, yet her 'personal' sphere still remains dominated by patriarchal norms. So even after successfully carrying out her duties as a people's representative, she is expected to return to take care of her family. The official duty hours of most of these elected women representatives start after 11 a.m., when all the necessary household activities have been taken care of. Importantly, however, often the 'public/private' boundaries are obfuscated. As a people's representative, the woman is expected to address the concerns of her constituency at any time of the day, even when her private family issues become a topic of public discussion and scrutiny, as seen in the case of Minoti. In the public sphere, the woman representative is expected to deliver and is often pressurized to perform better. The general tone of the people is also indicative of this, though in a contrary paternalistic manner, suggesting that reservation for women is necessary for their 'empowerment', to bring them at par with the 'male members of society'. In order to gain public or political acceptability, women need to acquire masculine attributes. Public spaces are, therefore, not always an arena of emancipation, but can be one of control and tokenism. Importantly, however, this public platform also provided these elected women representatives a space to put forth their individual and party differences whenever required. A kind of AGP-Congress tussle was visible between two members of the GP and they each vocally placed the merits of their cases. Though a very minor altercation, such discussions paved the way for the entry of women in political deliberation, allowing them to state their difference of opinion in public. Women are made to face patriarchal norms even in such situations, where many male members of the panchayat at this time rebuked them for having a 'cat fight', considered innate to the nature of women.

Milli Telli is a woman in her mid-40s, a social worker for many years, involved with people of the tea tribe in Dibrugarh. Her experience in active politics is a story that inspires a generation of young people in her area. From a marginalized background, and belonging to a tea tribe community, her quest for identity was a confluence of not only her private life but also the political aspirations of her community. Her background, however, never acted as an impediment to her aspirations of attaining better education or serving her community. In fact, she was the first female from her area to pass the matriculation exam. In 1992, with the introduction of reservations in the PRIs, Telli became the president of the GP. The subsequent dismantling of the PRI in the state was a major jolt to such upcoming women representatives who could find no more scope to prove their credibility on the political front. However, for Telli, the reinstatement of the PRI in the year 2001 provided her another opportunity when she was offered a ticket by the Congress party and went on to win as the president of the ZP. During that phase, her continuous engagement was on developmental issues and she travelled the whole district by herself to assess the situation. Speaking on the issue of women's reservation, Telli feels the need to engage more and more women in the process, but equally she pointed out the impediments in the way of such progress. She specifically stressed the fact that women representatives face more problems in performing their duties than their male counterparts. Most of the women, according to her, face these challenges not only because of social deprivation but also due to lack of education, which creates an impediment in understanding official procedures effectively and thereby requires someone else to help them out. Along with this hindrance, she also feels that the five-year term is too short to adequately train and develop expertise. Her insights repeatedly pointed out the growing frustration with the lack of effectiveness of PRIs, excessive bureaucracy and corruption at various levels, which ails the system in totality. However, while speaking of her own experience in the panchayat and the need for reservation, Telli believes that women need to have 'will power of their own' to make a mark in their respective fields, and could easily garner the support of people and be a part of power politics even without reservation.

Milli Telli belongs to a generation of women for whom empowerment was proposed both as a dream and a prerequisite for gender justice. She acknowledges the pressure on women to 'act as men' in order to mark their presence in grass-roots politics. While she abhors the gendered nature of society and the system in totality, on the personal front she has never allowed these to overshadow her sense of duty to her community. She, therefore, often posed as a challenge to a system that is in search of a female who will not abhor or contest the hegemony of males, whether in the private or public domain. Her voice for economic and educational uplift of women was loathed by many, and her concern for the need to address societal issues at large became debatable, though not many were able to openly contest her cause.

For many like her, Telli is caught in the continuous struggle of attaining an identity at two levels—the level of community, considering the political developments occurring in the struggle for identity by the tea tribes, and also at the individual level as a woman. Her political trajectory is reflective of her intense struggle for marking a space for herself in a site of power contestation dominated by male members of society. The last state assembly election was a major cause of disappointment for her when the Congress party refused to give her a ticket to contest the elections, thus stagnating her political career. This does not obliterate the fact that women like her, after proving their merit, challenge the patriarchal nature of politics. At the same time, it can in no way be concluded from such cases that essentialist understandings of male/female and powerful/powerless posited against each other can effectively provide the explanation for this outcome. Rather, it shows the rigid categorization in which the question of women's empowerment gets entrapped, and the need to transcend these binaries.

CONCLUSION

The questions which repeatedly arise are: Why do women need to prove themselves as capable as men? Even after succeeding in doing so, why do women remain a challenge to historically constructed social relations and gender hierarchies? The essentialist understanding of categories of both 'woman' and 'empowerment' has also led to the enactment of gendered differences, more emphatically where the women political actors are under continuous pressure to prove their merit by acting as male in the public arena.

One is often left to question whether women's empowerment, especially in a neo-liberal market economy, would ever be possible without enhancing women's intra-household bargaining capacity and access to financial resources, and without altering the gendered nature of society. The state essentially follows the demarcation of the public and the private spheres and finds it increasingly difficult to encroach upon the private sphere, which is often defined by relations of patriarchy, power and domination. Although the state is attempting to progressively open up the public/political sphere for women to compete in, ironically, it has failed to create space for women to challenge the patriarchal nature of the political sphere itself. The promise of empowerment has its own conception of 'public', where the changes are expected or intended to take place. The state, under the present regime, evolved as instrumental for good governance and policies, paving the way for active devolution of power to the grass roots. However, the inherent power discourse could not always be sufficiently stirred for the benefit of women. Further, neo-liberal ideology creates a marginalization effect at the intersection of power, caste and gender, which in turn adversely affects women. The promise of empowerment made by neo-liberal strategies does not aim at altering the power relations of society in favour of women, but rather makes it worse. The PRIs only recapitulate this dilemma.

NOTES

* The author would like to thank Professor Bhupen Sarmah for his critical comments on various drafts of this paper.

1. Data on women in national parliaments, 2014, http://www.ipu.org/wmn-e/world.htm (accessed on 3 November 2015).
2. 'State-Wise Number of Elected Representatives in Panchayats, 2013',https://www.google.co.in/url?sa=t&rct=j&q=&esrc=s&source=web&cd=1&cad=rja&uact=8&ved=0ahUKEwi-3bmA-9zQAhWBQo8KHa8hBnUQFggbMAA&url=http%3A%2F%2Frural.nic.in%2Fsites%2Fdownloads%2FIRDR%2F10.%2520Panchayati%2520Raj%2520Institution%2520PRI.xls&usg=AFQjCNHTopyPsINeODetDqfCDGflsy53Vw&sig2=b2yHKWswrIvkecFoVv9LmA (accessed on 3 November 2015).
3. The term 'tea tribes' denotes workers of the tea plantation who are descendents of different communities and tribes that migrated to Assam as labourers mainly during the colonial period. Many of them are recognized as Scheduled Tribes (ST) in their respective places of origin by the Government of India. However, in Assam they are not recognized as STs and are therefore fighting for ST status.

4. Personal interview conducted in July 2014 in Dibrugarh.
5. Names of all the respondents have been changed throughout this chapter. These interviews were conducted in the Zilla Panchayat and Gaon Panchayat offices in Sontipur district, and along with the target respondent, other women and many men also took part in the discussion.

REFERENCES

Baviskar, B.S. and George Mathew. eds. 2009. *Inclusion and Exclusion in Local Governance: Field Studies from Rural India*, Institute of Social Sciences. New Delhi: Sage Publications.

Brara, N. Vijaylakshmi. 2009. 'Brushed under the Carpet: Inclusion and Exclusion in Manipur', in B.S. Baviskar and George Mathew (eds), *Inclusion and Exclusion in Local Governance: Field Studies from Rural India*, Institute of Social Sciences. New Delhi: Sage Publications.

Buch, Nirmala. 2000. 'Women's Experience in New Panchayats: The Emerging Leadership of Rural Women', Occasional Paper No. 35, Centre for Women's Development Studies, New Delhi.

Chatterjee, Partha. 1989. 'Colonialism, Nationalism, and Colonialized Women: The Contest in India', *American Ethnologist*, 16(4): 622–33.

Chattopadhyay, Raghabendra and Esther Duflo. 2004. 'Impact of Reservation in Panchayati Raj: Evidence from a Nationwide Randomised Experiment', *Economic and Political Weekly*, 39(9): 979–86.

Committee on Empowerment of Women (CEW). 2010. *Empowerment of Women Through Panchayati Raj Institutions*, Third Report, Fifteenth Lok Sabha. New Delhi: Lok Sabha Secretariat.

Deka, Arunima. 2013. 'The Politics of Reproductive Health in Assam. A Study of Kamrup and Goalpara Districts'. Unpublished Ph.D. thesis, Centre for Political Studies, Jawaharlal Nehru University, New Delhi.

Dutta Hazarika, Sujata. 2005. *Examining Autonomy. The 73rd Constitutional Amendment in Assam*. Kolkata: Mahanirban Calcutta Research Group.

Economic and Political Weekly (EPW). 2002. 'Assam Panchayat Elections Finally', Editorial, *Economic and Political Weekly*, 37(02): 87.

Government of India. 1974. *Towards Equality: Report of the Committee on the Status of Women in India*. 1974. Ministry of Education and Social Welfare, Department of Social Welfare, New Delhi, December.

Jenkins, Laura Dudley. 2003. *Identity and Identification in India. Defining the Disadvantaged*. London: Routledge.

Kaul, Shashi and Shradha Sahni. 2009. 'Study on the Participation of Women in Panchayati Raj Institution', *Studies on Home Community Sciences*, 3(1): 29–38.

Mathew, George. 2003. 'Panchayati Raj Institutions and Human Rights in India', *Economic and Political Weekly*, 38(2): 155–62.

Nanivadekar, Medha. 1998. 'Reservation for Women: Challenge of Tackling Counter-productive Trends', *Economic and Political Weekly*, 33(28): 1815–19.

Pal, Mahi. 1998. 'Woman in Panchayat: Experiences of a Training Camp', *Economic and Political Weekly*, 33(4): 150–52.

Rai, Shirin M. 2002. 'Political Representation, Democratic Institutions and Women's Empowerment: The Quota Debate in India', in Jane L Parpart, Shirin M. Rai and Kathleen Staudt (eds), *Rethinking Empowerment. Gender and Development in a Global/Local World*. New York: Routledge, pp. 133–46.

———. 2007. 'Deliberative Democracy and the Politics of Redistribution: The Case of the Indian Panchayats', *Hypatia*, 22(4): 64–80.

Sarmah, Bhupen. 2006. *Rejuvenating Panchayati Raj: Ideology, the Indian State and Lessons from the Periphery*. New Delhi: Akansha Publishing House.

Scott, Joan W. 1986. 'Gender: A Useful Category of Historical Analysis', *The American Historical Review*, 91(5): 1053–75.

State Institute of Rural Development (SIRD). 2005. *A Brief Profile on Panchayati Raj in Assam*. Guwahati: SIRD.

Vyasulu, Poornima and Vinod Vyasulu. 1999. 'Women in Panchayati Raj: Grass Roots Democracy in Malgudi', *Economic and Political Weekly*, 34(52): 3677–86.

CHAPTER 3

Contested Space of Democracy in Assam: Women's Agency for Change

Dolly Phukon

The trajectories of Indian democracy are shaped by both elite politics and broad-based popular movements such as identity and ethnic movements, peasant movements, anti-development movements, ecological movements and women's movements, all with their own unique demands, ideas and aspirations. The broader Indian path towards democratization can be traced back to the movement for independence. Within the discourse on democracy and political agency, the contributions of women for social change and democratization should not be overlooked. Colonial modernity, which arose through the integration of the Indian state into capitalism associated with intensive agriculture, international commerce and manufacturing industries, no doubt also contributed towards creating space for women in the public sphere. During the colonial regime in India, gender emerged as the central issue associated with the social reform movement (Sen 2000). In the 19th century, when the East India Company enacted legislation regarding sati and widow remarriage (1829 and 1856), they used the position of women as a marker of societal progress made under their rule (ibid.). Paradoxically, it was also colonial influence that brought colonial consciousness to India, which later became the force behind the Indian national freedom movement. During that time there were numerous debates on women's education, property rights, the legal age for marriage and the duties of a wife, which brought about many changes in the outlook of women, both in India and in Assam (Phukon 2014). Within this context, this study analyses the journeys of the women of Assam towards agency for political change. This is done by investigating women's contributions to social and political change both pre- and post-Independence, covering women's contributions as social activists, freedom fighters, peacemakers, writers, and even armed combatants.

WOMEN'S MOVEMENTS IN ASSAM: THE PRE-INDEPENDENCE ERA

As in other parts of colonial India, British rule in Assam was justified (among other reasons) by the need to address women's issues. The British thus introduced reforms banning child marriage, the practice of sati (burning of the Hindu widow on the funeral pyre), and the need to establish schools for girls (Deka 2013). The reform movement in Assam was started by people like Gunabhiram Barua and Hemchandra Barua, who were inspired by the reformist ideas of Raja Ram Mohan Roy and fought for widows' right to remarriage. Some of them set examples by marrying widows or by giving their widowed daughters in marriage (Barooah 1993).

Influenced by progressive ideas during formal education, some educated Assamese women (mainly the upper-caste elites) started to form organizations known as Mahila Samiti (Women's Association) to promote women's welfare and fight against the prevalent customs that hampered women. Through the efforts of Debiprava Bhuyan and her daughter, Hemaprava Das, a Mahila Samiti was formed in 1915 in Dibrugarh, and under the aegis of Khagendrapriya Baruani another Mahila Samiti was formed in

Nagaon in 1917. Similarly, Chandraprava Saikiani formed a Mahila Samiti in Tezpur in 1919 (ibid.). Notably, the founding women belonged to the elite classes. The objectives of their organizations were primarily to teach skills such as weaving, cooking and other domestic work.

As the women's organizations spread in Assam, they included women who were actively becoming involved in the national freedom movement (Guha Ghosal 2005). Again, these women generally belonged to upper-caste and elite families. Among the dedicated women during the freedom movement were Pushpalata Das, Rajabala Baruah, Kanaklata Barua and Nalini Bala Devi (Phukon 2014). The name of the firebrand feminist and freedom fighter Chandraprava Saikiani is worth special mention. In the year 1925, a meeting of the Assam Sahitya Sabha (Assam Literary Organisation) was held in Nagaon, and she was invited to attend. During the session, she noted that the female audience was kept segregated on one side with bamboo curtains. As soon as she was given the chance to speak, instead of confining herself to Assamese language or literature, she spoke about the plight of women in society, and how they were not allowed to enjoy an equally dignified position compared to the men. She urged the women gathered in the meeting to break the curtains, destroy all barriers and sit with the people as equals. Her plea was so forceful that it instigated the women to break the barriers and throw them away. The day after the incident, the women who came to attend the meeting gathered with Chandraprava Saikiani and decided to form an organization under the All India Women's Association (ibid.). Chandraprava Saikiani, Hemaprava Das, Amalprava Das and Punyaprava Das hence joined hands with women from elite families, such as the Chaliha family from Sibsagar and the Agarwal family of Tezpur, to fight for the interests of women through the formation of women's organizations.

In order to boost the women's movement in Assam, Chandraprava Saikiani and her co-workers took the lead in the formation of a provincial women's organization in Assam, called the Assam Pradeshik Mahila Samiti (APMS). The APMS was formed in 1926, with branches across Assam, and it fought relentlessly to end the social injustices perpetrated against women. The APMS maintained a close relationship with the Congress party. Its leaders were inspired by the emotional call of Mahatma Gandhi, in which women were encouraged to join the national struggle. Although the APMS was initially concerned with issues like child marriage and widow remarriage, they also worked with reformatory and welfare work such as the promotion of girl's education. Gradually, they joined the national movement, playing an active role in boycotting foreign goods and promoting the use of handwoven khadi cloth.

According to historical accounts, the women of Assam are known for their economic potential as weavers, providing support to the family and the state in both precolonial and colonial Assam. In the Swadeshi movement, under the leadership of Mahatma Gandhi, women like Nalini Bala Devi and Mrinalini Devi undertook the task of weaving 500 khadi caps for the volunteers, which brought in huge appreciation for the weaving skills of the women of Assam from Gandhi, Rajendra Prasad and Subhas Chandra Bose (Deka 2013).

During their close involvement with the national freedom struggle, the women's movement in Assam diverted its attention towards supporting the development of an Indian national identity. In the process, they incorporated female figures from Hindu mythology, such as Sita, Savitri and Lakshmibai, into their ideals, aligning the movement with the central Hindu themes of womanhood.[1] Assamese women came out in hundreds and thousands to participate in satyagraha and various programmes of the Indian freedom movement. They took out processions, performed *Prabhat Pheris* ('welcoming of the new dawn'), destroyed liquor dens, boycotted foreign-made cloth and British-run educational institutions, and took part in other activities of the Quit India Movement, some even as members of the extremist wing Mrityu Bahini (NEN 2005).

Many women lost their lives, and many were jailed during the freedom movement of 1921–47 (Pathak 2008). Unfortunately, the contribution of the women of Assam towards the Indian freedom movement is little known and their sacrifice and valour have not been given due recognition (NEN 2005). Many women were killed while involved in active resistance, but few were declared martyrs. Within this context, the life and sacrifice of Dariki Dasi Baruah of Sivasagar is worth mentioning On 26 April 1932, a pregnant women's leader named Dariki Dasi Baruah died in Sivasagar Jail after her arrest during picketing on 1 February 1932. Even though she was pregnant, she was given six months of corporal punishment. Later, she suffered from dysentery, miscarried and finally died. During her stay in jail, even though the jail authorities tried to lure her into gaining her freedom by disclosing the secrets of her fellow demonstrators, she did not speak a word (Sharma 1988). Today, such examples are preserved only in the oral histories of the freedom fighters.

The history of the female freedom fighters in Assam remains unrecognized and almost lost. No magazines or newspapers have tried to focus on the exemplary contributions and stories of the women activists of Assam (ibid.). Thus it could be concluded that the early women's movement in Assam was intertwined and submerged under the pressure of the Indian national movement for independence. At the same time, it cannot be denied that women leaders of the independence movement in Assam created a space for women's agency towards change. This trend is highlighted in the work of women writers of Assam, published, among others, in the Assam Mahila Samiti magazine *Abhijatri* (first known as *Abhijan*), edited by Chandraprava Saikiani (Sharma 2005). In the writings of this period, authors such as Padmavati Devi, Ajali Tora Neog, Chandraprabha Saikiani and Nalini Bala Devi questioned patriarchy as well as colonial exploitation, highlighting social problems and gender relations, women's questions on education, widow remarriage, self-reliance, and women's political awareness (or awakening).

WOMEN'S AGENCY FOR CHANGE POST-INDEPENDENCE

Although the role of women in the national liberation struggle gave rise to organizations that articulated women's issues, post-Independence they lost momentum. Independent India and Assam witnessed a number of social movements starting from the communist movements, subnational movement, movements for ethnic assertion, armed combatants' movement demanding an independent Assam, and tribal statehood movements where women took part in different capacities, as supporters of militancy, peacebuilders and activists.

After Independence, women took active part in the communist movement during 1948–64 and the Indo-China War in 1962. Starting in the 1970s, there was a revival of the women's movement in Assam. This came in the wake of the report of the Committee on the Status of Women in India, *Towards Equality*, first published in 1974 (Guha, 1974). The report gave rise to a reconceptualization of the prevalent discourse on issues of gender and economic well-being, political participation, law, health and family welfare. Women's literary organizations were formed, which encouraged women writers of Assam including Nalini Bala Debi, Chandraprabha Saikia, Nirupama Borgohain, Mamoni Raisom Goswami and Hiranmayi Devi to initiate a feminist debate and consciousness through their literary works. Many of their writings questioned how women across class could secure their space as agents of social change. They further recorded the accounts of women's experiences, both the subjugated and oppressed women and upper-caste women, trying to unveil the shackles of patriarchal gender relations in the process of modernization, problems of widows, women labourers, and gender dilemmas between tradition and modernity. They often focused on situations where women characters revolt against patriarchy and play a proactive role in social transformation.

Within this context, it is necessary to recognize the role of the Assam Lekhika Samarooh (Assam Women Writers' Festival) in publicizing women's writings and encouraging women writers to write about women's issues. Associated with this, a group of women writers from Tezpur openly criticized the state's leading literary and cultural organization, the Assam Sahitya Sabha, for neglecting women writers. Consequently, the Assam Lekhika Parishad (Assam Women Writers' Organisation) was formed which later on fragmented into the Assam Lekhika Samaroh Samiti (Assam Women Writers' Block) and Assam Lekhika Santha (Assam Women Writers' Association). Another important quarterly magazine was *Ardha Akash* (Half the Sky), published by Nari Mukti Sanstha (Freedom for Women Group) formed in 1979, which mainly focused on atrocities against women. This magazine was dedicated to the development of the women's movement in Assam, with a special emphasis on its intellectual foundation. The development and publication of *Ardha Akash* was also a reflection of the conscious development of the feminist movement in Assam. The interdependence of the magazine and the movement was expected to lead towards a healthy growth of a gender-sensitized society. *Ardha Akash* provided a platform for discussing the important issues taken up by the women's movement in Assam. The magazine dealt with issues like women and law, the status of women in society, women and health, motherhood and childcare, atrocities against women, and the key debates in the women's movement. Another journal, *Aideu Jonaki Baat* (Moonlit Path) was published by the Working Women's Association of Dibrugarh. It tried to represent women's interests by presenting, besides the reports of women's activities, articles on problems relating to women artists and social workers, and poems and stories dealing with themes relevant to women, authored by both male and female writers.

WOMEN'S PARTICIPATION IN THE ASSAM MOVEMENT

The Assam Movement started as a protest directed against undocumented immigration and economic exploitation of the resources of Assam by the Indian central government. The agitation ended in August 1985, with the signing of the Assam Accord with the centre. Its leaders went on to form the Asom Gana Parishad (AGP) to engage in electoral politics. During the Assam Movement, women's organizations like the Sadou Assam Nari Sanstha, Mula Gabharu Sanstha, Assam Jagrat Mahila Parishad protested against cases of rape and domestic violence. These groups were closely affiliated with the All Assam Students' Union (AASU) and the Assam Movement. For instance, these organizations staged protests against the rape of rural women in Kamrup district by the Indian Army, and took up the Bhumuka rape case in Kokrajhar in Assam, where soldiers of the Indian Army raped an Adivasi woman in a forest village of Bodoland. In order to raise consciousness among the general masses of women, these women's organizations started publishing magazines for women, providing a platform for women to raise their demands and discuss their problems (Mahanta 1988).

Although the women of Assam had participated in both the Indian independence movement and in the Assam Movement in the post-Independence period, this was not out of concern for women's issues or a feminist agenda. The sexist attitude of the Assam Movement leaders was perceptible when they imposed dress codes in the colleges of Assam and made it compulsory for female students and teachers to wear the *makhela chaddar*, the traditional attire of the Assamese community. The contribution of women students within the AASU agitation was largely ignored, despite the fact that in many instances women formed 'human shields' between the agitating students and the armed forces (Phukon 2014). Moreover, organizations like Nari Mukti Sanstha, affiliated to the Communist Party of India (Marxist-Leninist) Liberation or CPI(ML), took up several cases of rape and murders of peasant women by landlords, creating a strong impact through the media (Mahanta 1988). Nevertheless, as affiliates of CPI(ML) their focus was on class struggle rather than women's issues. Party affiliations thus made it difficult for women to create a feminist forum or platform of knowledge to develop broader visions of root causes of gender inequality.

Women's cells or small women's groups were formed during the Assam Movement to mobilize women, who in turn helped the leaders of the movement with their outreach into rural areas. Further, these cells or groups tried to motivate rural women to join the movement. However, these women's cells were not free from gender bias, as they had little or no autonomy to raise questions concerning women's issues. When the Assam Movement came to an end after the signing of the Assam Accord in 1985, this paved a way for the leaders of the agitation to form a regional political party, the AGP. Later, when the AGP came into power, it nominated only two women as its candidates for state elections. Women activists were persuaded to join the women's wing of the AGP under the banner of the Assam Mahila Pradesh, but this wing remained subservient to the affiliated political party ideology, and did not take up issues related to women's dignity and entitlement as equal human beings. Women leaders and activists of the movement faced an identity crisis after the end of the movement, when they were again relegated to the private sphere. Women who felt a sense of liberation after breaking the patriarchal glass ceiling were confronted with their dual identity, that is, of woman leader and passive feminine wife, sister, daughter and/or mother. The contribution of women students within the AASU agitation was belittled and marginalized.

The Assam Movement had a disastrous effect on the emergence of an Assamese women's movement, as pan-Assamese nationalism also suppressed other minority movements including those of the different tribal or ethnic groups such as the Bodo, Karbi, Mishing, Tiwa, and the tea-garden community of Assam. Members of these groups were also forced to wear the traditional makhela chaddar during the Assam Movement, while the language, culture and customs of these communities were overpowered by Assamese mainstream meta-narratives. With the rising consciousness of ethnic identity and its preservation, each ethnic community of Assam tried to consolidate itself by forming sociopolitical organizations for demanding more autonomy, political, economic and cultural rights, and autonomous councils (Barua 2002). Along with these organizations, women's wings were also constituted to voice their demands—for example, Karbi Pragatisheel Nari Sanstha, Bodo Women's Justice Forum, All Assam Tribal Women's Welfare Federation, and Tai-Ahom Mahila Sangha. However, these lacked gender consciousness in their vision and were used basically as mobilizing agencies to reach out to remote areas and recruit women for the tribal cause.

In all movements for assertion of identities, women and their bodies were basically regarded as objects of honour and as performers of the traditions of the community. Women's common perspectives were thereby fragmented along ethnic intersections. The participation of women in subnational and ethnic assertions exposed them to public patriarchy, but the organizational capability of women as peacemakers or political actors remained under the banner of the political party. Nevertheless, participation in student unions and other organizations certainly boosted the women of Assam to defy certain patriarchal stereotypes.

In Assam, women's movements retained a sporadic and issue-based character. In both pre-independence and post-independence struggles, women were inspired by a sense of nationalism. However, when the movement ended they were again pushed back to their traditional sphere. Their participation was never recognized, nor was the space that was created for women in institutionalized politics. Rather, the myth was perpetuated that women were not interested in politics. The contributions of women went unreported, and their space in the movements was limited to that of mere victims in reports on the conflict situation (Phukon 2008). Meanwhile, women's quest for agency led some to join the insurgency movement called the United Liberation Front of Assam (ULFA).

Studies conducted by Paula Banerjee, Rakhee Kalita Moral (Banerjee 2001; Moral 2014) and the North East Network (NEN) highlight the gendered implications of armed conflict and also the prevalence of patriarchal practices in ULFA organizational networks. The case of the ULFA women as described in the book *Women, War and Peace in South Asia* (Banerjee 2001) clearly depicts gendered experiences within militancy. In an interview conducted by Paula Banerjee with female ULFA members in Sivasagar district, one of the respondents spoke of her tough life during training in the jungle and in camps in Bangladesh and Bhutan. According to her, men and women were given the same training, but women were rarely allowed to handle arms, and were assigned only a supporting role as informers and helpers in the transportation of arms from one place to another (ibid.).

In an interview that I conducted with imprisoned ULFA women, two of my respondents revealed that women were given special training in tailoring, weaving and medical aid, apart from weapons training. They were rarely assigned to participate in armed encounters, but were rather asked to transfer arms. Interestingly, they were not aware of being excluded from active participation as they felt that remaining sidelined would keep them safe from the police. However, the same exclusion would later obstruct them from attaining recognition and acquiring rehabilitation and post-conflict reconstruction facilities, which would have been important to the long-term struggle against societal taboos regarding women's military participation.

The interventions of women during conflict are varied. Women's organizations like the All Assam Progressive Women's Association and Kasturba Trust have protested against the violence committed by the army during counter-insurgency operations. Peace initiatives from women's groups like Matri Manch, Sajagota Samitis and Bodo Women's Justice Forum (BWJF) are of utmost importance. If we go back to the Assam Movement, there was a mass participation of women, such as in picketing and strikes, which contributed greatly to its success.

From this we can ascertain that patriarchy has manufactured consent from women that they are apolitical, in their individual struggles and in organizational efforts. Women have internalized the ideas generated by men that the domain of politics, where major decisions are taken, is exclusively for men and that women should concentrate on 'softer' issues. Male-dominated organizations have emphasized the role of women as mothers, wives, daughters and homemakers as sacrosanct and tradition-bound, suggesting that their participation in the world outside the home should be an extension of their primary role within it. Their political agency thus becomes marginalized.

WOMEN'S INTERVENTIONS FOR PEACE

Women of Assam have at times intervened for peace. Professor Mamoni Raisom Goswami, noted writer, scholar and Jnanpith Award winner, deserves credit for her role in helping ULFA leaders negotiate peace with the Indian government. ULFA gained notoriety as one of the most powerful militant groups in northeast India. Since 1979 it has been fighting for a separate Assamese homeland. During the last two decades, thousands of people have died due to the violent struggle. In order to suppress this outfit, the Government of India deployed armed forces in Assam and carried out massive armed operations, such as Operation Rhino and Operation Bajrang, leading to serious human rights violations. In the past, the Indian government has tried to persuade ULFA to sit down for talks, but there was reluctance to respond positively due to lack of confidence in the government. Through the initiatives of Prof. Mamoni Goswami, a peace process between the government and ULFA was initiated in the year 2004.

Prof. Goswami's efforts were unique in various ways. First, she was not a politician or civil servant but a renowned creative writer of national and international fame. Secondly, she happened to be an ex-colleague from Delhi University of then Prime Minister Prof. Manmohan Singh, who was also the Rajya Sabha Member of Parliament (MP) from Assam. It should also be noted that Prof. Goswami had personal experiences that equipped her with a greater ability to understand the pain and suffering of others. Her psychological orientation was tuned to the outcome of insurgency on society, and she was able to relate to the pain of upper-caste widows as well as working class women. As a harbinger of these experiences, Prof. Goswami expressed her own sorrow and joy through her creative writing, while keeping a focus on societal problems, making her very popular among readers. After many failed attempts to start peace negotiations since 1991, Prof. Goswami became known for breaking the ice between ULFA and the government in 2004.

Prof. Goswami's peace appeal was the outcome of her concern for the people of Assam who were suffering due to political violence between counter-insurgency forces and insurgents. The idea of writing about the suffering of the people of Assam came to her while she was working on the novel *Tej Aru Dhurile Dhusarita Prista* (Pages of Blood and Dust) in which she recounted the anti-Sikh riots of 1984 and the subsequent assassination of Indira Gandhi. With the aim of writing a novel on Assam, she set to work collecting first-hand data. Travelling in upper Assam and the interior villages of lower Assam, she met ULFA cadres in various meetings, interacted with local people in villages and transit camps, and was greatly touched by their stories. Prof. Goswami was so affected by these meetings that she was unable to write her book; instead, the humanist within her urged her to promote a dialogue for peace (Mishra 2011). Prof. Goswami was finally able to initiate a peace process in 2004, after receiving a positive signal from the then prime minister. ULFA first rejected the proposition from the Prime Minister's Office (PMO), but after some persuasion from Prof. Goswami, ULFA leaders sent Prof. Goswami a draft justifying the need to discuss the issue of sovereignty, which she conveyed to the government. She appealed to the government to deal with the problem by undertaking a humanist approach, asking the government to find out why the 'boys with guns in their hands' took the path of violence. Moreover, Prof. Goswami mounted pressure on New Delhi to control troops engaged in counter-insurgency operations against ULFA in view of the peace initiative, so as to create a congenial atmosphere to bring the rebels to the negotiating table. She also spoke on the role of civil society and stressed the need for extensive study of the problems in order to formulate a holistic plan for an amicable settlement. Due to her conscientious and untiring efforts, ULFA agreed to form a People's Consultative Group (PCG) with nine members, in addition to Prof. Goswami as its chief coordinator and Reboti Phukon as its coordinator. PCG was engaged in discussions with the central government, but peace talks held in October 2005, February 2006 and June 2006 failed as both the government and ULFA resorted to widespread violence and extortion drives (Mahanta 2013). Finally, ULFA and the government went into a temporary suspension of violence in August 2006. After the failure of the PCG's approach under Prof. Goswami's leadership, she continued her efforts on an individual basis, eventually becoming a stakeholder of the Sanmilita Jatiya Abhivartan (SJA) under the leadership of Prof. Hiren Gohain. Her initiative to edit the jailed ULFA militant Megan Kachari's poems built much trust with the insurgents. The resulting book, *Melodies and Guns*, is a composition based on the author's bygone days in the jungle, expressing a mixture of joy and sorrow, belief and distrust, and thoughts about loss and gain. The untimely demise of Prof. Goswami halted an important peace initiative backed by morality, ethics and good intentions rather than political motives.

Besides Prof. Goswami's peace initiative, there were certain sporadic peace processes initiated by women's groups such as Matri Manch, Sajagota Samitis, Mahila Shanti Sena and Bodo Women's Justice Forum. Matri Manch was formed by mothers whose sons had joined an insurgency outfit or were killed during encounters with police and military. Later on, many women who were not mothers were also motivated to join the movement. Matri Manch took up the issue of abuse of women and violence against women by both state agents and insurgents. In effect, this group never got the support of either the state or the insurgent groups, but was threatened to withdraw from active campaigns for peace. Due to the pressure, they were either marginalized or became targets of attack. The Sajagota Mahila Samiti often remains in a dormant state until an incident takes place, so they are less politically visible. However, whenever violence against women takes place, such as rape or police raids, members of the Samiti immediately organize, lead protest marches and agitate for human rights.

The MSS was formed in Bihar by a self-declared Gandhian, Acharya Ramamurti, who heads a non-profit organization in Bihar. Ramamurti has trained rural women in leadership skills, conflict resolution and prevention, and called these groups of women Mahila Shanti Sena or MSS. The women of the MSS deal with issues ranging from everyday village disputes to peaceful resolution of insurgency problems. Today, the MSS has trained over 50,000 women in Bihar and the northeastern states of Assam, Arunachal Pradesh, Manipur and Tripura. MSS volunteers have also been engaged in constructive work such as educating women, solving disputes related to family issues, land and water issues, and fighting social ills like alcoholism and gambling (Phukon 2009). During the days of inter-ethnic violence in Assam, MSS leaders displayed courage and determined leadership. They took out peace marches and kept a constant vigil around their communities and neighbourhoods. These women also used the MSS forum to negotiate for 'peace action'. They made efforts to 'transform' conflicts through viable income generating activities and livelihood opportunities (Banerjee 2008).

Another female-led peace group is the BWJF. This group concerns itself with issues of peace and human rights and took active part in initiating a Bodo dialogue on peace. Golapi Basumatary, the founder-secretary of the organization initiated and acted in negotiating peace through dialogue, but unknown assassins gunned her down and thus ended the initiative. The Forum continues to address the plight of the Bodo people in general and women in particular. In an address delivered by Anjali Daimari, president of the Forum, at the 6th Session of the United Nations Permanent Forum on Indigenous Issues in 2007, she opined that to protect the interests of the Bodos a mechanism should be developed to recover the alienated lands of the Bodo people from the clutches of the non-indigenous people in Assam and to restore the tribal belts and blocks created for safeguarding the indigenous Bodos and other tribal people (Phukon 2009). Daimari further stated that the Government of India should demonstrate sincerity and commitment to the ongoing peace process among various indigenous revolutionary groups by repealing the draconian Armed Forces (Special Powers) Act (AFSPA). She lamented that during anti-insurgency operations, security forces perpetrate violence against women.

CONCLUDING REMARKS

Women's movements in Assam are divided, having emerged out of a range of very different issues and interests such as nationalism, tribal identity politics, survival and ecological concerns, struggles against the state, and ethnic conflicts. Many women's organizations in Assam work as affiliates or under directives of political parties and government agendas, some even connected with insurgent movements. This offers little autonomous space and independent decision-making capacity.

Women have participated immensely in democratic movements, but still lack agency. They have played an active role in a range of political movements and also in insurgent outfits. However, leadership positions have remained out of bounds. Women cadres in ULFA were efficient emissaries connecting village to village, and communities to camps, helping to spread the outfit's mission more successfully than men, especially when the men were pushed further into the jungles and remained under constant surveillance (Moral, 2013). Thus, women's participation often emerged at a time of crisis, and when the crisis ended, women's activism, too, subsided. Moreover, female activist leaders are often seen to be absorbed into the state apparatus or in non-governmental organizations (NGOs) for greater networking between the state and grass-roots women's groups like the Mahila Samiti. It appears that post-colonial movements in Assam are based on exclusionist ideologies of ethnicity and nationality, which totally ignore pluralism and the rights of the 'other', and where women are also victimized.

Culture, tradition and religion can be powerful tools for organizing social movements, but they are also sources of disunity that have made it difficult for a united women's movement to emerge in Assam, despite women's networking across inter-group divides. For example, in the tea community, domestic violence and polygamy is regarded as an everyday affair, which leads to the naturalization of violence. Organizations in which many women are active are mainly social and woman-specific in nature. The struggle for women's rights is sometimes seen as exclusive and myopic, or less sensitive to the difficulties of tribal and minority women when (or if) they demand rights on their own behalf.

Women's movements rarely demand an end to gendered injustices in all domains of life, but are seen to be questioning narrow issues that are mere offshoots of structural inequalities. Further, women are deprived of recognition of their contributions to nationalist and ethnic identity-based and progressive movements for democratization in which women are used by the various affiliations. Scholars working on the status of Indian women consider women in the northeastern region to be more mobile and empowered than women in other parts of the country. This stereotype is internalized by women in the Northeast under the constructed imaginary of themselves as 'empowered' and 'having freedom of mobility' in contrast to the status of women in other parts of India. This has actually demotivated the 'empowered' women to launch a movement for the sake of their empowerment.

Although women's activism has had little impact on women's subordination in family and society, it has surely helped women defy certain patriarchal stereotypes by extending their activities beyond the domestic sphere. During the course of their activism they have obtained greater awareness of gender-based violence, which was addressed in the Indian freedom movement, the communist movement, the Assam Movement, and various ethnic movements in Assam. This can also be observed in women's activism for peace, which has provided useful learning experiences that have helped women towards greater political participation as well. Prominent in women's activism for peace is that it has initiated a new and different course for women's agency for change. Finally, a new feminist consciousness among women writers is challenging patriarchy in Assam, which is another encouraging sign of renewed women's agency for change.

NOTES

1. Sita, wife of Lord Rama (Hindu god and prince of Ayodhya), is one of the principal female figures in the Ramayana, regarded as the most esteemed example of Hindu womanly elegance and wifely virtue. After being abducted by Ravana, the king of Lanka, and rescued by her husband, she performs *agni-pariksha* (a test of fire) to prove her chastity and loyalty towards her husband.

   Savitri is a character in the epic Mahabharata. She is the wife of Satyavana. After his death, Satyavana was brought back to life by Savitri, after she pleased Yama (the god of death) with her illuminating speech on dharma, friendship, and just rule. Hindu married women need to fast in the name of Savitri for the well-being and long life of their husbands.

   Lakhsmibai or Rani (queen) of Jhansi was a leading figure in the Indian rebellion of 1857. For Indian nationalists she is a symbol of resistance to the rule of the British East India Company.

REFERENCES

Ardha Akash (Assamese Quarterly). 1985. April–June issue.

———. 1986. October–December issue.

Banerjee, Monica. 2008. 'Locating Civil Society in India's Northeast'. Paper presented at INTRAC Civil Society Conference, 3–5 December, The Netherlands.

Banerjee, Paula. 2001. 'Two Armed Patriarchies: Women in Assam and Nagaland', in Rita Manchanda (ed.), *Women, War and Peace in South Asia: Beyond Victimhood to Agency*, pp 111–12. New Delhi: Sage Publications.

Barooah, Jeuti. 1993. *Single Women in Assamese Hindu Society*. New Delhi: Gyan Publication.

Barua, Raju. 2002. 'Emergence of Women's Organization in Assam and their Progress', in Sivanath Barman et al. (eds), *Asomiya Nari: Otijya Aru Uttaran*, pp. 160–65. Guwahati: Student's Stores.

Deka, Meeta. 2013. *Women's Agency and Social Change: Assam and Beyond*. New Delhi: Sage Publications.

Guha Ghosal, Sarbani. 2005. 'Major Trends of Feminism in India', *The Indian Journal of Political Science*, 66(4): 25.

Guha, Phulrenu.1974. *Towards Equality: Report of the Committee on the Status of Women in India*. New Delhi: Department of Social Welfare, Ministry of Education and Social Welfare, Government of India.

Mahanta, Aparna. 1988. 'Emergence of New Women's Groups in Assam', in Neera Desai (ed.), *A Decade of Women's Movement in India*, p. 132. New Delhi: Himalaya Publication.

———. 1998. 'Women's Movement in Assam and Northeast India: An Assessment', in Narain Karna Mahendra (ed.), *Social Movements in Northeast India*, pp. 45–47. New Delhi: Indus Publishing Company.

Mahanta, Nani. 2013. *Confronting the State: ULFA's Quest for Sovereignty*. New Delhi: Sage Publications.

Mishra, Tilottoma. 2011. 'Indira Goswami: Brave, Gentle and Bold', *Economic and Political Weekly*, 46(53): 30–31.

Moral, Rakhee Kalita. 2013. *Living and Partly Living: Notions of Freedom, Politics Violence and the Women of ULFA*. New Delhi: Nehru Memorial Museum & Library.

———. 2014. 'The Woman Rebel and the State: Making War, Making Peace in Assam', *Economic and Political Weekly*, 49: 43–44.

North East Network (NEN). 2005. *Report on Women in Armed Conflict Situations*. Delhi: North East Network.

Pathak, Guptajit. 2008. *Assamese Women in Indian Independence Movement*. New Delhi: Mittal Publication.

Phukon, Dolly. 2008. 'Women and Politics of Peace Process in Northeast India', in Achutya Panda (ed.), *Situating Indian Women*, pp. 344–46. New Delhi: Abhijeet Publications.

———. 2009. 'Insurgent Movement and Gender Implications in Assam: Understanding the Role of ULFA and the Indian State'. Paper presented at the 21st International Political Science Association World Congress, 12–16 July 2009, Santiago, Chile. http://paperroom.ipsa.org/papers/paper 765. pdf (accessed on 14 June 2013).

———. 2012. 'Insurgent Movement and Gender Implications in Assam: Understanding the Role of ULFA and the Indian State', in Daisy Bora Talukdar (ed.), *Gender, Peace and Development in Northeast India*, pp. 80–86. Guwahati: DVS Publishers.

———. 2014. *Women, Democracy and the Media: An Analysis of Current Trends in Assam*, pp, 58–59. Guwahati: DVS Publishers.

Sharma, Dipti. 1988. 'Indian Freedom Movement: Assam's Women Martyr', *Prantik*, 7(24): 16–18.

Sharma, Prasad Govinda. 2005. 'Chandraprabha Saikiani', *The Assam Tribune*, 14 August.

Sen, Samita. 2000. 'Towards a Feminist Politics? The India Women's Movement in Historical Perspectives', The World Bank Development Research, Policy Research Report on Gender and Development, Working Paper No. 9, April.

CHAPTER 4

Demobilized, Dispossessed ... Disappeared? In Search of ULFA's Female Ex-combatants

Rakhee Kalita Moral

For most women rebels of Assam's 30-year old guerrilla outfit, the United Liberation Front of Asom (ULFA), the retreat from the base camps in the jungles and far-flung border territories along Assam's international boundaries with Bhutan and Myanmar was as beleaguered as their entry into the organization.[1] While not being a huge number in the cadreship, these women rebels constituted an important aspect of the rebellion and their status and present conditions after ceasefire and during the ongoing peace negotiations remain both an embarrassment and a challenge to the outfit and the state. Unable to settle the terms on which these female combatants and cadres can disband and reintegrate into civilian society, many of them are left to their own devices to resume lives at the margins, anonymously, in reinvented roles or even sometimes to simply disappear. As several insurgencies and non-state rebellions in other parts of the world have already demonstrated, the transition from camps to community has never been easy. The progression from the time of conflict to the cessation of hostilities towards 'peace' is a tenuous one. At this critical juncture, or for want of an exact term, in the 'post-conflict' moment, who is really responsible for these women who return home after 'war'? Who do these women turn to, the disbanded and disenchanted organization they once belonged to or the state, which is often belligerent and even intolerant? I argue that measures of transitional justice for this category of conflict subjects, often at the peril of social exclusion, have not been seriously formulated or adopted. Transitional justice apparatuses are still unfamiliar and untried notions in many conflict societies in India's Northeast as well as in other troubled regions both within the country and in its South Asian neighbourhood. For violence to end and real freedom to begin, it is perhaps necessary to first understand the difficult dynamics of transition for women who have been actors in armed conflict. Yet, in what seems to counter perceived and often stereotypical notions about women in conflict, this category of females has surmounted various odds and achieved significant agency in their post-conflict lives. The present discussion looks at how women's group initiatives and sometimes even solitary interventions have transformed the lives of such combatants of ULFA while arguably leaving them in various degrees of rehabilitation and reintegration into civilian life.[2] Did the women of ULFA experience empowering/disempowering moments in their combatant life or did they actually empower themselves in their transit from rebellion? In examining this transition I reflect on available mechanisms of legal accountability and the political pragmatics of accommodating them back into social life. And in discussing these from the context of ULFA's rebel women, I also ask can transitional justice bridge the gap between the two?

In the international arena too there has been much curiosity about women's participation in armed conflict and contrary to stock ideas in the prevailing scholarship on women seen primarily through the prism of victimhood, recent works in women's security studies reveal a great amount of active roles and patterns of 'empowerment' that turn the narrative around significantly (Shepherd 2008). Where there have been conditions of protracted conflict as in the Northeast with little or no third party mediation, unlike Nepal, for example, where former Maoist women rebels have found political agency after cessation of conflict, the unique phenomenon of women's reinvention of themselves is manifest in the growth, both organized and unorganized, of informal collectives of these rebel women demanding change, better livelihoods and, more importantly, sustainable peace (Banerjee 2008).

WHY WOMEN REBEL?

The Sanjukta Mukti Bahini Asom, the original name of the outfit popularly known as ULFA, first recruited its women in the late 1980s, almost a decade after they had formed their organization of armed resistance against the state. Significantly, the recruitment and mobilization of these women traces the somewhat familiar trajectory of being 'pulled, pushed and persuaded' into armed conflict histories in the wider South Asian region, and even beyond in Central and Latin America, home to several guerrilla movements (Viterna 2006). The women of ULFA, too, typically walked to the jungles, in circumstances that were often dictated by the need to follow brothers, kinsmen or partners into the insurgent fold, to ensure their own economic freedom, counter the prevailing state oppression and also to break free of conservative patriarchies even within what has been perceived to be a relatively more egalitarian society in the country. They defied traditionally chosen gender roles and abandoned their homes to join the rural guerrilla insurgency in a wave in the 1990s, arguably transforming attitudes towards womanhood in Assamese society, subsequently shaping both strategies and outcomes in social movements in the region. I argue that this emergence of the female combatant as a critical subject provides a particularly nuanced notion of the complex relationship between revolution and women's empowerment, typically cutting across geographies and cultural spaces.

Curiously, this tendency to join what was deemed as 'masculine', militant and high-risk revolutionary activities was a trend markedly dominant in the 1970s and 1980s in Latin America too when women guerrillas in El Salvador, Guatemala and Nicaragua touched an average 30 per cent of the membership (Chinchilla 1983; Luciak 2001; Thomson 1986). More significantly, for the case of ULFA itself, this fact was also true with the Maoist women rebels of Nepal in the mid-1990s who constituted almost 40–45 per cent of the total cadres, with women becoming key protagonists of the People's War in Nepal (Lecomte-Tilouine 2013). The path was evidently not always an easy one nor was it wholly free from the vacillation and doubt that ironically marked later stages of insurgent lives for these women who had chosen to rebel. In contrast to the propositions of the famous work, *Why Men Rebel*, the women rebels clearly had more complex reasons and their entry into militancy cannot be easily disengaged from either their gender or their relationship to male insurgents (Gurr 1970).

The 1990s proved to be a decade of great change in the body politic of ULFA, particularly because women entered the outfit in significant numbers following the two counter-insurgency operations led by the state against the rebels in 1990 and 1991, namely Operation Bajrang and Operation Rhino (Nath 2013). Yet, though the first of the official surrenders of ULFA's cadres began in the wake of these state-wide massive operations, it wasn't until the mid-1990s and later years of the decade that women began to pull out. The most notable disbanding from the organization, however, happened more than a decade later when ULFA's largest debacle took place in Bhutan in 2003 under Operation All Clear at the behest of the Royal Bhutan Army, purportedly with the close alliance of the Indian Army in a cross-border move to flush out ULFA rebels and a few other insurgent groups from northeast India, all of which had sought to camp on foreign soil (Moral 2014). This indeed was the first tipping point in the uncertain lives of the rebels enacted beyond the country's boundaries, the critical time of the wrapping up of the camps along the remote borderlands of Bhutan and Myanmar, signalling the imminent return home of former combatants. I shall examine here the woman rebel's confrontation with herself and society in her act of 'demobilization', besides her encounters with the more formal contours of the state and her struggle for justice. It may be useful to also briefly dwell on what the law provides under the circumstances for reintegration and resumption of life as a 'free' civilian.[3] Demobilization is a two-sided exercise and its efficacy also determines practices that are part of cease-fire and final peace agreements. It entails obligations on the part of the state and the combatants in a mutually accommodating manner meant to be executed with extensive logistical operations (Knight 2004).

The second signpost in ULFA's long and fragile period of negotiating both peace and freedom is the ceasefire, which, in conflict parlance, is the mandatory laying down of arms and cessation of hostilities that paves the way for transition from camp life in the jungles back to the community. ULFA formally declared a ceasefire with the Government of India in 2011 and erected, thereafter, a long and halting road to a possible resolution of the conflict. It is at this juncture that the experiences of the women cadres assume critical significance for patterns of empowerment/disempowerment that are revealed as their lives turn around and beyond conflict. What transpires in the 'designated camps' during ceasefire are readjustments amongst cadres and between male and female rebels as they tread the tricky path between demobilization from armed conflict and reintegration into society. The third and final moment I choose to hinge my discussion on is the present, the ostensible moment of the political resolution of conflict, wherein justice apparatuses are imperative while peace is being brokered by the state as the former rebels (by 'rebels' I refer to the *pro-peace* talks of ULFA) sit at the negotiating table with the government, abjuring from the rebellion and strife they had set out on more than three decades ago.[4] It is worth noting that ULFA's war against the state, like most contemporary wars in the region, is intra-state and therefore also protracted with no easy solutions. Since the earliest attempt by the former chairman, Arabinda Rajkhowa, in 1991 to negotiate peace, the rebel group has had a roller coaster ride over bumpy political terrain to find lasting and pragmatic ways to peace within the provisions of the Indian Constitution.

In the absence of many of the frameworks of transitional justice and reintegration, ULFA's former women cadres have thus remained, in the aftermath of war, a disorganized band of rebels, mostly sucked back into an ethos that has kept them at the social and economic margins over a period that has been marked by several dramatic turns in the history of the outfit itself. In 2003, a big contingent of former combatants was arrested and returned to Assam from the jungles of the Indo-Bhutanese border where the camps, safe havens of ULFA, along with other insurgent groups from northeast India, namely the National Democratic Front of Bodoland (NDFB) and Kamatapur Liberation Organisation (KLO) were flushed out.[5] In this move, when a sizeable number of female cadres from the camps was taken into custody, this group constituting at least 170 ULFA cadres, including minor children, fell into the net of the Royal Bhutan Army or the RBA (Panging 2010). These women cadres, who were arrested after the army operation concluded in late December 2003, were booked under the Unlawful Acts Prevention Act and then let off, found it difficult, if not impossible, to regain their space in the homes they had left behind.

The 'return' of these women from combat and the insurgency they had joined creates a new sociology of the complex phenomenon of women without fixed identities, former combatants whose suitability in life skills or conventional vocations, or even in the simple social ambit, is liable to be often questioned and, further, whose status in social domains remains ambivalent and problematic. The categories into which these former rebels may be broadly classified are three: (a) the demobilised, (b) the officially surrendered, and (c) those who straddle the lines and are neither surrendered nor in camps. There is a fourth, more fuzzy type of 'former rebel' who is nowhere identifiable and who often blurs into anonymity, who is difficult to track because of her wish to dissociate from rebel history and who lights out to other territories away from the dreary margins of civilian life to which most of the former rebels return. I take a closer look at these female rebels whose encounters with the state and society throw up narratives of ambivalence and suggest complex and unresolved issues in the post-conflict moments.

A LEAP OVER THE WALL

Unlike most other insurgencies, ULFA's 'demobilized' women are not always surrendered, hence making that distinction important among the rebels who return. In interviews conducted with more than four dozen former cadres of the outfit from whose testimonies I draw seminal ideas about the workings of the gender hierarchies within the outfit and the inequities of the post-conflict moment, it was not difficult to see a new radicalization of feminine roles in Assamese society, something which while not comparable wholly to the 'martial feminism' of Nepal's People's Liberation Army (PLA) does uncover an instinct that is shaped by a common liberating principle (Lecomte-Tilouine 2013). Thus women who leave the outfit, whether because of counter-insurgency drives, or because the moment of conflict is past, or still because they are disenchanted and dispossessed, do not demobilize in the official sense of the term. The United Nations (UN) mandates that for real peace to begin former combatants must be given amnesty, which is a condition that is tied to the processes of disarmament, demobilization and reintegration of rebels, technically referred to as DDR. It is also implicit that for amnesties to work former combatants must be accorded a fair measure of impunity that in turn facilitates disarmament and demobilization and psychological reintegration, attended by trust and goodwill (Patel and Greiff 2009). In the case of the ULFA women, the nature of the amnesties granted is often left to speculation for not having clear and mandated stipulations or benefits that are translatable in real terms or are equally distributed. So while one former woman combatant may have actually been compensated for the loss of her home while she was in the camps, another insurgent may have never received any dole from the state and could remain a destitute, homeless and penniless. Nor, as experts observe, are there any concrete and tangible measures for a comprehensive social contract that disarmament and demobilization are meant to be (Knight 2004: 499).

Second Lieutenant Meghali Kharghoria (alias Mamoni Kakoti), a former commissioned combatant of the 28th Battalion of ULFA which constitutes the prominent pro-talks faction, belonging to Sibsagar in Upper Assam, ULFA's home district as it were, clearly maintains that while some other females like her who returned have chosen to 'surrender', she is more comfortable knowing she can uphold some of the foundational ideologies of the outfit even as she is among those who have formally consented to negotiate the end of war by giving up arms and resolve differences with the Indian government. A beneficiary of the ceasefire agreement which entitles her to the irregularly disbursed Rs 3,000 monthly stipend to disbanded cadres in the interim period between ceasefire and peace, Meghali's is an empowered voice of these former women rebels whose soft speech and demure looks belie a certain cynicism with which she regards both the government's failure to address the issues of women's rehabilitation and her erstwhile organization's short-sightedness about the future of its cadres.[6] Her account of the destruction of ULFA's camps at Phukaptong and Merengphu villages in Samdrup Jongkhar in December 2003, along the Assam-Bhutan borders, and the travails borne by the women in their transit back to the home country suggests a firm resilience to the odds, a quality that sustains her over the long struggles of finding her way back into civilian spaces. Like Meghali, many women who survived the Bhutan raid, in which around 650 rebels were neutralized as 30 guerrilla camps were destroyed, have stories of courage and endurance to narrate. While these figures are disputed, most contemporary reports published in the press of the time carry stories of the displacement, though there is little by way of information on what happened to the women thereafter (Bhaumik 2009). She and several other former rebel women courted arrest, but as Meghali reiterates even now, more than ten years on, they refused to 'surrender'. Many of the ex-combatants scattered over different districts of Assam, for instance, those who returned after the Bhutan crackdown continue to trek to Nalbari, in western Assam, where the Royal Bhutan Army handed over the detenues (women and children in those camps alone amounted to more than 100) to the Indian side, to face hearings in judicial courts more than a decade after they were taken into custody. Besides, the case of those missing men, and as it is now widely believed, the case of one young woman recruit, who disappeared in custody, continues to be for most families one of the most unsettling of memories and truths to deal with, but more critically for those women who lost their husbands to an inconclusive fate (Moral 2013).

Are former combatants rejected by the societies they return to? What are the difficulties they face in seeking to go back to family and home? Studies and first-hand accounts have revealed that in Assam, unlike in many other Indian societies and elsewhere too, a woman who comes back from 'war' is not discriminated against greatly, though she may often be subject to scrutiny and surveillance. Haleh Afshar, for instance, observes that while there may be commonalities of experience that universally marginalize women in the post-conflict period, in Islamic societies, women, particularly in the Middle East and in Afghanistan or Palestine, encountered greater forms of oppression and ostracization for having been involved in militancy or for having dared to wield guns (Afshar 2003). Meghali, on the other hand, has gone back to her husband's home in an interior village of Lakhimpur in far eastern Assam, across the north bank of the Brahmaputra, and now lives with his family. As a unit of a guerrilla couple, she and her husband probably have the social sanction to live an ordinary and normal life in these rural agrarian societies, which saw and faced the ugly and raw brunt of counter-insurgency operations more than a decade and a half ago. Yet there are many other demobilized women who have single-handedly encountered hostile neighbours and judgemental elders to lead independent lives and plunge back into mainstream civilian life. For those who are wont to see the former rebel in the stereotypical role of 'war victim' or locate her as 'non-combatant' there is always the problem of dangerously overshadowing other more authentic voices that need to be recovered (Wibben 2011). Meghali and a host of former rebels from the Bhutan camps clearly indicate that their circumstances have created new identities out of their old ones, hyphenating them, nuancing stock images and releasing them from the traps of being always already circumscribed. In a manner that challenges earlier assumptions, these women have emboldened conflict narratives by their self-expression and mobility in their transition from camps to civilian boundaries definitively, so that the old paradigms of victimhood and suppression no longer hold out. Apart from joining in a rare intervention for justice and legal redress, in which the wives of six missing key cadres of the ULFA from the Bhutan operations of 2003 sought a writ petition of habeas corpus in the Guwahati High Court in 2005 in respect of their husbands, these women have mobilized in a new fashion to renew their attempts to empower themselves outside the insurgent fold.[7] Recent critical evaluations of ULFA have however undermined the importance of these women both in conflict and after it, reducing their description, for instance, to merely half a page in a book dedicated to understanding the outfit's mission. That these women have brought in new knowledge and factored in seminal social and cultural responses to the organizational modes of ULFA, being at once its critics and conscience, is easily missed by what are, often, traditional readings of revolution and rebellion in Assam's contemporary conflicts.

Between the critical moments of being at war and its strategic withdrawal from conflict, ULFA's female warriors, often erroneously recognized as the outfit's women's wing or '*nari bahini*',[8] have from time to time reinvented themselves in an attempt to survive their struggles. The outfit's unpublished constitution clearly mandates equal membership to male and female recruits (ULFA Constitution, n.d.).[9] The demobilized woman rebel has her own narrative of resistance and while she may not have emerged as a heroine of the war unlike her male counterpart, yet unlike many other outfits in South Asia where women cadres are large in number as, for example, the Maoists in Nepal where women make up a third of the membership or the LTTE, with a sixth being women militants who are part of suicide squads and carry out cold-blooded assassinations, the ULFA woman rebel despite her smaller representation enjoys on the face of it a greater degree of liberty with fewer risky operational responsibilities ascribed to a regular member. Consequently, the woman rebel who has crossed over to civilian life is invested with greater agency for change, is undeterred from making known her honest criticism of the outfit she once belonged to, and remains politically uninhibited because she is not bounden to the state in any other way except to remain disbanded from the outfit and is free to find herself any vocation she can fit into. Theoretically, this particular kind of ambivalence about the status of such demobilized cadres is actually enabling and arguably informs them with an empowering faculty as conversations with them reveal.

The state's indifference to the legal/juridical grievances of these women who remain entrapped in pursuing cases (pertaining to the National Security Act or the Unlawful Activities Prevention Act) pending against them year after year is in sharp contrast to the women's own initiatives to join collectives and surmount their condition. Shyamolee Gogoi, Minakshi Borborua, Hema Hanchepee, Anima Devi, Kabita Chakrabarty and Rupali Thakuria, all wives of ULFA leaders, who disappeared while ostensibly in custody, have renewed their pledge to approach the apex court in the country to bring about a conclusion to the unresolved 'disappearance'. A women's advocacy group in Jorhat in Upper Assam has recently taken up cudgels on their behalf to investigate the case again and knock at the doors of international agencies, if need be, to figure out ways to bring about justice. This is significant, as former male cadres, in positions of eminence and leadership, have rarely expressed adequate solidarity for these women who out of necessity have had to rouse support and strategy from within themselves. Such sorority amongst rebels and supporters, Maria Stern notes, is often productive in creating agency for women but seldom acknowledged. For, as she argues, 'when women organise in their own communities, whether to demand knowledge about the whereabouts of disappeared loved ones, to retrieve land taken from family or to garner support for widows, the fact that they organise as women raises suspicion' (Stern 2005: 31). As part of a women's collective, voluntary non-governmental agencies, like the one that runs from Jorhat under the zealous supervision of a gutsy young woman to intervene in sensitive legal matters in respect of the rehabilitation of former rebels, promise to offer a limited but necessary front against oppression and a forum for sharing of confidences. Academics, activists and voluntary women's groups have routinely explored the shared experiences of marginal women, whether they are economically disadvantaged, sexually exploited or politically and ideologically on the fringes of society. The Nari Adhikar Suraksha Samiti and the Asom Mahila Sachetan Manch, both women's collectives of the state, work on the common principle of accommodating such dispossessed women whose rights and safety are guaranteed within the framework of these organizations. It is not a coincidence that many former rebels have found suitable vocation in lending their energy and services to these advocacy groups where they are able to reinvent their agency from the camps and jungles and push to recover peace and stability for women like themselves. While organized rehabilitation and reintegration into community life has not been wholly planned or executed by the state machinery, it is apparent that former rebels have found meaningful agency in innovative ways, emulating unwittingly some of the key principles of the UNSCR 1325[10] by their participation in processes of reconstruction in the post-conflict period.

THOSE WHO STEPPED BACK

The separation of those who returned to voluntarily lead civilian lives and those who co-opted themselves to the state's own plans for rehabilitation drives a clear wedge through the erstwhile ULFA cadreship and the relationship that former rebels share with one another. The earliest of the surrenders of the outfit's members happened famously in a state motivated strategy that was initiated in 1992, at the behest of the then chief minister of Assam, Hiteswar Saikia. A detailed government document was later drafted relating to the surrender and rehabilitation of militants, which envisioned monetary compensation, residences and vocational training to ensure employment of former rebels and their eschewing of the militant way of life (Government of India 1998). While many of the state's well known insurgent personalities transited to the lucre and safety of civilian legitimacy, the period between the 1990s and the early 2000s also saw the rise of a bold new phenomenon in Assamese society, that of the SULFA (surrendered ULFA, in short). Yet, even as many former rebels in stellar roles stepped back and came home to the welcoming fold of state custody and civilian welfare, about 5,000 ULFA cadres were reported to have surrendered to the government by 1997, the non-visibility of the woman surrenderee remains enigmatic (Mahanta 2013). Her silence and absence in this canvas and the complete erasure of women rebels indicates a predominantly gendered view that prevailed around ideas of rebellion, armed conflict and violent resistance movements. Critics have argued that the number of women cadres was small and thus not salient to the inner dynamic or possible impact on the outfit's growth or image in its turbulent history. However, a closer look at the workings of the organizational structures and the everyday functions suggests a far more complex relationship between the outfit's male and female cadres and the roles the latter played in networking and strategic coordination of ULFA's policies and practices across the state. Some women's organizations of the 1990s like the Assam Mahila Kalyan Samiti, for example, were tacit overground support groups that fed the cadreship from time to time and women workers working for them, both trained and untrained, easily criss-crossed the several districts of the state, from west to east, in promoting publicity and recruitment drives for the outfit (Rajkonwor 2013).

In conversations with ULFA's former women cadres it is not difficult to sense the valorization of rebels who did not co-opt with the state. Thus, even after the official ceasefire of 2011 (an earlier unilateral ceasefire in 2007 declared by the Government of India after ULFA's 28th Battalion initiated a process for dialogue didn't yield much result by way of peacemaking), members of ULFA's pro-talks faction who cooperated with the state continue to revere those who didn't step back formally by way of official surrenders. The female surrenderee is, in this sense, persona non grata, and, as Cynthia Cockburn points out, cast in a post-conflict moment, which is 'vividly about male power systems, struggle and identity formations' where women encounter layers of exclusion and rarely get to participate politically (Cockburn 2007: 23). A travelling conflict feminist, Cockburn's work serves to remind the reader that like activists, women rebels too need to network amongst themselves to negotiate viable options and paths back to the community once war is over and the spoils of conflict actually begin to strike back. ULFA's strong pool of former female cadres concentrated in the Upper Assam districts of Jorhat, Sibsagar, Dibrugarh, Tinsukia and further up north in Lakhimpur regularly meet outside their former organizational contours to exchange fellowships, express solidarity and engineer new survival strategies as they chase pending legal tangles and devise ways of bettering lives. The hierarchy in this collective also builds on the binary of surrendered and non-surrendered rebels. The technicalities of the surrender consequent upon arrest of cadres complicate the voluntariness of giving oneself unto the law in adverse circumstances. Yet, members of the organization often rue the fact that some rebels seek to profit from alliances struck with the government, which in the typical view of a guerrilla must remain as the house of the enemy. In the words of one surrendered cadre, the compromise with government is 'mutually beneficial' as it aids the process of peace brokering and ensures safety and survival of the rebel who returns. However, feisty female rebels who support the outfit's bid to bring back peace and join the government in negotiating for the end of conflict maintain that surrendered rebels are stooges and lose the right to think, reason and debate on issues that involve the future of not just the rebels but the community as a whole. Further, the easy complicity that surrendered rebels have with the powers that be seems to take away from the integrity of former insurgents whose business they believe is to ensure that no genuine interest of the people is compromised even when rebels have abjured the path of violence and armed resistance.

In a recent demonstration of such independence, former ULFA cadre and wife of missing leader Major Ashanta Baghphukan, organizational secretary of the Central Committee of the Sanjukta Mukti Bahini Asom, Hema Hanchepee (alias Malini Engtipee) went on air in a local news channel to plead for a concerted enquiry into the case of the missing rebels in Bhutan on the eve of Prime Minister Narendra Modi's maiden visit to Assam in November 2014. Clearly, Hema's ability to voice the grievance of her tribe from the periphery of her position as a former female rebel of not much consequence, and who was heard across the state and beyond on television screens, was a crossing of borders in more ways than one. Was the moment of conflict therefore only a partial empowering of the female soldier? Did real empowerment come only when the cycles of being in conflict and out of it had been completed? For many rebels this indeed is for them the moment of self-discovery and a fulfilment of agency. Shanti Rajkumari (alias Tara Bujorboruah), the outfit's top female warrior, lieutenant by rank, and former ULFA chairman Arabinda Rajkhowa's niece, makes no bones about disenchantment and disillusioned dreams in the camps. Her grouse with the outfit's organizational restructuring and its bifurcation into military and political units in 1996 is clear as she vents her displeasure with several tactical flaws that it engendered within the body politic. Her other important criticism was directed towards the provision for family cadreship within the camps set up in Bhutan which she felt disrupted the discipline of guerrilla life and warfare. Yet, Shanti's ability to voice this vital concern ironically comes in the post-conflict moment, a time of greater realization and deeper conviction in the distance she has been able to put between the outfit and herself, despite her close affiliation to the top leadership.[11] In an interview with the author, in the Darrang district of central Assam, that is both surprising in its candour and insightful in detailing ULFA's organizational strengths and weaknesses, this senior former combatant harks towards a revisionist history of the outfit, something not many male leaders have been sensitive to put their thoughts to. A similar concern comes from prominent woman rebel and emancipated Nepalese Maobadi leader, and part of the Nepal Samyabadi Party, Hisila Yami (popularly known as Parvati), wife of Baburam Bhattarai, Maoist ideologue and former prime minister of Nepal, whose critique of the PLA and its gendered style of functioning is both an important intervention as well as a constructive history of the people's revolution in that country and of women's role in it (Lecomte-Tilouine 2013; Parvati 2006). Surrendered female ex-rebels of ULFA, on the other hand, are out of the revolutionary bind, as it were, and are emotionally relatively removed from the state of affairs that most demobilized women find themselves enmeshed in. While many female rebels surrendered between 1995 and 2001, the districts of Sibsagar and Lakhimpur registered the maximum number of official surrenders, with most of this category of former rebels now employed, and wholly absorbed in professional lives and often better placed in economic terms. Yet they are remotely involved in activities that occupy the 'demobilized' group, among them the fate of the disbanded outfit's political and ideological place in Assam's history or, for that matter, the progress in peace talks with the government, or in instituting solidarities for women's rights and welfare. The fat monetary packages that compensate surrendered rebels primarily explain their non-participation in such matters, but their insular nature is also not unconnected to the diminished internal regard for rebels who are thought to dissociate permanently from the fold.

After the official ceasefire declared by the ULFA pro-talks group led by Arabinda Rajkhowa in 2011, a new dynamic emerged within the outfit and among former rebels. The setting up of the 'cantonment' or designated camps in several districts to facilitate the transit of rebels to civilian mode within the modalities mutually agreed upon by the outfit and the government complicated the roles and responsibilities of former rebels vis-à-vis the overarching ideologies of the disbanded outfit. The designated camp is regarded as an important halfway house between a mobilized state and the dissolution of rebels. The advantage of a ceasefire camp in demobilizing rebels is however counterweighed by the risk of remobilization if peace is not implemented soon enough. Rebels who do not surrender but are circumscribed by the regimen of the designated camp into discipline and duty within the four walls of the cantonment are likely to be oppressed by these semi-permanent enclosures. Many women rebels in fact leave the designated camps for what they feel is a 'replication' of the life of the camps in the time of conflict, as indicated in conversations with combatants who have been candid about expectations and hopes in the run up to peace. Further, more than a dozen female rebels have confessed that they do not regularly receive the Rs 3,000 interim stipend promised by the government to the outfit for each member. On the other hand, it is widely alleged that many young couples not greatly involved in the organization stay on in the designated camps simply to be able to 'live together' while single women leave the cantonment (Interview Meghali Kharghoria 2014).

Women in this regard have been more innovative and independent, and several combatants earn and eke out modest livelihoods by raising poultry or setting up small businesses while continuing to pay for legal expenses to move their pending cases in session courts that are hundreds of miles away from where they live. For those who have no real homes to return to, sometimes a friend or a cousin's home provides refuge. Sociological theories that women subjects lose their specific identities in pursuit of revolutionary goals do not always ring true, especially after the conflict, and most women guerrillas who experience partial blurring of gender distinctions and a certain degree of masculinization claim that that their gender reinforces their 'outsider' status post-conflict and brings increasing need to seek new and innovative methods of reinventing themselves (Molyneaux 1985;

Randall 1982). The more recent move by ULFA's women rebels towards a concerted fuelling and mobilizing of public opinion to be included as peace negotiators or members of the talks that have been brokering peace with the Government of India since the first ceasefire declaration in 2007 draws attention to their continued attempt to break out of the mould. In the first state-wide civil society intervention for long-term peace, 109 organizations, activists and public intellectuals chalked out modalities for the Indian government and ULFA to find measures and a resolution to the long-standing grievances of the rebels and the people of the state. The Sanmilita Jatiya Abhivartan (United National Convention) led by Professor Hiren Gohain in 2010 submitted a charter of demands in which the inclusion of former women cadres at the negotiating table was a key condition to settlement of the insurgents' fate (Gohain 2010). Does the state then not have a greater responsibility in finding more permanent solutions for this category of citizens in ensuring their rehabilitation and reintegration back into the community? Do transitional justice measures need to be formally put in place where none seem to exist even as ULFA and the government periodically huddle together to find ways to lasting peace in the state?

WHERE HAVE THE REST GONE? WHAT'S IN A NAME?

Jeff Goodwin, in his classic work on the way states fuel revolutionary activities, ponders on the role of women in the post-conflict moment as he argues that a repressive state can mobilize anti-state dissent (Goodwin 2001). For every 10 former women rebels that are traced to either their parental homes or the new arrangements in which women live in small rented tenements alone or with partner/spouse from the organization, there are one or two rebels who are usually not found. This points to another familiar trend in the reorganized lives of former women rebels in which some ex-guerrillas prefer to merge into the anonymity of ordinary daily life. Many demobilized women rebels fail to furnish details or whereabouts of their former compatriots as they sometimes lose track of their present circumstances. There are subtle hints that a few even plunge back to the jungles and return to active combat, disappearing from the radar of visibility. A young woman rebel of the Kamrup district, belonging to ULFA's lethal Enigma base unit, who was in active frontline combat and escaped narrowly from being ambushed in the Bhutan crackdown of 2003, on the other hand, is today, for example, an ordinary householder who does not wish to be drawn into discussions on the outfit's future or on her own involvement with it. Having surrendered in early 2009, she quietly 'disappeared' from the scene, and after her marriage assumed a new identity and now leads a completely transformed civilian life having severed all communication with other former rebels and compatriots from the outfit. None of her former fellow cadres knows where she is and there are no telling clues about her either. Earlier, between 2007 and 2009, this rebel, then in her mid-20s, had made available to the author several accounts of her life in the camps and given interviews that drew heavily from a detailed diary, written painstakingly in her neat and tiny hand, of those years spent at combat training and the travails of her 'escape from the Royal Bhutan Army dragnet'.[12] Had this rebel found her real vocation after withdrawal from the outfit in happy partnership with her husband, in dramatically altered identities, or were the memories of the guerrilla camps too fraught to even recollect?

The practice of blotting out earlier insurgent experiences does suggest the possibility that some women rebels consider their lives in the jungles disempowering and even regard them as moments of coercion and misplaced faith in a cause that was ultimately futile. The safer life of marital conjugality and domestic bliss prevailing over the hard and sometimes wasted sacrifices of insurgent life is indeed the subject of a former Nepalese Maoist, Tara Rai's, diary, 'Chhapamar Yuvatiko Diari', who chose to 'make love rather than war' (quoted in Lecomte-Tilouine 2013: 361). Did the ULFA women also reject their pasts or are their present lives mediated impossibly through their insurgent experiences? Besides, several women rebels who were martyred, in army encounters or through atrocities and rapes committed on them by counter-insurgency forces, have disappeared into ULFA's unwritten history with little or no records left of them and it took the efforts of a pro-talks leader of the 28th Battalion, a major player in the peace-brokering exercise, to put together a carefully documented list of some 17 women who fell to guns or were raped and killed, the earliest in 1991.[13] From whatever can be obtained as information on these unfortunate women, their families seldom count their fated lives as glorious or empowering, given the decline of the rebellion in later years into a fractious ragtag band of opportunists at the worst, and a hollow airing of disenchanted passions by sentimentalists at its best. More surprisingly, nor does the outfit institutionally deify or hold those brave young women who staked their lives in reverence or ceremony. Significantly, yet another novel mode of reintegrating into mainstream society is seen in the deradicalization of several former woman rebels whose long years of guerrilla life leave them disappointed in the heavy scrutiny of militarized life, and who choose to blur into the crowds. Yet such narratives are hardly representative of combatants' later life, as the experiences of several former rebels remobilizing into women's rights groups and voluntary collectives indicate. Militant pasts train women to assume untypical roles and adopt unique measures of social engineering in post-conflict times for peace and rehabilitation, as many of the above accounts reveal. As former rebel Shyamolee, wife of missing ULFA cadre Prakash Gogoi, put it recently: 'The community is above the individual and what I have learnt from rebellion is to put our pasts behind, join forces together and work for a stable and peaceful future.'[14] Enrolled in an undergraduate Arts programme at a college in Doomdooma in Tinsukia district of Upper Assam under a new name, Moni Moran, she now looks to completing her education, while schooling her own 12-year-old daughter, refashioning herself in preparation for a job whereby she can pick up the threads of her pre-rebel life. She is without regret for her past and still hopeful. The future, she indicates, is clearly one that has extricated itself from her life as an insurgent, and one that looks at herself as an agent of change, even as she believes that her long and difficult trek along the road not taken readied her for the challenges ahead.

NOTES

1. A self-styled rebel group, founded by a set of young men at Sibsagar in Upper Assam in 1979, the United Liberation Front of Asom, or, ULFA has been regarded as an outfit severely critical of the Indian state, confronting it with separatist tendencies until more recent times when it declared a ceasefire. Prominent as a guerrilla organization of Assam, along with other insurgencies in this part of the country, its emergence in the postcolonial moment via armed resistance is embedded in the larger geopolitical, sociological and intellectual contexts of the northeastern region.
2. The ethnographic data for this study was based mainly on long years of research on the female combatants of ULFA in the period after the ceasefire, beginning provisionally in 2007, until recent times. Most statements by the women alluded to here are drawn from interviews, conversation and correspondence with them conducted over the last four or five years. This study also depends on documents and unpublished material that some former rebels offered the author to read and are deemed as private papers and not quoted verbatim from.
3. In addition to removing the symbols of a combatant's military life, to prepare them for civilian freedom, such as their weapon, uniform and rank, demobilization activities, in the normative sense, include a survey of combatants' needs and aspirations, medical examinations, counselling, initial reintegration packages and transportation to the community of choice.
4. ULFA's body politic, like most insurgencies, underwent a decisive split in the late 2000s when hardliners pulled out of the peacemaking process, led by its self-styled commander-in-charge, Paresh Baruah, still at large beyond the borders of the country, and came to be redesignated as ULFA (Independent) in contrast to the larger group of moderates in the outfit headed by its erstwhile chairman, Arabinda Rajkhowa, who is currently negotiating peace with the Government of India.
5. In 2003, following a series of diplomatic parleys between Bhutan and India, the Indian Army and the Royal Bhutan Army (RBA) joined forces to flush out insurgents from the Bhutanese territory where several militants from Northeast India had found refuge, as the government of India took stringent steps to hunt down the non-state rebels. ULFA's camps were the

central target in these exercises that were carried out towards the end of the year leaving the outfit suddenly in shambles, with several dozens of its cadres displaced and some of the prominent leaders missing.

6. Interviews with Meghali, December 2009 and September 2014.
7. One of the signposts in the ULFA timeline featuring its women cadres is the 2005 writ petition admitted into the Guwahati High Court, W.P. (Crl) No. 17 by petitioner, ULFA cadre Gyanoma Moran, alias Shyamolee Gogoi, who led a series of such petitions by five other women cadres over the next year with respect to the custodial disappearances.
8. Pradip Gogoi, former vice president of the outfit, declared emotionally that ULFA's women cadres were comparable to the royal Ahom army's women's wing that boasted of legends such as Mula Gabhoru, Joymoti and other royal Ahom queens (Interview: Guwahati Central Jail. December 2007).
9. ULFA's constitution clearly lays down that every cadre is a member of the outfit and not differentiated in terms of gender.
10. The United Nations' Security Council Resolution 1325 was adopted by the Security Council at its 4213th meeting, on 31 October 2000. Resolution 1325 was the first formal and legal document from the Security Council that required parties in a conflict to prevent violations of women's rights, support women's participation in peace negotiations and in post-conflict reconstruction, and protect women and girls from sexual and gender-based violence primarily.
11. Personal conversation, September 2014.
12. Interviews with author in 2007 and 2009. Unpublished diary (in Assamese).
13. Mrinal Hazarika, ULFA pro-talks leader, in April 2014.
14. Gyanoma Moran (alias Shyamolee Gogoi), in several conversations since 2007, and in April, September and November 2014.

REFERENCES

Afshar, Haleh. 2003. 'Women and Wars: Some Trajectories towards a Feminist Peace', in H. Ashfar and D. Eade (eds), *Development, Women and War: Feminist Perspectives*, pp. 178–88. Oxford: Oxfam.

Banerjee, Paula. 2008. *Women in Peace Politics. South Asian Peace Studies*, vol. 3, New Delhi: Sage Publications.

Bhaumik, Subir. 2009. *Troubled Periphery: Crisis of India's Northeast*. New Delhi: Sage Publications.

Chinchilla, Norma Stoltz. 1983. 'Women in Revolutionary Movements: The Case of Nicaragua', in *Revolution in Central America*, edited by the Stanford Central America Action Network, pp. 422–35. Boulder, CO: Westview.

Cockburn, Cynthia. 2007. *From Where We Stand. War, Women's Activism and Feminist Analysis*. London: Zed Books.

Gohain, Hiren. 2010. *Agnigorbha Asom aru Xubho Uttoronor Proseshtha* [Burning Assam and the Pursuit of a Happy Transformation]. Guwahati: Ashok Press.

Goodwin, Jeff. 2001. *No Other Way Out: States and Revolutionary Movements (1945–1991)*. Cambridge: Cambridge University Press.

Government of India. 1998. Scheme for Surrender-Cum-Rehabilitation of Militants in the North-East: Government of Assam www.satp.org/satporgtp/countries/india/states/assam/documents/papers/surrender.htm

Gurr, Ted Robert. 1970. *Why Men Rebel.* Princeton: Princeton University Press.

Knight, Mark. 2004. 'Guns, Camps and Cash: Disarmament, Demobilization and Reinsertion of Former Combatants in Transitions from War to Peace', *Journal of Peace Research*, 41(4): 499–516.

Lecomte-Tilouine, Marie. 2013. *Revolution in Nepal. An Anthropological and Historical Approach to the People's War.* New Delhi: Oxford University Press.

Luciak, Ilja A. 2001. *After the Revolution: Gender and Democracy in El Salvador, Nicaragua, and Guatemala.* Baltimore: Johns Hopkins University Press.

Mahanta, Nani Gopal. 2013. *Confronting the State: ULFA's Quest for Sovereignty.* New Delhi: Sage Publications.

Molyneaux, Maxine. 1985. 'Mobilisation without Emancipation? Women's Interests, the State, and Revolution in Nicaragua', *Feminist Studies*, 11(2): 227–54.

Moral, Rakhee Kalita. 2013. *Living and Partly Living: The Politics of Freedom and the Women of ULFA*. NMML Monograph no. 31 (New History and Society Series), New Delhi: Nehru Memorial Museum and Library.

———. 2014. 'The Woman Rebel and the State: Making War, Making Peace in Assam', *Economic and Political Weekly*, 49(43/44): 66–73.

Nath, Manoj Kumar. 2013. *ULFA: Xeujia Xopon, Tez Ronga Itihax* [ULFA: Green Dreams, Blood-red History]. Guwahati: Aank Baak.

Panging, Tushar. 2010. *Operation All Clear.* Guwahati: Bonbahi Prakash.

Parvati. 2006. 'Ten Years of People's War and the Question of Women's Liberation', in *People's War... Women's War?* Two texts by Comrade Parvati of the Communist Party of Nepal (Maoist) with a Commentary by Butch Lee. Kersplebedeb: Pamphlet edition, pp. 1–12.

Patel, Ann Cutter and Pablo de Grieff. eds. 2009. *Disarming the Past. Transitional Justice and Ex-combatants.* New York: Social Science Research Council.

Rai, Tara. 2010. *Chhapamar Yuvatiko Dairi* [Diary of a Young Woman Guerrilla]. Quoted in Lecomte-Tilouine, Marie. 2013. *Revolution in Nepal. An Anthropological and Historical Approach to the People's War.* New Delhi: Oxford University Press.

Rajkonwor, Kaberi Kochari. 2013. *Issa Anissa Sottweo Kisu Katha* [Despite Wishes and Restraints, a Few Things]. Guwahati: Aalibaat.

Randall, Margaret. 1982. *Sandino's Daughters.* London: Zed Books.

Shepherd, Laura. 2008. 'Power and Authority in the Production of United Nations Security Council Resolution 1325', *International Studies Quarterly*, 52(2): 383–404.

Stern, Maria. 2005. *Naming Security, Constructing Identity: Mayan Women in Guatemala on the Eve of Peace.* Manchester: Manchester University Press.

Thomson, Marilyn. 1986. *Women of El Salvador: The Price of Freedom.* Mexico City: Comision de Derechos Humanos de El Salvador (CDHES).

Viterna, Jocelyn. 2006. 'Pulled, Pushed and Persuaded: Explaining Women's Mobilisation into the Salvadoran Guerrilla Army', *American Journal* of *Sociology*, 112(1): 1–45.

Wibben, Annick T.R. 2011. *Feminist Security Studies.* New York: Routledge.

CHAPTER 5

Gendered Citizenship and Representation: Women's Contributions to Peacebuilding in Naga Society

Anungla Aier

Conflict and violence associated with the cultural practice of head-hunting among the Naga tribes have been largely instrumental for the development of the traditional ethos and customary practices that strengthened patriarchy. This is also clearly visible in the gendered landscape of Naga society today. Throughout the known history of the Naga people, conflict and violence have always been a part of their experience. To better understand the above observation, mention is made here that military and administrative reports of the early colonial encounter show that the Nagas were war tribes. This is corroborated by the oral tradition of the Nagas themselves. These tribes were practising headhunting imbued with concepts of fertility, valour and honour, around which were built not only the major cultural markers of identity, but also the gender roles and power equations between men and women. The authority and decisions of men were unquestioned for security reasons, while the power relations between the genders were always to the advantage of men. Patriarchal values were infused into all the different levels of customary practices and the manner in which society was organized.

Today's Naga society represents an interesting blend of traditionalism and modernity. Cutting across the many problems of development and changing quality of life that confront most developing societies, issues of gender remain among the most pressing and yet least attended and understood. The challenge is further deepened because Nagaland is the site of the longest ethnic political movement in India, starting soon after World War I and turning into a full-fledged armed conflict between the new Indian state and the Naga army in the early 1950s. Though the nature of engagement with the movement has changed, the fact is that the conflict still remains unresolved and technically the movement continues. Today, the situation is even more complicated and unpredictable due to the division of the movement into various factions which are based not so much on political ideologies as efforts to maintain territorial control. Undoubtedly, there is always an air of unspoken tension, and frequently also the eruption of violence between different factions as well as between insurgents and paramilitary forces. Thus the prevailing situation in Nagaland presents us with a cultural precondition of stringent patriarchal values and a history of violence and protracted conflict, side by side with repeated crimes against women and gender-based discrimination. In these prevailing circumstances, multiple questions arise concerning gender and empowerment, especially if we try to unravel the different layers of conflict and processes of peacebuilding in the local community. In this chapter, the discussion will focus on the construction and practice of citizenship, and how it impacts women's contributions to peacemaking processes in Naga society.

WOMEN AND CITIZENSHIP

The term 'citizenship' as used here may not conform strictly to the political and legal definition of the term, as its usage in this chapter is in accordance to local usage. I feel that this is justified considering the fact that in all the Naga tribes, the identity of every individual is rooted in their belonging or citizenship of their native village, which traditionally was an independent political unit, and till today each village has a certain degree of autonomy and the powers to exercise legal authority over its citizens through customary law courts. Given the centrality of the concept of gender in the way societies are structured, although the notion of 'citizenship' in itself may be gender neutral, in practice the interpretation of it is hardly gender neutral wherein women are almost always put in a disadvantageous position, whether in family life or the workplace, and whether in governance, development, conflict situations or peace building. To illustrate this viewpoint, this chapter begins by tracing the concept of citizenship in Naga society, and how perceptions about citizenship determine the manner in which the rights and responsibilities of men and women are defined in practice.

The structure of Naga society is organized around a system of kin-based divisions of society into agnatic clans, which stand in exogamic relation with one another. The identity or personhood of both men and women in each Naga tribe is drawn from membership in the constituent tribal villages, and citizenship in the village is determined by claims of descent from a particular kin group (see Figure 5.1).

Naga society is thus a kin-based segmented society, and the clan is the central theme around which the gamut of social and political life revolves. A person is born not only to a set of parents, but also to the clan unit. The construction of his or her social identity is primarily drawn from membership in the clan unit. In this scheme of identity construction based on clan membership, a woman occupies a less significant position as she finds her identity and responsibility shifted to that of the husband's clan after marriage. In the case of men, however, they are born to a particular clan and remain attached to it throughout their lives. In the case of a woman, her membership in her birth clan is marginal because she gets affiliated to her husband's clan when she marries.

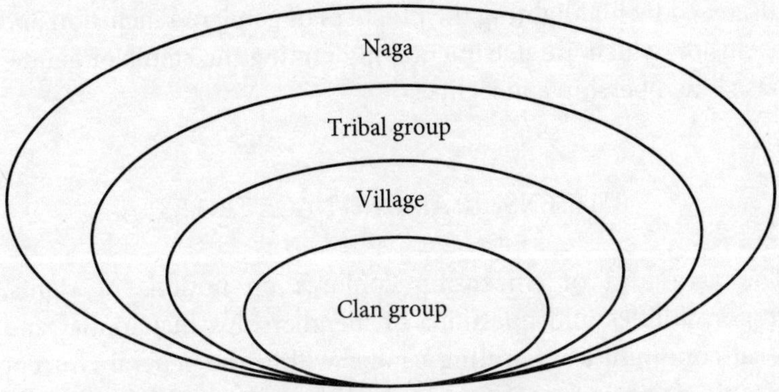

Figure 5.1 The relationship between units that make up Naga society

Her responsibilities are for all practical purposes transferred to that of the husband and his clan. She obtains access to the lands and resources of the husband's clan, but she continues to be identified by her birth clan. This suggests that her position in the clan she marries into remains marginal. Due to these prevailing structures of kinship and identity, the position of women in society can best be described as fragmented and marginal. Reasons such as these are frequently cited to justify why women representing the clan in any official or formal capacity are not accepted or recognized. As observed by Aier (2008), it is arguable that such restrictions on women are imposed mainly because the patriarchal clan recognizes only male ancestors, and therefore only men have the right or honour of representing the clan in any social capacity. Aier further opines that the construction of gender identity within the strictly patriarchal system of Naga society draws its inspiration from various oral traditions and narratives that immortalize and revere male ancestors as progenitors, whereas female ancestors are pushed to the background or simply forgotten. This perhaps legitimizes the patriarchal structure of society and the internal arrangement of power between men and women. The notions of gender identity and the recognition or de-recognition of such gendered identities within the local concept of citizenship is further discussed by highlighting the practices of gendered inclusion and exclusion which are detrimental in defining the status of gender based membership and rights.

CITIZENSHIP AMONG NAGA TRIBES

The very idea of citizenship conjures up notions of rights, responsibilities and questions of memberships in national and local communities. Locating gender within the general concept of citizenship is paramount in developing an understanding of the nature of citizenship as membership in a community and shedding light on the patterns of inclusion and exclusion that shape such membership. In Naga society, two different terms are used to designate village membership or belonging: 'people of the village' and 'citizens of the village'. Since the terms used vary from tribe to tribe due to linguistic differences, I make reference here to the terms used by the Ao and the Sangtam tribes. Among the Ao tribe, the term used for 'people of the village' is *yimer* and in Sangtam the equivalent terms are *kilongri* or *yanglangrü*. These are inclusive terms that include all men, women and children, and any other people who are residing in the village or have their original roots in the village, even though they are not physically residing there at present. The second term, *senso* in Ao and *süro nyetsarü* in Sangtam is a more exclusive term with a biological and territorial connotation. The literal meaning of both the terms can best be described as meaning 'birth people'. Both terms in essence are gender-neutral, much as the term 'citizen' is gender-neutral. Traditionally, every Naga village has what can best be described as a 'citizens' forum'. Such citizens' forums are known as *senso mungdang* (Ao) and the Sangtam call it *süro nyetsarü* and all the men by default are members of such forums but the same rights are not extended to women even though they are by birth members of the same social group. The gendered connotation of the term comes clearly unveiled at the practice level because women are clearly not considered as members of citizens' forums, such as *senso mungdang or süro nyetsarü.* Among the Lotha, a more gendered term *potsüng* is used to define who have the right to attend a citizen's forum. The term *potsüng* can literally be translated as a man (*po*) who is of the seeds (*tsüng* or *atsüng*). An adult man from each household of all the constituent clan groups of the community is required to attend the meetings of a citizen's forum whenever the call is made by the local authority of the village. A woman headed household in such a situation cannot be represented since a woman can never be considered as a *Potsüng.* However, if she has a son, her household can be represented through the son. In such meetings, political and social issues of critical importance to the community are discussed, and decisions made. The decisions and declarations given by such citizens' forums are binding on all the members and defaulters are penalized. Traditionally, women are not allowed even to enter the premises where the men are gathered and such citizens' meetings are taking place. Even in today's times, participating in such gatherings is out of the question for women.

Another inference of citizenship can be drawn from the traditional decision-making institution of the Ao tribe, which is called the *putu Menden.* The constitution of this *putu menden* follows strict customary practices of clan representation. Once nominated by the clan and inducted into the p*utu menden*, the person holds the position as a *tatar* (member of the *putu menden*) for a specified period. A *tatar* represents the clan and there will be as many *tatar* as there are clans in the village. The number of *tatar* for each clan as well as the tenure of office is decided as per customary practices, and so it varies from village to village. Their status and authority is supreme, similar to that of a cabinet council in a democratic system.

Traditionally, and even at present, Ao customary law does not permit women to represent the clan in the *putu menden.* So far there is not a single Naga village where women have been given the privilege to become a member of such traditional political institutions of the village, and no woman has been appointed as a member of a customary court such as the *Dobashi.*[1] Women are thus excluded from clan meetings and they are not allowed to act as a representative of the clan. This supports the assumption that they are considered to be marginal members of the clan, though they may carry the name of the clan as their surname. That women are not given full membership in their respective clan group is evident by the fact that they are not considered a citizen (*senso* or *süro* n*yetsarü*) and are barred from citizens' forums. The consequences of such customary practices effectively disempower women by preventing them from participating in decision-making processes.

The distinction between female and male members of society as 'citizens' and 'non-citizens' with differential rights and access to structures of power and decision-making reminds us of the observations made by Ruth Lister, who stated that the answer to the question posed by Sylvia Walby 'Is citizenship gendered?' has to be a resounding 'yes'. She noted that citizenship has always been gendered in the sense that women and men have stood in a different relationship to it, to the disadvantage of women. Yet, for much of its history, 'a veil of gender-neutrality has obscured the nature of this differential relationship' (Lister, 2001: 323). As seen in the case of Naga society, it is evident that women and men have always stood in a different relationship with regard to the conception of citizenship, as a consequence of which women and men have had different rights and unequal access to decision-making and power.

CITIZENSHIP AND REPRESENTATION

The practice of citizenship involves real people struggling for recognition, rights and inclusion in policy agendas in located situations. As stated by Barbara Hobson and Ruth Lister (2001), citizenship is perhaps the concept in which the exclusion of women has been most firmly imprinted within its historical template. In the case of Naga society, one of the central agendas of Naga women's activism over the last few decades has indeed been for recognition and equal treatment. Hobson and Lister's 'historical template' is clearly visible in the continued practice of gendered citizenship as elaborated above, where women's citizenship remains unrecognized, and, consequently, women are not even considered legitimate or rightful representatives of the community. The existence of such cultural bigotry is one of the fundamental obstacles to the inclusion of women, whether in politically relevant institutions and committees of the government or civil society organizations that are in a position to negotiate and make political decisions on behalf of communities.

One of the more recent developments in Nagaland is the growth of mass-based non-governmental organizations (NGOs), at both the tribal level and the pan-Naga level, cutting across different tribal groups. Each tribal group has a tribal organization such as the Ao Senden, Angami Public Organization, Sumi Hoho, Lotha Hoho, Yimchunger Tribal Council, and the United Sangtam Likhüm Pümji. As many as 15 such tribal organizations had been founded at the time of writing. At the higher inter-tribal level there are organizations such as the Naga Hoho, Eastern Naga People's Organization (ENPO) and Nagaland Tribes Council (NTC). At all levels of the structure—although in essence these organizations represent groups that include both men and women—in terms of representation, the inclusion of women is not uniform. For instance, in some tribes two or more representatives of the tribal women's organizations become members of the tribal union by default, though this is not practised in all the tribes. If we take the Ao Senden (the apex tribal organization of the Ao Nagas) as an example, despite the fact that it stands to represent the Ao community as a whole, in reality it is an all-male forum. Women are not recognized as members of the organization, and they are not allowed to attend the meetings. In particular cases, if women's issues are to be discussed, the women's organization may be invited to share their opinions and give suggestions, but women are not expected to be actively involved in the deliberations and decision-making.

All these mass-based organizations (at tribal as well as inter-tribal levels) are structured in the same way as the village-level organization. At the tribal level, members are representatives of the constituent villages and at the subsequent inter-tribal level, members are representatives of the tribal group (see Figure 5.2).

Tribal representatives to the inter-tribal organizations are always men. Thus, in the deliberations and decisions made at the tribal or inter-tribal level, the voices of women are not represented in all the tribes. All men of the respective tribes are by default members of the tribal organization, which nominates and approves tribal representatives to the higher pan-Naga organizations. In such a structural set-up, the chances of women being recognized as legitimate representatives of their people with authority to negotiate and participate in decision-making is slim. The key challenge for women's empowerment and public participation continues to be the breaking down of structural obstacles built upon the traditional construct of citizenship.

Though women are excluded in the mass-based tribal organizations, they have been very active in informal spheres. Here, women have been responsible for broadening and exploring the limitations and ambiguities of notions of equality and equal rights of men and women. Today, there is recognition that the experiences and needs of men and women are different, and that women have been denied rights and privileges enjoyed by men. One of the main achievements of the women's movement

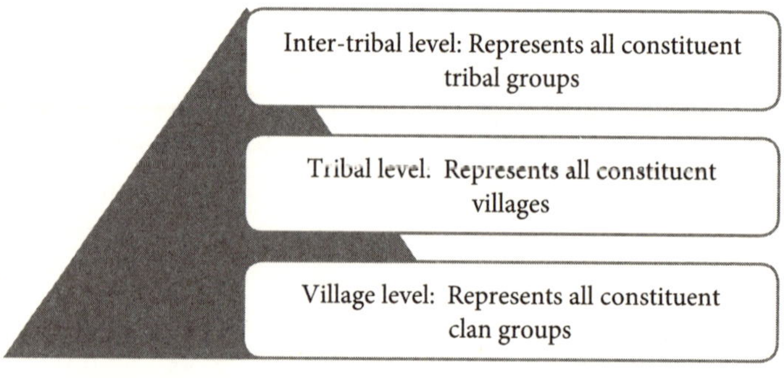

Figure 5.2 The hierarchy of representation

in Nagaland is the growth of women's organizations at the tribal and inter-tribal level, following the same pattern as the all-male tribal organizations described above. Thus alongside the tribal organizations we find women-exclusive organizations such as the Watsü Mungdang, Sümi Totomi Hoho (STH), Lotha Eloi Hoho, Angami Women's Organization and Konyak Nyupuh Sheko Khong, to name a few. Similar women's organizations have been set up among all the tribal groups in the last two decades. Also, parallel to the all-male inter-tribal organizations, there are women's organizations cutting across tribal divides such as Naga Women's Hoho, Naga Mothers' Association and Eastern Naga Women's Organization. By setting up women's organizations similar to those where women are excluded, Naga women have been creating new political spaces by making visible the real experiences of women living as an excluded section of the community. This is also seen as a strategy of working with the powerful male-dominated institutions to change the rules and demand recognition and a means to voice their concerns. Nonetheless, the political spheres where women were not traditionally accepted or recognized still continue, women's organizations are still subject to the dictates of the tribal organizations which are controlled by men, and they can still be controlled by the all-male tribal organizations.

Drawing an inference from the experiences of the Ao women's organization (Watsü Mungdang), it is stated that activities of women's organizations against crime and violence and their demand for recognition of their rights as a bonafide citizen of the community remain a continuing struggle against the patriarchal system. This is clearly exemplified by two incidences in which the women's organization was reprimanded sternly for taking their own decisions. One incidence was the case of a girl who was raped and molested in Mokokchung town on 10 October in 2011. The perpetrator of the crime was identified, and a local women's group took a confession from him. They then called for a public meeting in the town centre, where the culprit was paraded and was made to publicly confess to the crime he had committed. After several days, the women's organization was summoned by the apex Ao tribal organization, the Ao Senden, and was reprimanded for calling the public meeting without their consent thereby causing defamation to the village of which the culprit was a citizen. The Ao Senden suspended the women's organization. However, the women's group defied the suspension order and continued functioning and kept their office open thereby inviting the disfavour and anger of their apex tribal organization.

In another incidence, the Naga Mothers' Association organized a state-wide 'Black Day' on 1 October 2012 in protest against the failure of the government of Nagaland to implement a bill prescribing that one-third of the seats in the state's municipal councils are to be reserved for women (see also Aier 2012: 51–60). However, in Mokokchung the 'Black Day' could not be observed because the Ao Senden declared that no such protest day would be allowed. When a media house enquired why the Ao women were not participating in the movement, they replied that Ao women extended their solidarity with the protest but were unable to observe the 'Black Day' due to a ruling by the Ao Senden forbidding them to organize and observe the 'black day'. After this the women were again reprimanded by the Ao Senden and pressurized to take back their comments in the media.

It must be noted that all these events were taking place among one of the most educated and progressive tribes in Nagaland. At the level of interpersonal relationships and domestic affairs, women in Ao society enjoy as much liberty as any of the men, and sometimes it is the women who control family affairs. However, in the public sphere women are not given the necessary space and recognition. The Ao women's experiences echo the experiences of all Naga women to a larger or lesser degree. It is clearly evident from experiences such as these that the real structures of gender-based oppression and subordination are directly linked not with the formal interpretation of citizenship but with the actual practices of citizenship where power relations between the genders are displayed by denying women the right to decide for themselves and to be accepted as equal representatives and members of the community. Formal equality does not guarantee structural equality between women and men. Rather, it obscures and legitimizes real inequalities between women and men which emerge unmistakably only when we unpack the practices of citizenship rights, as revealed by Naga women's experiences.

WOMEN'S ROLE IN PEACE NEGOTIATIONS

Notions and practices of citizenship impact the legitimacy of a person's or a section of the population's right to represent the community. In the Naga case, as this study shows, this right is denied to women. The historical trajectory of women's contributions to peace has been defined largely by the exclusionist practices of citizenship. In the pre-colonial period when headhunting was practised as ritualized warfare, women played crucial roles in perpetuating conflict as well as making peace, even though they were not physically involved in the act of war or in peacemaking. For instance, women were known to prefer suitors who were acclaimed for their headhunting skills. Success in raiding an enemy village would be feted by the women by weaving and presenting the victorious men with warrior cloths, and composing songs glorifying their deeds. Women were also known to have provoked conflict by going to enemy villages singing about the greatness of their village and their warriors, thereby challenging and inviting confrontation or war. At other times, however, women were known to use their position as the caregiver to broker peace between rival groups. Stories about Naga women peacemakers such as *Pukrelia*[2] (Manchanda 2004: v) are confined to some Naga tribes in Manipur, but there are no references to such traditions among the Naga communities of Nagaland.[3] However, in times when the enmity between two villages became unbearable, women who were married to men from the rival village would try to persuade their respective men to stop the enmity and enter into peace agreements with each other.

Among the Chang Nagas it is known that when different clans of the same village waged war against each other, the women who were married to men from the rival clan would mobilize other women and walk up and down the road between the inter-fighting clans so as to stop the men from killing each other. It is for roles such as these that women have sometimes been described as 'bridge-makers'. However, formal or official messages were sent only by men, and on the agreed day the men of the different clans and the village elders would meet and carry out the necessary peace ceremonies. What is common among all the Naga tribal groups is that only men could come to the peace negotiations and the deals were made based on the deliberations of men only. From a feminist perspective, what is significant in such narratives is that despite the role women played in creating the space for peace negotiations they were excluded from participating in peace dialogues. The rationale of such practices is also clearly linked with the practice of citizenship. Since women's citizenship was perceived as temporary and floating (as explained earlier), they were not accepted as legitimate representatives of the community with the authority to negotiate and make decisions on their behalf.

During more than half a century of armed conflict in Nagaland, several peace initiatives have been pursued (Srikanth and Thomas 2005; Swu 2013), without women's voices ever being heard. In the recent past, however, some changes to this pattern are visible and women are slowly gaining recognition. These changes are perhaps happening because the terms of reference for peace and the nature of engagement with peacemaking activities have changed as well. During the last two decades, the situation took a turn for the worse with the escalation of intra-fratricidal conflict between rival Naga political groups. As the situation worsened, the conflict became more complex and multilayered—between Nagas and the Indian state, between rival Naga political groups, and along tribal fault lines. In the 1990s, due to a growing sense of urgency, women's groups such as the Naga Mothers' Association became increasingly vocal about the need to stop the bloodshed. Many women's groups hence began to mobilize for peace.

Women's activism distinguished itself by taking a non-political peace stance, drawing mainly on religious and humanistic approaches to peace. Women's activism for peace started informally. One of the strategies was to work closely with local churches and organize prayer days for peace. Another was to organize mass protest rallies of women demanding peace and an end to bloodshed. Such visible activism alongside the not so visible personal counselling and consultations brought about attitudinal changes recognizing the importance of women in the peacemaking processes. And, for the first time, two women—one from Nagaland (the former president of the Naga Mothers' Association) and another from Manipur (representing the Naga Women's Organization of Manipur)—were inducted as members of the Forum for Naga Reconciliation (FNR), a forum that plays a key role in the Naga peace process today. According to Reverend Dr Aier, the advantage of having women as negotiators is that they are better able to factor in humanistic factors in their arguments at the peace table, and they can also be more patient.[4] The recognition accorded to women's activism for peace by including women in one of the highest platforms of peace negotiations in the state is a major achievement for women. In a society where women are still not recognized as legitimate representatives of the tribe, village and clan units, which are at the core of Naga society and identity, for a woman to be given recognition as a peace negotiator is greatly empowering. This is because at the peace table where the majority are men, women members are in a position not only to voice the experiences of women, but, more importantly, they are in a much wanted enabling environment where women are able to negotiate with men on equal terms.

Women have also been called upon to mediate in situations where the men could not go, as when women's organizations have been approached to intervene to avert violent confrontations. In very volatile situations, the presence of women may have the effect of bringing out the humane side of the protagonists. Several incidents can exemplify this. For instance, in 2005, representatives of the Ao Senden were summoned and confined by the militant group National Socialist Council of Nagalim, Isak-Muivah faction (NSCN, IM) in their headquarters at Camp Hebron. The captives were threatened at gunpoint in connection with issues of taxation. Members of the Watsü Mungdang then stood up and asked whether NSCN (IM) were fighting for the good and peace of the land, or for money and power? They asked what right the NSCN (IM) had to kill the innocent who were just trying to protect the people? The women argued and negotiated for the release of the Ao Senden members. If a man had spoken as the women did that day the situation would have turned very ugly, but since it was women who gave voice to reason and compassion the tension was defused.[5]

Women's groups have also actively resisted intimidation by armed militants. For instance, when two female church workers were molested and threatened by NSCN (IM) cadres in Zunheboto district in 2013 the apex Sumi Naga women's organization, Sümi Totomi Hoho or STH, mobilized itself. Together with the public and other organizations, such as the students and tribal organizations, they demanded justice for the victims and appealed to the NSCN (IM) leaders to take disciplinary action against their cadres. This was ignored and no action was taken. Consequently, the public decided to overrun the camp where the perpetrators resided, but the women's group representing the mothers, sisters and wives of the men in the camps tried to stop the confrontation, pleading not to use arms, but talk with one another and come to an understanding. The women's group went up to the entry gate of the NSCN (IM) camp, but they were denied entry and forced to retreat under threat of being fired upon. Thereafter, from 27 to 30 December 2013, civil society volunteers attacked the designated NSCN (IM) camp and kept it under siege. There were several deaths on both sides, and the siege ended only after the armed cadres of the NSCN (IM) fled the camp.

Another incident took place in Mokokchung town in 2004, after intimidation by National Socialist Council of Nagaland, Kaplang faction (NSCN-K) cadres led to a fight between the cadres and local boys of a neighbourhood of the town. In further altercations, one 12th standard student was shot dead. The general public, women leaders and elders of the town saw this as the last straw in a series of violent, intimidating and oppressive acts that has spanned almost a decade, meted out against the public by the armed group. The citizens of the town rose up against the militants and attacked their camp. The result was a total uprising of the town's people against the group, compelling them to flee the town. This was ground-breaking action taken by the entire town, including men and women. In the aftermath of this event, there was a lot of tension among the town's people fearing retribution from the armed cadres. Mokokchung being the district headquarter of the Ao tribe and as the largest tribal body of the district, the Ao Senden took the responsibility of guarding the town, defusing tensions and dealing with any retaliatory action from NSCN (K). Since Mokokchung is the administrative centre of the district, the town is also multi-ethnic and the situation was developing towards tensions along tribal fault lines.[6] Realizing that all the citizens of the town must stand united to avoid the situation turning into a communal conflict with tribal politics, the women's groups of the town's different wards,[7] together with the Watsü Mungdang leadership, did what they could to spread the message that this was a common problem of all the citizens, and not just the Ao tribe. As one woman stated: 'I am a teacher and I used my students' connections to reach out to their parents and through them their community.' Another woman said: 'I am married to a non-Ao man and through my marital connections we reached out to my husband's community.' According to the women, members of other tribes and communities started attending and participating in the public meetings after they were thus mobilized. Despite this, women's activism in the informal sphere failed to gain recognition. As one of the women leaders stated:

> As women we do a lot of mobilization work because we can do it and we are also expected to. We were with the men in all the critical times, but women are still not nominated or included in formal committees empowered to represent the tribe or wards or villages.[8]

According to women participants in a group discussion about the incident:

> The men don't know what we have done, and even if they do they will not acknowledge that our background work of networking with other communities also contributed to the one voice, one stand of the town's public during such dire times. For almost a month after the incident, each neighbourhood ward set up public vigilante groups to guard the ward day and night. During this period the Watsü Mungdang instructed their ward units to take care and support the groups guarding the ward in whatever ways they could. And the women did it by providing food and refreshments, firewood from our kitchens during the day and even at night-time. But in a major public meeting called by the Ao Senden, some male members accused the Watsü Mungdang of not showing their support by not even providing tea and refreshments for the men guarding the wards.[9]

The experiences of the women as narrated here indicate that one of the strengths of women in peace negotiations is their ability to take advantage of their social networks and neutrality as women. Since women do not have the legitimate right to represent the tribe, they can approach others more freely and bring the message of peace for common good on a personal level beyond community controversies. For example, women married into another tribal group have better access to their husbands' community and can communicate the concerns of the 'other' party without any political or tribal implications. Another dimension of women's peacebuilding is the informality of their every day activities such as talks around the hearth and facilitating communication. For instance, women of different groups are known to rally together on common issues of safety of their children and the sick and communicate these to the menfolk in their community, thereby persuading them to stand with one another for their common concerns.

Both men and women suffered tension, fear and worries during the unfolding conflict between the town residents and the armed militant cadres of the Naga political group, and later, both men and women were involved and engaged at their own social levels to bring about normalcy and peaceful co-existence among the people in the town. However, in the aftermath of the conflict, when reconciliation meetings were brokered between the tribal unions and the NSCN faction, the women's groups were not invited to participate and denied the opportunity to voice their concerns and sufferings. The Naga experiences show that women's initiatives to bring warring rival groups to the negotiating table is well recognized and even encouraged. However, when official peace negotiations take place, women are rarely nominated to the all important peace committees, which apparently bears a link with the traditional notions of citizenship and the differential rights of men and women to represent.

CONCLUDING REMARKS

One of the lessons we learn from the experiences of Naga women is that the contributions of women to peacebuilding processes is as multilayered as their experiences of conflict are complex. They are complex because women have to deal not only with the problem of bringing a peaceful solution to the conflict, but as women's groups they do not function independently, but always have to work in close consultation with the apex tribal organization. The apex tribal organization, which is essentially a man's organization, even has the authority to stop a women's group from functioning. This was clearly exhibited by the experiences of the Watsü Mungdang when the Ao Senden issued a declaration banning it and stopped the collection of fees from members, even prohibiting the women from conducting a peaceful procession in protest against the non-implementation of the state government's own Women's Reservation Bill.

The other lesson is that women's activism for peace is normally informal, and women also depend a lot on personal networks for mobilization. In this regard they have the advantage of appropriating the 'mother' image and appeal for the common good of all. Since women's approach to peacebuilding is usually non-political, it has the ability to create more space for negotiations. Time and again women have proven that they are no less capable than men in their ability to mobilize, create the right environment and even negotiate a peaceful solution in difficult situations. Yet these contributions often go unrecognized and remain undervalued because they take place outside official high-level fora. Often, at high-level discussions and deliberations, women are not included or nominated as members of peace delegations or committees authorized to speak on behalf of the community. Such exclusion and under-representation of women has been associated with the trivialization of women's experiences and sufferings. In the Naga context, when we unpack all the arguments for excluding women from representation, the fundamental question of the practice of gendered citizenship emerges. This is because no Naga clan, village or tribe would allow women to represent them politically in the public arena. What we find here is that discourse on citizenship has to do with the identities people deploy in everyday life (Hobson and Lister 2001: 27; Stevenson 2000). This is clearly visible in the ways in which gender identity is defined by the social and political spaces that men and women occupy in Naga society, and the ways that this impacts their efforts to broker peace.

Feminist thinking is responsible for redefining the concept of 'citizenship', not in its narrow sense of the 'right to vote', but in the sense of *entitlements, rights, responsibilities* and *agency*. This definition of 'citizenship' of having agency as free subjects has meaning only, if we give substantive content to it (i.e., the means and the mechanisms by which formal equality can be realized for citizens). The Indian Supreme Court has ruled that if one does not have substantive equality then one does not have equality at all (Sen 2003: 24). On the question of equality, society is organized along the fault line of gender, which is basically a social and cultural construct of 'categorizing, and symbolizing power, of hierarchically structuring relationships among different categories of people and different human activities in a manner symbolically associated with masculinity and femininity' (Mazurana and Proctor, 2013: 2). Drawing a distinction between the status of being a citizen, and 'doing' citizenship by seeing it as a social role and behaving accordingly, is very important. Gender, race and class, and other aspects of identity determine the degree to which people are able to participate in governance, and shape decisions that have an impact on their lives. How this plays out in practice is very context-specific, making it critical to begin working on citizenship with a grounded, concrete analysis of the reality of women's lives in particular localities (Sweetman et al. 2011: 349). While the idea of citizenship today is based on the idea of universality, 'what it means and how it is experienced is not' (Ibid.: 350). In the present study also it is found that the notions of *entitlements*, *rights* and *responsibilities* that are the elemental features distinguishing a citizen from a non-citizen are definitely not the same for men and women.

From the perspective of understanding citizenship as a social and political status that involves rights, especially the right to represent, and as a practice involving political participation, it is clear that women in Naga society are denied the full rights and status of a citizen. Gendered political practices in which women are denied equal political rights as citizens show up clearly in the exclusion of women from all important leadership positions of political significance. Whenever there is a question of representing a particular tribe or political group, women fail to get nominated or be selected as representative members in the delegations or committees. The socio-cultural construction of gender that feeds the practice of gendered citizenship is found to be a vital facet of women's disempowerment.

NOTES

1. The institution of the Dobashi court, introduced by the British, is a district-level court under the deputy commissioner. It has judicial powers to arbitrate based on the customary law of a particular tribe.
2. *Pukrelia* is a tradition in which women holding Y shaped sticks are known to burst forth between warring clans in an effort to stop them from killing each other.
3. According to this tradition, whenever women were married outside of their birth villages they acted as peace messengers. On the other hand, there are also narratives of such women acting as spies.
4. Personal communication, interview conducted in March 2013.
5. As narrated to the author in December 2012 by the women who went to negotiate with the NSCN (IM) to release the men.
6. In 2013, the author met with several women and men and conducted several interviews. The men also said that initially the other tribes who were also citizens of Mokokchung were not very forthcoming, perhaps due to apprehensions over possible retaliation. Initially, they did not attend the public meetings called by the Ao Senden, although they were equally affected.
7. The town is divided into 10 blocks called wards. Each ward has its own ward council that takes care of the general welfare of the residents and the internal law and order situation of the ward. The ward councils consist of men only.
8. As stated by the president of the Watsü Mungdang, Mokokchung town, in an interview conducted on 10 April 2013.
9. Mokokchung, April 2013.

REFERENCES

Aier, Anungla. 2008. 'Folklore, Folk Ideas and Gender Relation Among the Nagas', *Eastern Quarterly*, 5(2/3): 87–95.

———. 2012. 'Culture, Customary law and Gender: An Overview of Emerging Issues in Nagaland', *Journal of the Asiatic Society*, 54(2): 51–60.

Hobson, Barbara and Ruth Lister. 2001. 'Keyword: Citizenship', in Jane Lewis, Barbara Hobson and Birte Siim (eds) *Contested Concepts; Gender and Social Politics*, pp. 1–54. https://www.researchgate.net/publication/242461255

Lister, Ruth. 2001. 'Citizenship and Gender', in K. Nash and A. Scott (eds), *Blackwell Companion to Political Sociology*, pp. 372–82. London: Blackwell.

Manchanda, Rita. 2004. *Naga Women in the Peace Process*. Kathmandu: South Asia Forum for Human Rights (SAFHR).

Mazurana, Dyan and Keith Proctor. 2013. 'Gender, Conflict and Peace'. Occasional Paper, 15 October, World Peace Foundation.

Sen, Gita. 2003. 'Feminist Politics in a Fundamentalist World' (Keynote address), in Maitrayee Mukhopadhyay (ed.), *Proceedings of the International Conference on Governing for Equity: Gender, Citizenship and Governance*, pp. 24-26. Amsterdam: KIT Publishers.

Srikanth, H. and C.J. Thomas. 2005. 'Naga Resistance Movement and the Peace Process in Northeast India', *Peace and Democracy in South Asia*, 1(2): 57–87.

Stevenson, N. 2000. *Culture and Citizenship*. London: Sage Publications.

Sweetman, Caroline, Jo Rowlands and Lina Abou-Habib. 2011. 'Introduction to Citizenship', *Gender & Development,* 19(3): 347–55. DOI: 10.1080/13552074.2011.636591

Swu, Scatu. 2013. *Hails and Blames: A Brief Account of Naga Independence Movement.* Dimapur: Heritage Publishing House.

CHAPTER 6

Gendered Power Systems and Peace Politics in Nagaland*

Rita Manchanda and Seema Kakran

LONGKHUM VILLAGE, NAGALAND, AUGUST 2013

The fabled Naga village democracy was at work, as 150 Naga men, belonging to two clans of the Ao Nagas, had gathered in the *Morung* (meeting hall) to settle a dispute over hierarchy and status. Opposite them, but beyond earshot, we sat in the home of Moatula (an alias), an active member of the Ao tribal women's body, Watsü Mungdang, discussing the organization's struggle to assert women's entitlement to quotas in the Mokokchung district metropolitan and town councils. Naga women's opposition to their exclusion from governing bodies—traditional and modern—has polarized Naga society. But here her daughter, on vacation from Delhi University, saw nothing contradictory in the juxtaposition of the two meetings, ours and theirs. So normalized was the practice of gendered exclusion that she took no notice of it. In Longkhum village, a Naga student of theology who had accompanied us told us that her family is still regarded as an 'outsider', despite a century

*A modified version of this article will also appear in the journal *Cultural Dynamics.*

of residence there. But the young woman had the last laugh—'The men harp on about safeguarding tradition, but are quick to don a tie-suit, whereas we women remain faithful to Naga dress, for all formal occasions.'[1]

Our request to take photographs of the 'elders' inside the Morung elicited a prompt refusal; we weren't allowed a closer approach either. This brought to mind the traditional proscription against Naga women walking past the Morung, lest snatches of the conversation of men fall upon women's ears and be garbled in the retelling. Ironically, during the conflict and ceasefire aftermath, Naga women became valued couriers, trusted interlocutors and channels for indirect communication between the top leaders of rival factions.

The Longkhum encounter provided a dramatic counterpoint to our research pursuit—to explore the empowering potential of Naga women's practice of peace work against the broader canvas of the dynamics of the relationship between gender, ethnicity and nation in the context of the peace politics of the Naga conflict-peace continuum in the Northeast.[2] Naga women—who through their decades of peace work at the village and state level had emerged as stakeholders in the peace process—were now questioning their gendered exclusion in the public sphere (both modern and tribal). Seventeen years of ceasefire had accelerated the growth of a social grouping that approximates to a nascent 'new middle class'[3] of educated professional women and men. This small but influential educated, professional social grouping, which straddles both the traditional tribal institutions and modern socio-economic structures, is expanding the Naga public sphere and reshaping its society and politics (Manchanda and Bose 2011).

We contend that 50 years of Naga statehood and market penetration, galvanized further by the long cold peace, is producing a new order of elite stratification which is not only reworking the relations within traditional tribal hierarchies, but also class, youth and gender relations. A new generation of educated and professional tribal women has emerged—a generation in which many of the women are linked with national and international women's movements, and are seeking more equal modes of imagining citizenship (Aier 2014). Importantly, there is convergence between the modern and the traditionally rooted women's associations. The coalescing of these social developments has produced new assertions and contestations, especially in the area of (a) Naga women's exclusion from decision-making, (b) customary law and traditions that trivialize violence against women, and (c) expanding property rights for women, which is more latent.

The patriarchal backlash targets Naga women as threatening Naga community identity by undermining Naga customary laws and practices, which are integrally related to that identity and constitute the ideological foundation of the Naga national struggle. We argue that the tensions inherent in the relationship between gender, ethnicity and nation are coming to a head as a consequence of the intense social and political churning in Naga society, particularly telescoped in the last 17 years of ceasefire and 'pacification' (Francis 2010).

Feminist scholarship has drawn attention to the complex ways in which the ideological construct and practices of 'nation' and 'ethnicity' intersect with patriarchy (de Mel 2001; Enloe 1993: 250; Yuval Davis 1997). Gendered narratives of the nation state and of autonomies have focused particular attention on the ways in which male and female differences are reinforced post-conflict. Indeed 'new' states (especially ethnically organized entities) have formulated rights and obligations that have strengthened the masculinity of the public sphere and the femininity of the private sphere (Moghadam 2000). In the Northeast, a majority of peace accords supposedly resolving ethnonationalist conflicts, including the 1960 agreement creating Nagaland state, specifically guaranteed customary laws and practices to govern land and social relations.

Scholars have showed the ways in which the reification of tradition and customary laws in these self-governing states/councils has turned women into 'internal minorities' in the

Northeast (Bhattacharjee 2002: 133; Chakraborty 2008). However as Samir Das, a student of peace accords, reminds us:

> Women's democratic struggles are in many ways embedded in ethnicity and ethnic movements and the success of their struggle depends not so much on their ability to stand alone (for that is what seldom happens in any society) but very much on how they steer and negotiate their way through conflict between their gender identities as women and as members of some particular ethnic communities. (Das 2008: 56)

As discussed in this chapter, there is nothing to suggest that the women leaders believe in the possibility or even desirability of pursuing an autonomous woman's agenda—unaffected by indigenous/ethnic or nationalist ones. As feminist scholar, Cynthia Cockburn emphasizes: '[W]e are always not just women but a woman who has to deal one way or another with "being" a Serb, an English woman or an Indian' (Cockburn 2008: 287). This has implications for the ability of women to forge cross-community peace politics (Manchanda and Potter 2012).

SINGULARITY OF THE NAGA MOVEMENT AND NAGA WOMEN'S EMPOWERMENT

Our choice of focus on Nagaland in the conflict-affected sociopolitical landscape of the Northeast was influenced by a complex set of factors. The Naga 'national' movement is the 'oldest' self-determination struggle against post-independence India's efforts at nationally integrating communities which are ethnically and historically separate from the Indian nation. Also, it is paradigmatic of the effective limits of both the Indian state's militarist counter-insurgency strategy, and the flaws in the peacemaking strategy of 'Integration through Internal Re-organisation' as articulated in a succession of flawed peace accords (Chadda 2002). In particular, the 1960 Naga peace accord laid the template for the grand strategy of power sharing and devolution of power to territorially focused, ethnically delimited autonomies. The strategy succeeded in dividing the national movement, but establishing a Naga state did not end the violence. Three decades later, the Indo-Naga Ceasefire Agreement of 1997 is the Indian state's latest démarche in peacemaking.

More importantly, from a gendered perspective, Naga social dynamics provides an opportunity to examine within the overall social churning in traditional hierarchies and structures of authority the opening up of spaces for reworking gender relations. Also, while there is a rich narrative of women's groups at the forefront of the struggles against state militarization in the Northeast, defending human rights and building peace, the Naga women's trajectory is singular in that it demonstrates the scope and limits of peace politics being empowering and enhancing women's rights. Admittedly, as L. Basanti Devi's chapter in this volume shows, both the organizational ethos of the Meira Paibis and the political meaning of the movement are being contested and redefined especially after the 'success' of the movement in shaming the Indian state on the Armed Forces (Special Powers) Act (AFSPA). Manipur scholar-journalist Pradip Phanjoubam, writing about the Meira Paibis earlier had reflected that, powerful as the movement was, it would not be able to outgrow its grassroots foundation. 'The abundance energy, talent, enterprise all remain too raw to be able to transform into instruments needed to carve out respectable and equal spaces in the bargains and negotiations for power in modern political institutions' (Phanjoubam 2008: 101). Evidently, the Meira Paibis' loose coordinating structure is changing and getting more formalised. However, we argue that the crucial issue is the degree of vulnerability to instrumentalization by both civil society and state.

In contrast, the journey of the Naga women's groups has taken them from village-based grassroots tribal organizations to apex bodies such as the Naga Mothers' Association (NMA) and Naga Women's Union (NWU). Moreover, from being a women's group concerned with witch-hunting, drug peddlers and 'prostitutes', the NMA has reimagined itself as frontline 'peacekeepers' and stakeholders in the peace process, integral participants in all civil society initiatives such as the 'Forum for Reconciliation'. We argue that the NMA is demonstrating its capacity to translate its local power into formal authority in the public sphere. The NMA's transformational journey is mirrored in the changes in the working style and thinking of the NMA as revealed in the contrasting response of two professional women belonging to two different generations. The journalist Monalisa Changkija, in the 1980s, declined to join the NMA, feeling alienated from its activities and functioning style. Two decades later, Professor Rosemary Dzuvichu is a consultant with the NMA, and is steering the campaign of the new generation of educated, professional tribal women challenging women's exclusion in decision-making.

This chapter explores the shifting forms and expressions of Naga women's agency, from motherhood politics to women's rights assertion. It teases out their shifting agendas—from subsuming gender consciousness in an identity-based mobilization to pushing for inclusion and equal rights that challenge customary practices; from an apolitical engagement to political activism for transforming the nature of inequality, exploitation and exclusion. We examine the thesis that ethnonationalist mobilizations instrumentalize and marginalize women and explore the possibility of an emancipatory democratic politics in the Naga context (Nongbri 2011).

The chapter supplements existing literature on the issue with intensive interviews conducted in August 2013 in Nagaland (Dimapur, Kohima, Wokha and Mokokchung) with a wide range of civil society groups: NMA, Watsü Mungdang, Lotha Eloe, Naga Hoho, Ao and Lotha Public Organisations, women in public administration, the police, the church, and Naga women politicians, educationists, journalists and non-governmental organizations (NGOs). Unfortunately, our conversation with the women of the National Socialist Council of Nagaland (NSCN) in Camp Hebron remained too rudimentary to tease out an analysis. Finally, the authors bring to the study years of participatory research engagement and advocacy work in the Northeast.

WOMEN IN NAGA TRADITION

In Naga tribal society, women are said to have enjoyed more freedom of movement and choice than the caste-ridden Hindu women subject to layered socio-religious oppression. As Christopher von Fürer-Haimendorf, an Austrian ethnologist, observed:

> Many women in the more civilized parts in India may well envy the women of Naga Hills their high status and their free happy life; and if you measure the cultural level of a people by the social position and personal freedom of its women, you will think twice before looking down on the Naga as savages. (Xaxa 2008: 114)

Contemporary Naga women, like the anthropologist Dolly Kikon, are challenging the myth of the high status of Naga women in casteless egalitarian tribal societies. Traditionally, Naga societies were geared to readiness for war and masculine war-like qualities were valorized. Women were debarred from touching a weapon or participating in public life. According to Dolly Kikon:

> Every Naga woman has experienced humiliation and insults from the men on the basis of her womanhood. These men are not outsiders or strangers. They are their 'respected' uncles, cousins and in some cases their fathers and brothers who never fail to remind them about the predestined inferior roles that have already been slated out for them. (Kikon 2002: 179)

While there is no overt discrimination on the birth of a girl child, it is significant that the Ao boy child is welcomed by the clan 'as one of ours', the girl child as 'one of theirs'.[4]

While customary laws and practices differ among the more than 40 Naga tribes, a patriarchal bias is common. For instance, the Lotha Nagas believe men possess six kinds of strength and women five, which make them unsuitable for responsible jobs. Lotha women were not allowed to go past a public hall where the elders conferred lest they overheard the discussion and in 'gossiping' about it distorted it. The Angami Naga male was given credit for his extramarital affairs, with his status rising according to the number of his relationships. Women accused of adultery were punished by physical defacement of the nose, slicing off the heel or cutting off their hair. The Zeme Nagas consider it derogatory to eat the meat of an animal killed by women. The Mayon Nagas of Manipur, for example, consider women to be 'unprincipled and unreliable' because they do not have a permanent clan; their clans change into that of their husbands when they marry (Nag 2006).

The material reality of Naga women's lower status is that women have no inheritance rights over community or clan lands. This is despite the Naga woman's proactive role in the *jhum* (shifting cultivation) economy. While customary law differs among tribes and there is no codification, the common practice is that women cannot inherit immovable property, though they can lease land for use during their lifetime and a father can 'gift' acquired wealth to a daughter during his lifetime, which remains hers till death, after which it reverts to the 'male' heirs. A widow remains in her husband's family as guardian of the minors but cannot inherit his property. With regard to divorce, an Ao husband can take his wife's ornaments and also claim a penalty of a head of cattle and repayment of the bride price from his wife's family and a fine from her lover. In case of rape, traditional courts encourage settlement and fine the rapist (or even murderer) a pig or two.

This is not to deny that indigenous sociocultural systems provided greater freedom of movement and choice to women. There was choice in matters relating to selecting partners, divorce and widow remarriage, and once the man had identified the field for jhum cultivation it was the woman who decided on the division of labour of the collective engaged in clearing the field, and women had multiple economic roles in the house and community (National Commission for Women [n.d.]). As long as there was common ownership of property resources, women had some control over livelihood and freedom of movement was assured. Moreover, as our Naga male interlocutors emphasized, the gendered public-private divide made women sovereign in the home but excluded their participation in the Naga village tribal authority or in the tribal courts (as judge). The colonial encounter and the interface with the Baptist Christian missions not only strengthened the patriarchal ethos, it also introduced aspects of Victorian morality to Naga culture.[5]

THE SOCIAL UPHEAVAL OF CONFLICT

The Naga nationalist struggle for survival required the mobilization of the whole community. Every Naga was involved. Every Naga was 'suspect'. Churches were desecrated, villages razed, 'rice barns' and field crops burnt. The counter-insurgency strategy uprooted and herded people into 'strategic hamlets', keeping them on subsistence rations, making them do forced porterage, and imposing collective fines and punitive curfews at harvest time. Those identified as relatives of 'undergrounds'—women, children and elders alike—were herded into concentration camps, beaten and starved (Manchanda 2004: 4).

As in many identity-based struggles, it was the women, the purveyors and reproducers of the community, who were targeted and their bodies became the symbolic terrain of battle. Sexual torture was widespread and impunity absolute. A rare exception in breaking the silence was the initiative of Yangerala Ao and Watsü Mungdang, the Ao tribal women's organization. Persuading four rape survivors to testify, the women appealed to the National Human Rights Commission to set up an Inquiry Commission into the violence perpetrated by the Indian Army in Mokokchung market on 27 December 1994. Soldiers of the Manipur Light Infantry and Assam Rifles had, in a reprisal attack, fired at post-Christmas shoppers. Nine people were shot dead, and 89 shops and 48 houses looted and gutted. Women were stripped and sexually assaulted. Yangerala, a medical doctor and Mokokchung district director of health, had personally examined 15 of the rape victims and confirmed sexual violation (Khala 2003).

It is beyond the scope of the chapter to detail the gendered narrative of violence and devastation which has been elaborated elsewhere (Manchanda 2004). However, an analysis of the scope of gendered power shifts and the possibility, 'post-conflict',[6] of the emergence of more inclusive and equal societies requires some contextualization. The ceasefire saw women overturning gender stereotypes, breaching the public-private divide and creating the conditions for women with moral authority at the local level laying claim to formal politics. The social impact of women joining the armed groups seemed to have been minimal, although the chairperson of the National Socialist Council of Nagaland (Isak-Muivah) (NSCN [IM]) women's wing, Salim (an alias), claimed that women made up 20–30 per cent of the armed cadres. However, far from being role models, Rosemary Dzuvichu, advisor to the NMA, dismissed the women cadres as school dropouts with low capacity.[7]

WOMEN'S PEACE WORK

Narratives of her-story of the Naga conflict are strewn with incidents of women shielding men, physically lying on the road, blocking trucks loaded with the village boys from driving away. Bloody reprisals for militant ambushes would see women in the villages beating a drum to sound the alert, rushing to form a wall between the security forces and their men. A village woman of Jotsoma (The village of the legendary Angami Phizo, the father of Naga nationalism) spoke with pride:

> When the Indian Army came, it was women who stepped forward between the soldiers and villagers. It is only women who can intervene. We constantly had to talk to the army. We mothers would go to the warring factions, walk to their camps and plead with them not to kill each other, not to harass villagers. (Manchanda 2004: 37–38)

From the start of the conflict in the 1950s till now, the time of ceasefire, Naga women have used their bodies as human shields to block state forces and NSCN armed cadres from clashing. In the 2010 stand-off at Mao Gate on the Nagaland-Manipur border,

Naga women for days outfaced the Manipur armed police in a protest sit-in, prayers and marches. In the 2009 Shirui siege, Naga women physically interposed their bodies to avert clashes between the Assam Rifles and the NSCN. 'We're just doing our job as peace keepers', the women told the exasperated commanding officer, as they constituted a firebreak for 15 days and nights in relays of 50 women (Haksar 2009). The Assam Rifles had laid siege to an NSCN (IM) camp in Manipur (technically outside the ceasefire regime) and the villagers were caught in the middle.

In conflict, Naga women's bodies became the terrain on which war was waged—to be brutally assaulted and mutilated to teach the community a lesson, to humiliate it for failing to 'protect' the women, and to spoil the reproducer of the community. In turn, Naga women used their bodies to confront a more powerful opponent by shaming the 'protector' authority (the state) and embarrassing the soldiers to stop them from breaking their physical cordon. They leveraged their helplessness as women to gain access in threatening situations to negotiate release of sons and husbands. Both aspects are part of an integral patriarchal script. Women no less than men have internalized this patriarchal script. Such strategies reinforce stereotypes of gendered subordination and raise troubling questions about the empowering and disempowering aspects of the politics.

Social sanction for Naga women's peace activism is rooted in their traditional role as peacemakers between warring villages from the headhunting days when a *demi* or a *pukrelia* would step forward in the midst of battle and halt the violence. Its contemporary version is the apocryphal story of Neidonuo Angami, then president of NMA, intervening between two fighting factions in Phek district and saying, 'Listen to your mother before you kill your brother' (Manchanda 2004: 43).

Spiralling fratricidal violence in 1980 and the 1990s pushed the welfare-oriented Naga women's organizations into taking responsibility for stopping Nagas killing Nagas. Every morning bodies were lying unclaimed in the bazaars and the people were too terrorized to come forward to claim them. At this time, the NMA, in alliance with the churches, came forward to perform a funeral ritual—according the body a dignified funeral wrapped in the tribe's shawl—affirming the value of life. In 1994, the NMA launched a 'Stop all Bloodshed' campaign with non-partisan 'Peace Teams' fanning out to the district headquarters to urge an end to the violence. Through tribal affiliation, the mothers reached out to the tribal segregated factions listening to their grievances like a 'mother' and talking them into reconciliation. Nearly a decade later, with the 'unity' question back in the foreground and stymieing the peace process, the NMA, at its 7th General Assembly in 2003, would again call for national reconciliation. As factional violence surged in 2006–8,[8] the NMA and its Manipur-based sister organization, the NWU, which was formed in 1994, became core members of the influential civil society initiative—Forum for Naga Reconciliation or FNR (2008). NMA's peace work is focused on keeping channels of communication open between rival factions, from the top leadership to the cadres.

It is significant that some of the most influential pan-Naga civil society organizations—NMA, NWU and Naga Hoho—are of recent vintage (1984, 1994 and 1998 respectively). While they derive their authority from the traditional tribal institutions, the two apex bodies straddle both the traditional and modern worlds, and their changing composition reflects the generational shifts in social stratification in Naga society. In understanding the morphing of the NMA from welfare to peace activism, and then to focusing on strategic rights, 1994 is a key evolutionary moment. According to Kheslie Chisi, former president of the NMA: 'The situation demanded it.'[9] Also, the pressure from the churches was significant.

Attention should also be drawn to the ideational influences of organizations like the Naga People's Movement for Human Rights (NPMHR), which had important connections with democratic rights-based movements in India and internationally, for example, the Asian Indigenous Peoples' Pact. NPMHR by then had emerged as a nodal body, even challenging the constitutional validity of AFSPA in the Supreme Court (1987–97). Naga human rights activists had participated in the Vienna Human Rights Conference in 1993. Also, ideas about civil society and its potential for peacebuilding were spreading across borders, especially from Sri Lanka's conflict, borne on the shoulders of visiting Indian human rights activists (Manchanda and Bose 2015a).

MOTHERHOOD POLITICS

Mobilizing around 'motherhood' provided the context for women's everyday micropolitics. It positioned their intervention in the public sphere as a stretching of their traditional roles as reflected in the use of phrases such as 'kitchen politics' to reach out to armed factions against violence. Local leaders would be invited for a meal in the kitchen, the heart of the Naga home. Also, as mothers they could scold errant sons. 'Who are you fighting for? Not for the 50–70 of you, but for us, not for your today but for our tomorrow', Yangerala Ao reprimanded young NSCN cadres against enforcing protracted curfews that disrupted schools and businesses (Manchanda 2004: 39). The NMA claimed that as mothers they are trusted by all sides. 'For women there are no factions. We are still united. It is the men who have misunderstandings. Struggle for power has divided them', said Jotsoma, village woman elder (ibid.: 42).

By depoliticizing women's activism, 'motherhood' politics undermined their ability to assert their right to be part of decision-making institutions. Defending that strategic choice, Neidonuo Angami was stoical: 'We have our roles to play as mothers, they theirs' (ibid.: 28). That gendered division of labour meant, according to Dr Akang Ao, deputy speaker of the Naga Hoho, that 'we call them (NMA) when there is an issue of concern to them. When it is Hoho business, there is no need to call them' (ibid.: 21). It ghettoized women as speaking only on and for women. Importantly, the new generation of NMA leaders holds up as role model Rosemary Dzuvichu's mother, once a nominated (but voting) member of the Kohima Village Council who was outspoken and not just on women's issues.[10] It should be added that, in the 1990s, NMA's reorientation from a social welfare organization to one engaged in peace politics, albeit couched in motherhood politics, provoked vociferous comments about social transgression.

That reaction may explain why NMA held back while its sister organization in Manipur, the NWU, boldly pursued a women's rights agenda, reflecting the concerns of the professional women who were its office-bearers. Its General Assembly resolutions asserted women's rights on marriage, divorce, private property and representation in the United Naga Council (UNC). The different working styles of NMA and NWU are a reminder of the very different political contexts in which the two women's groups operate (Ray 2000).

SUSTAINING THE CEASEFIRE AND PEACE PROCESS

In July 1997, the Government of India signed the Indo-Naga Ceasefire Agreement with the dominant armed group, the NSCN (IM), providing for unconditional political negotiations at the highest level. On the political front, however, talks got stuck on the demands for exceptional autonomy or shared sovereignty and integration of the divided Naga habitat. The unity question proved equally contentious. Persisting fratricidal violence has torn apart Naga society, with Naga killing Naga after the Naga National Council (NNC) split over the Shillong Accord in 1975. Moreover, at the time of the ceasefire agreement, while NSCN (IM) was the dominant nationalist group, NNC and the Khaplang group, the NSCN (K), enjoyed wide support with the latter controlling swathes of territory. For various reasons, the government chose to enter into separate ceasefires with the two NSCN factions,

Isak-Muivah and the Khaplang group, further fomenting factionalism. Naga 'civil society' played a crucial role in sustaining the peace process when the ceasefire was under strain from multiple conflict lines: inter-factional, inter-community (Naga-Meitei, Naga-Kuki) and moderate 'integrationists' vs radical 'independentists'.

That the ceasefire has held these 17 years has a lot to do with the peace work of the Naga social organizations in creating a society-wide consensus in support of the peace process, monitoring ceasefire violations, providing early warning and building reconciliation amongst the factions. In understanding the dynamic role of Naga civil society in the peace process, it is appropriate to acknowledge the influence of civil society activists from mainland India who persuaded the NSCN collective leadership of the value of civil society's potential in peacemaking (Manchanda and Bose 2015a). One of the earliest initiatives was an experimental peace audit that enabled an interaction with a cross-section of the stakeholders (including women) of the Naga and Chittagong Hill Tracts (CHT) peace accords. Held in Kathmandu in 1999, the peace audit also brought into the dialogue a leading peace activist from Sri Lanka (Perera 1999). Central to the civil society discourse was the argument that in asymmetric conflicts the support of civil society groups could provide strategic depth to NSCN (IM) negotiations vis-à-vis the more powerful Indian government.

What finally overcame the NSCN leadership's diffidence was the success of an open meeting focusing on human rights, justice and the Naga peace process in Kohima in March 2001. It brought together a panoply of 40 Indian and Naga civil society groups. NPMHR, with its origins in India's post-Emergency civil society effulgence in Jawaharlal Nehru University, served as the link with mainland Indian civil society. The massive support for the peace process expressed by all Naga groups cutting across tribal lines, business people and professionals at the Kohima meeting impressed the NSCN collective leadership of the value of keeping the civil society informed, and the need to cultivate an overground support base.

PROMOTING UNITY AND ACCOUNTABILITY

During the long ceasefire, the NMA and other social organizations insulated the peace process from 'spoiler' machinations (Kumar and Murthy 2002). The NMA joined other Naga social organizations and the churches in a 22-member Action Committee to independently monitor the ceasefire. The Action Committee pushed for inclusion of independent observers in the formal ceasefire mechanism, which though accepted[11] foundered over questions of their autonomy.[12] However, it did secure the inclusion, in the Ceasefire Ground Rules in 2001, of civilian security concerns of injury and property damage.

The most important role of the NMA and the NWU was to keep open the channels of communication between rival factions, widen the ambit of the ceasefire to encompass NSCN (K), and end factional violence. In 1999, four representatives of NMA and NWU enabled indirect talks between the top leaders of NSCN (IM) and NSCN (K). Four women representatives of NMA and NWU trekked across the Myanmar border to the NSCN (K) camp and met Khaplang at his headquarters in Saiging district in Burma. On their return, they briefed 16 top NSCN (IM) leaders. Naga women, who were not previously trusted to carry messages, had become trusted interlocutors.

At every significant consultation, the collective leadership of NSCN (IM) included women's groups such as NMA and NWU. Fierce turf wars between the NSCN (IM) and NSCN (K) factions saw a spike in factional violence in 2006–8. Concerned at the dangerous drift, NMA and NWU joined other Naga social organizations and the church to launch the FNR, a non-partisan civil society initiative. Above all, NMA has sought to bridge the social disconnect of the collective leadership, by directly appealing to Th Muivah, the group's top leader, in Delhi, for instance, to act against armed cadres involved in assaulting women, and to root out the culture of impunity. Confronting the NSCN (IM) leadership was a new generation of educated professionals, 'mothers' who had come a long way from the grass-roots level, and who were connected nationally and internationally via the Internet with Amnesty and the Indigenous Women's Forum.

SHIFTS IN SOCIAL STRATIFICATION: REIMAGINING EQUALITY AND INCLUSION

The peculiar characteristic of the Naga conflict, and indeed several other armed struggles in the Northeast, is that endemic cycles of war coexist with the parallel trajectory of the Indian state's peacemaking via the creation of self-governing 'ethnic' homelands and special federal arrangements. Fifty years of Naga statehood has entrenched modern structures of governance, elected lawmakers and political parties. They coexist with the traditional tribal structures of authority and the more recent and competing avatars such as the Naga Hoho and NMA. Also, the protracted ceasefire has produced the overground presence of competing armed groups and their rival 'governments in waiting'. In addition to these intersecting circles of power, there is the oppressive dominance of the security forces and the corrupting impact of their non-accountable security-related expenditure (Longkumer and Jamir 2012).

State and market penetration has produced a widening circle of stakeholders in the existing Indian state system—political leaders, the salaried, contractors, lease holders of natural resources, educationists, and civil servants, among others. The political economy that sustained the communitarian societies of the borderless world of the Naga is rapidly transforming (Manchanda and Bose 2015a: 38). While formal land reforms have not taken place, communitarian ownership is giving way to privatization of land and property. The ceasefire has accelerated the conditions for the growth of a new middle class. This postcolonial middle class has emerged from a different relationship with the Indian state than the 'middle class' colonial elite that spearheaded the Naga national movement and was anchored in traditional tribal structures (Misra 1983).

In this context, a new order of elite stratification is unsettling tribal hierarchies. Importantly, many of the new initiatives for resolving the old problems that have gridlocked Naga society—the FNR and the Committee for Alternate Arrangement—are being steered by men and women who inhabit the 'middle class' space of Naga society in terms of their urban location, education and professional occupations. They are exposed to democratizing ideologies and networks, national and international. This small but influential educated and professional social grouping which straddles both traditional tribal institutions and modern socio-economic structures is expanding the Naga public sphere, reshaping its society and politics (Manchanda and Bose 2011).

Earlier, the conflict had brought women into the public sphere, engaging in micropolitics. The ceasefire expanded the middle space for non-partisan engagement. Moreover, it is in the civil society sphere that women are present in large numbers as opposed to their absence in formal politics. Alongside, a new generation of educated, professional Naga women who straddled the traditional and modern, regional and national, collective and individual is confronting local patriarchies embedded in customary laws. We argue that the coalescing of these social changes has created a context in which the women's question has emerged as symbolic of reworking social hierarchies around three sites of inequality—discriminatory adjudication practices in customary law, inclusion in decision-making structures, and (at least latently) property rights.

Customary law does not entitle women to property rights. However, as Nagaland's senior-most woman civil servant, Additional Chief Secretary Banou Jamit, ruminated: 'The crunch will come once this generation of professional women create wealth and are blocked by the men of the clan from disposing it'.[13] Already, Monalisa Changkija, owner and editor of *Nagaland Page*, observed that her uncle and nephews were expecting her to pass on the newspaper business to her maternal nephews, the clan heirs, not her daughters who belonged to another clan. Sensitivities on the issue of property rights are extreme, as evident in the male pathology about Naga women marrying outside the community and alienating clan land. This anxiety drives the opposition of the Lotha (Wokha) Tribal Authority, faced with Lotha women marrying migrants from mainland India, setting up matrilocal residence and taking on Lotha names.

WOMEN IN PUBLIC LIFE

In northeast Indian societies, the public space is generally the monopoly of men. Customary practices and traditions that define the Naga way of life across diverse tribes extol the participatory village republics, but exclude Naga women, who are streamed into the tribal women's organization, safeguarding culture and social welfare (Das 2011). Among tribes that follow hereditary principles, such as the Sema, there are accounts of a woman *Gaonbora* (village head) in the 1970s, wearing the traditional red shawl, staff in hand, performing her duties. Rosemary Dzuvichu's mother, an NMA advisor, was a nominated member of the Angami Public Organisation, but with voting rights. The current NMA president has been member and vice chair of the Kohima Municipal Council.

More recently, under pressure on quotas for women, the Naga Hoho proposed 'nominating' two women to the Naga Hoho collective. 'Once that becomes the practice, the resistance too will weaken to women's equal participation', explained Chuba Ozukum, secretary of the Naga Hoho.[14] Rosemary Dzuvichu, who is steering the campaign for women's quotas, dismissed it as perpetuating the selection of proxy women without voting rights.[15] The UNC in Manipur too has been experimenting with the nomination option. The nominee of the Maring tribe, a woman was elected secretary of the welfare department. Since the 1990s, the NWU has been lobbying for women's political rights challenging their 'ceremonial' presence symbolizing Naga identity. A major breakthrough was when the Moyon Naga Council gave the women's tribal body the right to vote in the elections and a

Moyon woman became Speaker of the Council in 1997. But these advances have been difficult to sustain and efforts to amend the UNC Constitution continue to be resisted.

In Nagaland, women are missing not only in the traditional tribal structures of authority, but also in the modern structures of state politics. The Nagaland state assembly has an unbroken record of 11 legislative assemblies never electing a woman from its 60 seats. In Nagaland, only 25 women have stood for any election in 50 years. As for Lok Sabha elections, the single exception to the male bias was when Rano Shazia represented Nagaland in 1977. Women are relied upon to do door-to-door campaigning, distribute cash inducements to voters (a routine practice) and act as poll agents, and yet they are not considered worthy contestants. Khegholi Aaomi, a Congress party worker (whose husband was a minister), was rudely rebuffed by the state party unit bosses when she indicated an interest in contesting elections. At the insistence of the central leadership she was given a ticket to contest from Dimapur in the 2008 assembly elections, but she withdrew her name as there was no party support. In the 2013 elections the party offered her a ticket. This time she refused. '[The] Congress was losing. I didn't want to be made a scapegoat.'[16] 'The money question is what holds women back', said Monalisa Changkija, owner and editor of the daily *Nagaland Page*.[17] Women have no property rights, and like the men cannot use their property to get money to fight elections. She explicitly linked the demand for quotas with property rights. However, the Joint Action Committee on Women's Reservation strategically delinks the two.

Against the backdrop of discord over women's quotas, two women contested the 2013 assembly election—Yangerala Ao (independent) from Mokokchung, the state's most literate district, and Rakhila Lakiumong (Bharatiya Janata Party) from Tuensang, the most backward. The Naga People's Front, the 'nationalist' ruling front, put up no woman candidate, a reminder that ethnonationalist political parties tend to be hostile to the entry of women in formal politics (Mahanta 2002; Manchanda and Bose 2015b). 'Had Yangerala been able to break the glass ceiling and become the first woman to be elected MLA, it would have been the ideal resolution of the bitter struggle over quotas', observed Banou Jamit.[18] She did not win, and was not even supported by 45 per cent of the electorate, the women (Shrinivasan 2013). Evidently, Naga women have so internalized patriarchal exclusion that they will not vote for a woman. 'That is why reservations are necessary', Abokali Jimomi of *Youth-Net* emphasized.[19] Significantly, grass-roots women are more supportive of quotas than professional women like Jamit and Hushili.

The states of Nagaland, Mizoram and Meghalaya and two districts of Assam are exempt from the purview of the 73rd Amendment of the Constitution due to existence of local self-government bodies: village councils and village development boards (VDBs). Nevertheless, several VDBs have dynamic women secretaries. Sizeable funds (from centre and state) flow through the VDBs and particularly through urban and metropolitan councils. The experience in the cash-modest VDBs has been that new women members raise uncomfortable questions about auditing funds, though none of the women village councillors or bureaucrats interviewed believed women were less corrupt.[20] Ironically, in the midst of the heat and noise over quotas, Nagaland has been quietly implementing 25 per cent women's quotas in the VDB (Nagaland Village and Area Councils Act, 1978).

CONSCIOUSNESS AND CONFIDENCE OF WOMEN AS POLITICAL SUBJECTS

Political settlements resolving identity-based struggles have as their core the guaranteeing of customary laws and practices. In the Northeast, a majority of ethnic peace accords, including the 1960 agreement creating Nagaland state, constitutionally guaranteed (Article 371A) customary laws and practices governing land and social relations. In Nagaland, women are challenging sociopolitical exclusion and calling into question the adequacy of the traditional all-male tribal system of arbitration and reconciliation that they feel trivializes crimes against women. And from the backdoor has come in the contentious question of the property rights of Naga women. It is within this context that Naga women want to initiate a debate on Article 371A.[21] The decision-making committees that at a particular moment in history determined the inclusion of 'all' customary laws, including those that perpetuated the suppression of women, excluded women's perspectives and those perspectives need to be brought back now.

The social upheaval of conflict has pushed women through their human rights and peace work into the public sphere. The long ceasefire further expanded the middle space for civil society, including women's activism. The possibility of women translating that activism and recognition in the informal sphere of politics into authority in the formal sphere of representative politics (modern and traditional) will be the measure of the empowering potential of peace politics in Naga society today. Already apparent is the quality of new-found assertiveness of Naga women as political agents within an overall context of reimaging equality and inclusion in Naga society, 'post conflict'. It is evidenced in the generational difference between the consensual style and content of the politics of former NMA president, Neidonuo Angami, and the greater assuredness in the articulations of the current office-bearers of NMA and their advisors. Significantly, Angami has been ambivalent if not negative on the demand for women's quotas and inclusion in decision-making structures.

Asserting Rights: Quotas for Women

The Naga women's challenge to unequal gendered relations has got catalysed around women's claims to quotas in urban and metropolitan councils, which technically are outside the purview of customary laws which govern Naga village life and exclude women in decision-making. The debate has got framed as positing the 'traditional' world of the Naga in opposition to the hegemonic influences of 'modern' India; the recourse of the 'cosmopolitan' Naga women to Indian courts is pitted against the customary ways of reconciliation.

India's third tier of government, the local self-governing institutions, was not extended to the 6th Schedule areas. In 2001, the Nagaland government enacted the Nagaland Municipal Act, extending the 73rd and 74th constitutional amendments (1992) to Nagaland's metropolitan and urban councils. Five years later, 33 per cent reservation for women was incorporated in the Nagaland Municipal (First Amendment) Act, 2006. However, since its adoption no elections have been held despite the expiry of the terms of 19 existing councils. Elections in Mokokchung were disrupted in 2008 due to fierce opposition by Naga tribal associations. In 2009, the council of ministers, citing a threat to law and order, indefinitely postponed elections across Nagaland. Naga Women's Joint Action Committee took their case to Guwahati High Court. Despite a favourable court order of October 2011, the urban development minister continued to procrastinate, paving the way for repealing the amendment. Women's organizations then appealed to the Supreme Court.

In September 2012, the Nagaland state assembly unanimously adopted a resolution declaring the 2006 Amendment in violation of Naga customary laws guaranteed under Article 371A.[22] This was on the direction of the Naga Hoho and the Eastern Naga People's Organization (ENPO). Invoking the government's obligation to uphold the traditional landholding system and customary laws under Article 371A, they called on it to promptly withdraw quotas for women. The critical salience of the women's challenge is evinced in the fact that Article 371A has been invoked only twice, once when Nagaland claimed special rights to control its oil resources, overriding the government's claims (Suan 2013), and, second, on the issue of reservations for women.

As Yansathung Kyong, chairperson of Wokha village tribal authority, cautioned: 'All these social changes—women in decision making bodies—will destroy our identity, our communities. It's against our customary law and practices'.[23] The Lotha women's organization is an active member of the Joint Women Committee for Reservations. The emotionalism associated with the discourse on the women's quota as well as the perceived gravitas of the social challenge implied by the women's demand for inclusion is evident in all its complexity in the still evolving crisis over municipal elections in Mokokchung district. The Ao women's organization, Watsü Mungdang, has been at the forefront of confronting the opposition of the Ao tribe elders and their organization, the Ao Senden, in contesting municipal elections in 2008 and 2009. In question was no simple binary opposition of tradition versus modernity or of youth versus elders. For instance, the head of the Ao Senden is Dean of Social Sciences, Mokokchung University, and belongs to the new generation of the professional 'middle class' (as do office-bearers of the Naga Hoho). His wife, an office-bearer of Watsü Mundang, is also well-educated. These heads of Naga tribal authorities are more open to women's equal participation. Are they constrained by the need to carry the older generation with them?

Rosemary Dzuvichu, who has been steering the campaign of the new generation of tribal women challenging women's exclusion in decision-making, attributes more material motives to the Ao Senden and Naga Hoho's opposition:

> The Naga Municipal Act provides that the majority of state and central funds will go to the towns and municipalities for development. With no elected councils, the state government continues to hold all the funds. Their circle of cronies in the bureaucracy and the tribal Hoho share in the non-accountable wealth. With women coming in, who are not their wives, mothers and sisters but candidates put up by mobilized women's groups, obviously they are hostile.[24]

The crisis in Mokokchung came to a head ostensibly over the Watsü Mungdang taking the 'law' in its own hand and punitively shaming an Ao tribesman who had raped a girl from the Chang tribe (see Aier, this volume). The women feared that if left to the customary arbitration procedures the rapist would have been absolved by giving a pig or two. The Ao Senden upbraided the women for interfering and excommunicated them for a year. Social relations were grudgingly re-established at the intercession of the church. The incident exposed a widening social rift, cutting across the women's demand for inclusion in decision-making and settled power networks, and challenging discriminatory customary laws that trivialize violence against women.

Asserting Rights: Tribal Courts

The women's challenge to the tribal courts has prompted a fierce backlash. The onslaught of modernity and the market has already undermined the clan's ownership of common resources and unsettled the basis of authority of tribal hierarchies of power. Increasingly, the continuing salience of the tribe as a social organization of society has come to rest on its dispute resolution mechanism and practices. Not surprisingly, tribal elders are resisting any erosion of their adjudicatory role in managing social relations, especially gender relations. However, the new complexities confronting Naga society, especially in expanding urban centres such as Dimapur, are calling into question the adequacy of customary justice mechanisms. A social culture of impunity for crimes against women has been further reinforced by protracted militarization and non-accountability, making justice a remote prospect.

National Crime Research Bureau (NCRB) statistics for 2013 suggest that Nagaland has the lowest rate of crimes against women in India. However, under-reporting is likely and there are accounts of Naga women confronting multiple insecurities due to the presence of the Indian Army and its armed cadres, in addition to incidents of wife-beating, incest, etc. (Kikon 2014). Arguably, social cohesion of village society has acted as a deterrent to sexual violence, though with urban growth incidents of violence against women are increasing. 'Domestic violence, we've never heard the men talk of it', say the women.[25] Also, few cases come to light as women are reluctant to approach the tribal courts. 'Why approach the tribal elders' arbitration courts to be told: "It's your fault, you must have asked for it". Probably the guy will be given a warning, he may pay a fine. Then life goes on', explained Monalisa.[26] The people who sit in the customary courts are all men. There are no jails, only punitive fines, excommunication and expulsion. Shame and humiliation is 'punishment' for sexual violence. There are often attempts to hush up these matters. Akum Longchari, founder of *Morung Express*, was more succinct: 'There is a culture of impunity in customary law. Those in positions of power, get away with it. What is convenient is termed customary!'[27]

CONCLUDING REMARKS

In the early ceasefire years, when peace politics was overwhelmingly male dominant and fragile, the NMA's political strategist Neidonuo had held back from commenting on the political agenda, saying 'the decision has to be theirs [leaders], our job is to take advantage of ceasefire period to create a peaceful atmosphere so that a permanent solution may follow on what they decide' (Manchanda 2004: 71). Arguably, the position was a tactical one, much like the mobilization of motherhood, aimed at retaining the trust of all sides. 'The solution should come from our leaders. Not from an ordinary mother like me. If I give a decision they may not accept it' (ibid.: 71).

In a situation of ceasefire normalized as 'peace', the new generation of Naga women office-bearers are more assertive about insinuating a more direct voice in peace consultations, calling into question the consequences of men deciding for both halves of society. The historical experience of all-male committees determining how Naga society should be run has shown that the absence of women's perspectives has meant that their interests are ignored. It is a tight balancing act negotiating the thin line between upholding community identity and enhancing women's choices and rights. The NMA suggested, as an entry point, joining forces with the women of the NSCN (IM), but their assessment of the women was not inspiring. However, the Naga women have shown that they are determined to not lose the moment of agency and they are resisting the pushback.

Naga women have travelled a tumultuous journey, from the conservative outlook of the early founders of the NMA, such as Sano Vamuza, presiding over the 'mothers' taking punitive action against drug peddlers who had 'wasted' their sons and daughters to the sophisticated peace politics of consensus pioneered by Neidonuo Angami and the conversion of a women's welfare organization into a strategic stakeholder in the Naga peace process. The NMA has emerged as a body led by educated, professional women who are recasting Naga women's agency in a more assertive rights-based politics. These gendered shifts reflect the changing social dynamics of Naga society as it renegotiates a realignment of status, authority and power relations in the long ceasefire and cold peace. It is in that context that the women's question has become central in the social unpacking of tradition and customary law in the confrontation with modernity and market.

NOTES

1. Interview with Ayangla Longchar at Longkhum village, Mokokchung, Nagaland, 30 August 2013.
2. India's 'Northeast'—a cluster of seven states—is a complex mosaic of ethnic tribes and communities that make up 4 per cent of the country's population and covers over 7 per cent of its landmass. The region's geographic unity is a legacy of the colonial construct of the 'northeast' as a segregated 'frontier' region, eliding its huge diversity.
3. Leela Fernandes' study *India's New Middle Class* provides many explanatory resonances helpful in understanding the constitution of such a social group and its working through the civil society sphere as opposed to the sphere of electoral (majority) politics. While civil society space is often conflated with the middle class sphere, however, as Fernandes argues, social movements like Narmada Bachao Andolan can through struggle expand and even transform the sphere of civil society, and indeed make the middle class heterogeneous.

4. Rosemary Dzuvichu, interviewed by Manchanda, New Delhi, 5 March 2014.
5. Interview with Monalisa Changkija, Dimapur, 26 August 2013.
6. The notion of 'post-conflict' needs to be problematized, especially in view of the historical experience of continuing militarization after peace settlements. While violent conflict is said to have ceased, there can be no presumption that the 'peace' is not violent.
7. Rosemary Dzuvichu, interviewed by authors in Kohima, 9 August 2013.
8. South Asia Terrorism Portal (SATP) Data from tables of 'Annual Fatalities in Terrorist Violence in Nagaland, 1992–2011' listed in South Asia Terrorism Portal, http://www.satp.org/ (accessed on 11 November 2014).
9. Kheslie Chisi's communication to Manchanda, Kolkata, 8 November 2014.
10. NMA president, Abeu Meru, interviewed by Manchanda and Kakran, Dimapur, 29 August 2013.
11. Text of Government of Nagaland letter communicating message received from the Ministry of Home Affairs, Government of India, 11 February 1998 (Nuh and Lasuh 2002: 477–78).
12. Text of Core Committee Convener and Naga Hoho to the Ceasefire Monitoring Cell, Kohima, 18 February 1998 (ibid.: 479–80).
13. Banou Jamit, interviewed by authors, Kohima, 28 August 2013.
14. Interview with Chuba Ozukum, Kohima, 28 August 2013.
15. Ibid.
16. Khegholi Aaomi, interviewed by the authors, Dimapur, 27 August 2013.
17. Monalisa Changkija, interviewed by the authors, Dimapur, 26 August 2013.
18. Banou Jamit, interviewed by the authors, Dimapur, 28 August 2013.
19. Abokali Jimomi, interviewed by the authors, Kohima, 28 August 2013.
20. This observation was made by women in several interviews and discussions including a discussion with several members of Watsü Mungdang, Mokokchung, 30 August 2013.
21. Article 371 A of the Indian Constitution guarantees protection to the customary laws and practices governing tribal land and social relations. This Article has been used only twice in legal jurisprudence; once to counter the demand for quotas for women in local political bodies.
22. The Article states that no Act of Parliament in respect of Naga customary law and procedure shall apply to the state of Nagaland unless the Legislative Assembly of the state by a resolution decides to adopt it.
23. Yansathung Kyong, interviewed by the authors, Wokha, 29 August 2013.
24. Rosemary Dzuvichu, interviewed by the authors, Kohima, 29 August 2013.
25. Focus group discussion with Watsü Mungdang officer-bearers and members, Mokokchung, 30 August 2013.
26. Interview with Monalisa Changkija, Dimapur, 26 August 2013.
27. Akum Longchari, interviewed by the authors, Dimapur, 26 August 2013.

REFERENCES

Aier, Anungla. 2014. 'Gendered Citizenship, Representation and Peace Negotiations in Naga Society'. Paper presented at 'Gender Empowerment and Conflict in South Asia' conference, Kolkata, 25 November.

Bhattacharjee, Sukalpa. 2002. 'State, Insurgency and Wo(mens)'s Human Rights', in R.R. Dhamala and Sukalpa Bhattacharjee (eds), *Human Rights and Insurgency: The North East India*, p. 133. Delhi: Shipra Publications.

Chadda, Maya. 2002. 'Integration through Internal Reorganisation: Containing Ethnic Conflict in India', *Ethnopolitics* 2(1): 44–61.

Chakraborty, Anup Shekhar. 2008. 'Emergence of Women from 'Private' to 'Public': A Narrative of Power Politics from Mizoram', *Journal of International Women's Studies*, 9(3): 27–45.

Cockburn, Cynthia. 2008. 'Drawing Lines Erasing Lines: Feminism as a Resource in Opposing Xenophobia', in Paula Banerjee (ed.), *Women in Peace Politics*, South Asian Peace Studies, vol. 3, pp. 274–88. New Delhi: Sage Publications.

Das, N.K. 2011. 'Naga Peace Parley's: Sociological Reflections and Plea for Pragmatism' *Economic and Political Weekly*, 66(25): 70–77.

Das, Samir. 2008. 'Ethnicity and Democracy Meet When Mothers Protest', in Paula Banerjee (ed.), *Women and Peace Politics*, pp. 54–77. New Delhi: Sage Publications.

de Mel, Niloufer. 2001. *Women and the Nation's Narratives*. New Delhi: Kali for Women.

Enloe, Cynthia. 1993. *The Morning After: Politics at the End of the Cold War*. Berkeley, CA: University of California Press.

Francis, Diane. 2010. *From Pacification to Peacebuilding: A Call to Global Transformation*. London: Pluto Press.

Haksar, Nandita. 2009. 'Machiavelli's Ceasefire and the Indo-Naga Peace Process', *Mainstream Weekly*, 47(16). http://www.mainstreamweekly.net/article1276.html (accessed on 12 December 2016).

Khala, Khatoli. 2003. *Armed Forces Special Powers Act and its Impact on Women in Nagaland*. New Delhi: WISCOMP (Women in Security, Conflict Management and Peace).

Kikon, Dolly. 2002. 'Political Mobilisation of Women in Nagaland: A Sociological Background', in Walter Fernandes and Sanjoy Barbora (eds), *Changing Women's Status in India: Focus on the Northeast*, pp. 174–82. Guwahati: Northeastern Social Research Centre.

———. 2014. 'Memories of Rape, Cultural Impunity and Politics of Agency in Nagaland'. Paper presented at 'Gender Empowerment and Conflict in South Asia' conference, (Calcutta Research Group [CRG] and Peace Research Institute [PRIO]), Kolkata, 23–26 November.

Kumar, Ram Narayan and Laxmi Murthy. 2002. 'Five Years of the Naga Ceasefire'. A report. New Delhi: The Other Media.

Longkumer, Lanushahi and Toshimenla Jamir. 2012. *Nagaland*, Status of Adivasis/Indigenous People's Land, Series 6. New Delhi: The Other Media and Aakar Books.

Mahanta, Aparna. ed. 2002. 'Human Rights for Women', Human Rights and Women in Northeast India, pp. 245–53. Centre for Women's Studies, Dibrugarh University, Dibrugarh.

Manchanda, Rita. 2004. *We Do More Because We Can: Women in the Naga Peace Process.* Kathmandu: South Asia Forum for Human Rights (SAFHR).

Manchanda, Rita and Tapan Bose. 2015a. 'Endgame in the Naga Peace Process', in Rita Manchanda, Tapan Bose and Sajal Nag (eds), *Bridging State and Nation: Peace Accords in India's Northeast*' pp. 35–126. Sage Series in Human Rights Audits of Peace Processes, vol. 2. New Delhi: Sage Publications.

———. 2015b. 'Gender and Ethno-nationalist Struggles', in Rita Manchanda (ed.), *Making War, Making Peace: Conflict Resolution in South Asia*, pp. 138–66. Sage Series in Human Rights Audits of Peace Processes, vol. 1. New Delhi: Sage Publications.

———. 2011. 'Expanding the Middle Space in the Naga Peace Process', *Economic and Political Weekly*, 66(53): 51–60.

Manchanda, Rita and Antonia Potter. 2012. 'Who's that Girl…', NYT Quarks blog, October.

Misra, Udayon. 1983. 'Naga Nationalism and the Role of the Middle Class', in J.B. Dutta Ray (ed.), *The Emergence and Role of Middle Class in the NE.* Uppal Publishers.

Moghadam. 2000. 'Transnational Feminist Networks: Collective Action in an Era of Globalization', *International Sociology*, 15(1): 57–85.

Nag, Sajal. 2006. 'Her Master's Voice: Women in Peacemaking and Genderisation of Politics in Fighting Her Own War: Women and Peace Making in Northeast India', in C.J. Thomas Prasenjit Biswas (ed.), *Peace in India's Northeast; Meaning Metaphor and Method*, pp. 208–228. Delhi: Regency.

National Commission for Women (NCW). n.d. 'Tribal Customary Law and Women's Status: An Introduction', in *Customary Laws in North East India: Impact on Women.* A study conducted by North Eastern Social Research Centre, NCW. http://ncw.nic.in/pdfReports/Customary%20Law.pdf (accessed on 26 November 2016).

Nuh, Rev. N.K. and Wetshokhrolo Lasuh, compilers, 2002, *Naga Chronicle I*, Delhi: Regency Publications.

Nongbri, Tiplut. 2011. 'Exclusionary Practices: The Marginalisation of Women in State and Public Policies', *Summerhill IIAS Review*, pp. 38–47.

Perera, Jehan. ed. 1999. 'Peace Process in Nagaland and Chittagong Hill Tracts', SAFHR Paper No. 5, South Asia Forum for Human Rights (SAFHR), Kathmandu.

Phanjoubam, Pradip. 2008. 'Challenges before the Women's Movement in Manipur', in Anuradha Dutta and Ratna Bhuyan (eds), *Women and Peace. Chapters from the Northeast*, pp. 99–108. Delhi: Akansha Publishing House.

Ray, Raka. 2000. *Fields of Protest: Women's Movement in India.* New Delhi: Zubaan.

Shrinivasan, Rukmani. 2013. 'Nagaland may get first women MLA', *Times of India*, 19 February.

Suan, H.K.K. 2013. 'Adding Fuel to Fire', *The Hindu*, 9 August.

Yuval Davis, Nira. 1997. *Gender and the Nation.* London: Sage Publications.

Xaxa, Virginius. 2008. *State, Society & Tribes: Issues in Post-Colonial India.* New Delhi: Pearson Longman.

CHAPTER 7

Meira Paibis: Forms of Activism and Representation of Women in Manipur

L. Basanti Devi

The present study enquires if all women in Manipur are Meira Paibis, and explores the meanings of being a Meira Paibi (literally 'woman torchbearer'). The media (national and local) have portrayed the Meira Paibis as iconic figures, valiantly defending the victims of atrocities committed by state security forces. Behind the scenes, however, there are internal debates about their identity. This chapter looks at the changes in the Meira Paibi movement, particularly after the killing of Thangjam Manorama and the subsequent protest by elderly 'mothers' in front of Kangla fort in 2004.

The *ima* (mother) remains the core identity of the Meira Paibi movement. However, the Meira Paibi identity is a matter of concern among the women and organizations who have been taking part in the movement. From a relatively loose understanding, and less organized sense of a women's movement, the women involved have found a need to define who the Meira Paibi really are. This study starts from this point, and explores the debate and divergent ways of understanding and mobilizing among the key women's organizations involved in the movement. It mainly explores the pedagogical aspects of building and sustaining the Meira Paibi as a political identity. The chapter investigates two key organizations, namely Poirei Leimarol Meira Paibi Apunba Manipur (hereafter PLMPAM) and Nupi Samaj or the All Manipur Women's Social Reformation and Development Samaj (hereafter Nupi Samaj). The data collected for this study is largely made up of interviews and informal interactions, field observations of organizational activities in connection with memorable events by the concerned organizations, and their pamphlets circulated for publicity.

Several studies have addressed motherhood as not only the motivating identity for women's social action, but also as a key to their protest against human rights violations. Walker (1995) conceptualized motherhood as a social identity derived from membership in a social group. This identity could be instrumental to other political roles. For instance, the case of the Madres de la Plaza de Mayo in Argentina shows that although mothers began organizing themselves to address the conditions that made them unable to be mothers, they also came to address broader human rights issues (Femenía 1987; Schirmer 1989; Ma 2004). They resisted the dictatorship and transformed women's view of Argentinean society and their agency in it. They even challenged the traditional ideology of motherhood; an ideology most commonly found in the moral discourse of the military (Femenía 1987; Fisher 1995). This is similar to the role of the Meira Paibi mothers in Manipur, who extended their role in the family into the public domain to protest against human rights violations and to safeguard the sons and daughters of their community.

Studies of motherhood in the Indian context often approach it as a justification for the exclusion of women from all avenues of power, position and creativity in the public domain (Bagchi 2010; Krishnaraj 2010; Lakshmi 2010). However, it is also true that feminist scholars have approached motherhood as a source of political activity (Umanski 1996). In the term motherhood the value of caring for the other or childcare has become the source of political activity in the public sphere. This may be thought of as an empowering approach to motherhood, perhaps even rejecting the value of caring or the work of mothering as an extension of patriarchal control of women in the public sphere. Reger (2002) maintains that although motherhood is conceptualized as a historically constructed ideology that provides a gendered model of behaviour for all women, even those who have not given birth or raised children, women's organizations have approached motherhood differently, thereby shaping feminist identities differently. However, in our context, although it will be shown how women's organizations in Manipur approached motherhood beyond the familiar image of child-caring to that of defending the rights of sons and daughters, even while speaking the language of democratic rights and dignity, it will be erroneous and imposing to say that these women's organizations are informed by the above feminist perspectives. Rather, our study has attempted to understand the ways in which they themselves define and debate with each other.

Studies of the Meira Paibi movement have understood the mothers in protest as a celebration of the autonomy of women (Banerjee 2008), and a challenge to patriarchy and the patriarchal mindset of state security forces (ibid.; Chakravarti 2010; Mehrotra 2009). However, recent studies have contested this view, arguing that Meira Paibis rather than posing a challenge are reinforcing patriarchy (Brara 2002; Yengkokpam 2012). Some also argue that while motherhood could be an effective strategy in conflict-ridden societies like ours, it could also limit the space and scope of protest (Haripriya 2012). While these works may be useful as a point of departure, this chapter discusses whether the Meira Paibis and their idea of motherhood already represent a fixed, consensual or non-debatable identity. The question is also why there has been an increase in women's organizations taking Meira Paibi as their identity, and, simultaneously, why efforts have been made to delimit this identity. Despite much publicized acts of protest, the women's organizations that play leading roles in the movement evidently feel the need to redefine the Meira Paibi, and debate the diverse ways of understanding this identity.

In this chapter, motherhood as the source of political activity is not assumed as an already defined, fixed or non-negotiable identity, without any organizational and political challenges. Hence, motherhood is seen as an identity that continuously has to be redefined, as the movement is looking for sources for empowering their acts of protest, keeping into account changes, both in the structure of the state and its practices, the nature of women's organizations, their responses, and the relationship among them. The pedagogical aspect of identity is emphasized to understand the dynamic nature of identity and of debate among the women's organizations in their concern with motherhood as a political identity.

MEIRA PAIBI ORGANIZATIONS

In this section I discuss how the Meira Paibi movement developed under the Nupi Samaj and PLMPAM. Nupi Samaj was registered in 1978 under the Societies Registration Act, 1860 (as published in the Gazette of India, 1960), while PLMPAM was registered in 1986 under the Manipur Co-operative Societies Act, 1976. Both organizations have local branches or sister organizations in Manipur. Historically, the Meira Paibis emerged as a mass-based movement, known as Nupi Kanglup in the 1980s. In the beginning there was no need for leadership by a formally established women's organization. Today, the movement is formalized in that it is coordinated and mobilized through the agency of the two aforementioned registered women's organizations. However, this does not represent a complete break from the social role associated with the early Meira Paibis: the role of women safeguarding the sons and daughters of the community. Rather, the formalization meant that participants in the movement introduced offices of president, secretary, treasurer and advisor. Moreover, they set up state-wide monitoring cells through a grass-roots network of local women. Looking at the level of networking and activities since the 1990s, the expansion of the organization of Meira Paibis has increased not only in Manipur but beyond the state borders as well, such as in Hozai, Assam. The grass-roots form of organization brought many informal local women's groups into the relatively more organized network. There is a strong historical presence of informal women's bodies in Manipuri society. These informal organizations have catered mainly to social and economic needs. For instance, Manipuri women have a long history of informal credit associations. Though some still remain traditional, others have registered for welfare purposes or as a credit-based organizations under the The Manipur Society Registration Act 1989 of the state government. In brief, over time, the above two key organizations not only opened their own new branches at the grass-roots level, they also linked up with already mobilized informal bodies of women. This link between the larger and more formal body of women, like the above two, and the grass-roots organizations serve as an important resource in times of major protest activities.

Figure 7.1 shows the basic structure and networking system of the Meira Paibis.

Mode of communication is another vital element of the organization of the Meira Paibis. Here, mutual trust depends on constant meetings at the state and local levels. PLMPAM, for instance, have regular meetings (weekly, monthly and annually), and yet the frequency of these meetings varies according to the

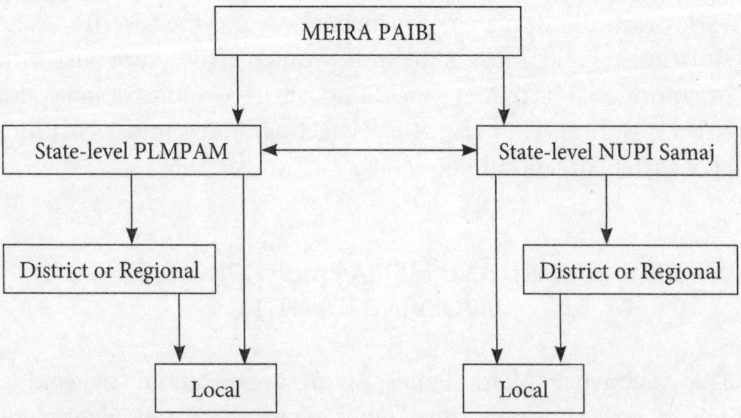

Figure 7.1 Meira Paibi organization and networking

leaders' perception of the current level of tension. At times, the women at the local, district and state levels encounter difficulties in keeping everyone informed. However, the most interesting feature of the Meira Paibi organization is the manner in which the women get together. Here, again, the traditional ways of communicating among women are retained. Historically, in times of need, all one needs to do is pick up a stone or a pebble and hit it at the nearest electric pole. The message is then loud and clear, that a meeting is called for, and all the women in that particular *leikai* (locality gather together in the premises of the local club. If at all the situation requires the attention and cooperation of adjoining neighbouring bodies, then the message is sent across in the same manner and so on and so forth. In times of acute social or political crisis, at least one woman from every household participates. With the entry of mobile phones, communication among the Meira Paibi 'imas' has become much easier than before. Most of the Meira Paibi leaders now use cell phones to communicate with each other.

Leaders are selected on the basis of their experience and the trust they have developed with the rest of the members of a group. The most active members are elected consensually to act as office-bearers. Mandated by peer pressure and community status, membership is universal, but the extent of participation varies with the women's own inclination and the severity of the situation at hand. Most of the time, women activists are busy with organizational activities, including sit-in demonstrations and street meetings. They also attend meetings and seminars of other civil society organizations.

NISHABANDHI AND MEIRA PAIBI: CONFLICTING OR EVOLVING IDENTITY

The emergence Meira Paibis as an organization triggered a debate on two fronts: one, on the meanings and identity of Meira Paibi; and, two, on the continuity and discontinuity with previous women's mobilization under the banner 'Nishabandhi' (prohibition of *nisha* or an intoxicant such as alcohol, drugs, and so on). There are two popular views on the meaning and identity of Meira Paibi. According to one view, the Meira Paibis came into being in the late 1980s, and more particularly in the 1990s, as a form of women's mobilization against wrongs perpetrated by the security and police forces and, later, also against the violence of non-state actors. According to another view, the mothers were already mobilized locally during the late 1960s and 1970s as Nishabandhis, fighting against social evils like drug abuse, locally prepared alcohol, and domestic or community violence, continuing their role as mothers even as Meira Paibis. While PLMPAM nurtures strictly the first view, the other is generally understood as true of any mother in a situation of social and political concern. This second view also continues to be accepted by the members of Nupi Samaj, though they also increasingly show preference for the first view.

In both the above narratives of the mobilization of women, the central personality is the mother (ima). The role of ima has been transferred from the family to the public space. Ima in a daily social environment carries both biological and social meanings. Biologically, it means one who has given birth to a child, and who cares and nurtures it. Socially, it means one who looks after the family either in the presence or absence of a husband, and engages in several relationships with others by virtue of kinship and belonging to a family. When a woman becomes a mother, she is acknowledged and enjoys relative relaxation in many areas where normally women are restricted in Meitei society.[1] Meira Paibis have increasingly become associated with this sense of mother. This has become the identity of the activist ima. All the women whom I interviewed were addressed as 'ima', but not every ima is a Meira Paibi.[2] The Meira Paibis are mostly women who are past childbearing age. They are women who no longer carry the physical burden of motherhood and their social and cultural constraints are lighter as well. However, the title of 'ima' as used by Meira Paibis carries a broader connotation than the mother who is the bearer and caretaker of children. The term carries the meaning and identity of the mother of a larger mass of people who are allegedly tortured, killed and raped. During an interaction, Ima Shakhi and Ima Memma from Apunba Manipur Kanba Ima Lup (AMKIL) (an organization closely associated with Nupi Samaj) expressed that they are the mothers of all, whether insurgents or army. They viewed the role of mothers as rescuers of people from police and army personnel. Hence, 'ima' ultimately becomes the identity of women in the act of protesting. Motherhood is a means through which women are mobilized across various age groups. This means mobilization of women as mothers who start taking collective action against alleged atrocities and inhuman treatment of civilians by agents of the state. This sense of motherhood may be understood as the political ima.

The political ima is largely the product of an anti-state stance, taken by the leading members of Meira Paibi organizations such as PLMPAM. Political imas have come to refer specifically to Meira Paibis. However, this is differentiated from another category of women, called Nishabandhi. The ex-president of Macha Leimai (a close associate of Nupi Samaj), Kh. Ibetombi Devi, distinguished the Nishabandhis from the Meira Paibis. She identified one distinct difference in that Meira Paibis emerged from women's encounters with state forces, while Nishabandhis emerged out of their encounter with 'social diseases'. To her, another basic difference is that Meira Paibis work to safeguard the sons and daughters of the community (*pari imom*).[3] But some women leaders still think that the Nishabandhi movement is relevant and they actively carry out such work, though they differentiate themselves from the Meira Paibis.

The work of Nishabandhi has acquired a different organizational name, the All Manipur Anti-Drug Association or AMADA. AMADA has its headquarters in Imphal. This organization carries out activities that stop the production and sale of local wine and the use and sale of drugs. While carrying out fieldwork, I met the secretary of the district branch of AMADA (Bishnupur district,

Manipur). She differentiated AMADA from the Meira Paibis. To her, AMADA works for the health of society to save the young generation of Meiteis from drugs. She would not mind associating with the police and army personnel, or departments of the state government while carrying out her organizational activities. I found that both PLMPAM and Nupi Samaj would likely also distinguish their organizations from AMADA, particularly because the work to stop the use of drugs, though appreciated, could be an area of state appropriation of the role of Meira Paibis.

It is here that the Nishabandhis and Meira Paibis emerge both as distinct historical phases and as distinct areas of the women's movement in Manipur. Both the PLMPAM and Nupi Samaj would differentiate the Meira Paibis from an organization like AMADA. According to the PLMPAM, I noticed an increasing concern to limit the identity of the Meira Paibi ima to the one who takes up the issue of the state's violation of human rights. There is an effort to distinguish this identity of Meira Paibi from social reform work, such as that of AMADA. Rather, the political mother is at the core of the Meira Paibi. It was this sense of motherhood that manifested itself in the events following the killing of Thangjam Manorama. I discuss those events in the next section.

THE NUDE PROTEST

The mother as the key political figure was manifest in the 2004 'nude protest' after Thangjam Manorama Devi was killed by the armed forces. This incident was a matter of extreme concern for the Meira Paibi imas, and their protest against the killing was also a turning point in the Meira Paibi movement. Thangjam Manorama was arrested by the Assam Rifles on the accusation that she was an 'explosive device expert' of the banned People's Liberation Army (PLA), one of the insurgent groups in Manipur. She was found brutally killed in custody at a place in Imphal East. The Meira Paibis believed that Manorama was raped before she was killed, a charge that was strongly denied by army authorities. The murder of Thangjam Manorama led to huge mobilization of imas. Anandi, Managing Trustee of the Just Peace Foundation, informed me that soon after they received information about the case, about 50 elderly women activists held a meeting on the night of 14 July 2004. On the following day (15 July), a selected group of 12 activists staged a dramatic protest against the alleged rape and murder in front of Kangla fort in Imphal. Further, I was informed that the women took off their clothes in public, carrying long white banners bearing the slogan: 'Indian Army, Rape Us', and shouting 'Rape us, kill us, take our flesh'. There was also the voice of the imas shouting: 'We are all Manorama's mother, mothers of a raped daughter'.

During my interaction with the imas (Nganbi, Memma, Ramani, and Momonleima, among others), they gave the following accounts of their protest on that day. As described by Momonleima (who later became convenor of another women's group, the Sharmila Kanba Lup), the imas went to the hospital where the body of Manorama was taken for a post-mortem. There, at the hospital morgue, Ima Momonleima felt like her own daughter had been killed in a most inhumane manner. She was shocked when she saw the dead body of Manorama. She asked, 'Why do we stay so calm in the name of Meira Paibi? We are not passive Imas. We don't want the Meira Paibi Imas who are active only at the public platform [giving] speeches.' Ima Gyaneshwari felt that this was a do-or-die situation for Manipuri women (Teresa 2009: 32–33). Loitam Ibetombi Devi explained: 'Our humiliation was beyond endurance', while Ima Ramani added, 'Our anger shed our inhibitions on that day. If necessary we will die—commit self-immolation to save our innocent sons and daughters' (ibid.).

Despite the possibility that any observer of their protest may interpret their actions as showing leniency towards the insurgent, these women were defensive of their position as the performing mothers. After all, Manorama was alleged to have been an explosive device expert of the People Liberation Army (PLA). Ima

Taruni, one of the leaders of Meira Paibi (Nupi Samaj), said that Meira Paibis are often called the 'mothers of insurgents', noting that insurgents were after all the sons and daughters of vegetable vendors and fisherfolk (Veda 2005: 33). Ima Sakhi, Ima Randhoni and many other Meira Paibi imas often expressed to me during my fieldwork the thought that both insurgents and civilian boys are their sons and that they are performing the role of a mother.

Many of the nude protesters expressed mixed feelings about their protest. On the one hand they felt anguish, anxiety and hatred towards the state, while on the other they felt love and compassion for the children. The feeling of motherhood here is significant, for it was the courage of a mother defending her children which these women channelled in order to be able to come out for the nude protest at Kangla. As expressed by Ima Nganbi, vice president of Apunba Manipur Kanba Ima Lup (AMKIL):

> We could not sit back and be silent any more after the Manorama incident. We felt there was no purpose to life if we had to live without prestige or respect. We can't live like this. All of us women in Manipur are mothers of women who have been raped by security forces. We want to fight to protect our prestige and the removal of black laws like AFSPA.[4]

Ima Nganbi reportedly went for the protest full of courage, strength and spirit, maintaining that she was the first ima who had shouted their slogan in English: 'We are all Manorama's Mother'. According to Ima Gyaneshwari, women were always insecure, forever at risk of molestation by security forces. Hence the protest was meant to teach a lesson not just to the security forces but to the whole world, as an act of power, courage and strength. The Meira Paibis took care to refute rumours that the protest was orchestrated and said that they reacted 'just as any mother would when her daughter was killed or raped'. They explained: 'Ordinarily Manipuri women don't take off their shawls but there was so much of pain and anguish in our heart that we forgot our shame' (Veda 2005: 34). This is described in their journal *Ichemma 'Meitei Nupi Ekai Khangdaba Natte, Masagi Ekaiba Yonthoklaga Mashagi Amasung Majatigi Ekaiba Kannaba Hotnajabani; Marin Pandabishingnadi Pakngamgadaba Natte'* ['Meitei women know the embarrassment of being nude in public, but to save the pride and honour of a collective society they are not shy of doing it'][5] (Phuritsabam 2004: 3). It was felt that women confronting and challenging the army/state in the nude was the ultimate form of resistance that they could perform. However, some observers viewed the nude protest as a challenge to the patriarchal structure of Manipuri society. The nude protest was seen as an act of resistance not only against the Armed Forces (Special Powers) Act, 1958 (AFSPA), but also against the entire masculine militarized machinery that has been unleashed in the process of conflict. The women consciously created a collective expression of rage, challenging the concentrated, brutal patriarchal power (Mehrotra 2009).

Different interpretations and opinions came up after the protest. Some said that the imas protested on behalf of all women, and particularly the younger generation of women; others said they did it for all sections of society. They were seen as defending their daughters, but the reaction was against violations suffered by several generations. The public protest was their reply, their challenge. It was a message of enduring, endless resistance. On the other hand, there were some who questioned why the attention was given only to the case of Manorama Devi. For instance, the people from the hills contended that no one talks about the late Reverend Jamkholet Khongsai who was also a victim of brutality by the Assam Rifles at the time. But during the course of my interactions, I was informed that the Meira Paibis have also been involved in saving the lives of the people in the hills. The contention was aroused only because of the existing political divide between the hills and the valley-based civil society organizations in the state. However, it is also true that Meira Paibi as an identity seeks to transcend differences of interpretation when it comes to challenging the state and its security forces.

Meira Paibi imas chose a creative way of protesting (see Dey in this volume). They challenged the perpetrators and demanded transparency and accountability for crimes carried out by the security forces. The imas understood rape as an issue of women's rights and integrity, taking a very different view than the usual patriarchal perspective of rape as a source of shame and dishonour to the family and community of the victim. The imas were concerned with social relations, not the gendered relationship between male and female. The focus was therefore not on the victim, but directly on the perpetrators, the Indian Army.

While many would agree with the above interpretations, some of it would be problematic for others. It is commonly agreed that the nude protest challenged the state and the perpetrators of violence, but not everyone would accept that it was equally a challenge to the patriarchal structure of society. For instance, a certain section of social activists whom I met during fieldwork maintained that in their opinion the Meira Paibis were not specifically concerned with the question of women's rights, even though they talk about the concerns and security of the women.

Keeping in mind the above interpretations, the nude protest can be seen as a communitarian defence through the medium of the mother's body. It is important to note that the body presented in the protest is the body of the community at large. This is because the mothers whom I interviewed felt that the 'rape and killing' of Manorama is a violation of the dignity of the entire community. More than the defence of the community and the dignity of its women, the protest also contributed to shaping the identity of the Meira Paibi. In my interaction with the Meira Paibi mothers, I was explained that the most essential characteristic of the ima can be found in the saying '*Khunaigidamak Meira Paibigi Ehou*', or 'Meira Paibi movement is for the society'. Hence, the idea and identity of mother as Meira Paibi represents a mother who cares and safeguards her sons and daughters. This is the heart of motherhood in the context of this study. We now turn to how this idea and identity of the 'mother' as Meira Paibi took its course following the Manorama incident.

CELEBRATING AND CONSTRUCTING MOTHERHOOD

Following the protest, the imas' image of motherhood had a greatly positive and motivating effect on the larger community, and in spreading the ideas of the Meira Paibi imas. Imas themselves are proud to say that they all are 'Manorama's mother'. The local and national media exposure had immense value for other imas as well. The 12 women (mothers or imas) who went nude received fame and recognition from their own communities and from society at large. When I interviewed activists such as Ima Mangol and Ima Sakhi, they expressed their need to do something that can make good history for future generations, just like the work done by imas of the past: in the first and second Nupi Lan (literally, women's uprising) in 1904 and 1939. These mothers of the past are the role models against whom they measure their courage and strength. Historical and mythical characters become the source of their 'mother' identity. It is clearly evident from their actions and activities that women are not passive victims, but active participants in their own identity construction.

When I interviewed these imas, they showed a distinctive character and expressed proudly that they were a part of that nude protest. For instance, Ima Ramani told me: 'The women's struggle has shaken the army authorities as well as the state government.' Ima Nganbi and her colleagues are also glad that their protest had an impact. It led to the opening up of the Kangla fort to civilians. The fort was once the palace of the Manipuri king, a vast area surrounded by a moat. In 1891, after the Anglo-Manipuri war, the British Army occupied it and after India gained its independence the Kangla fort was taken over by the Assam Rifles. On 20 November 2004, after 113 years of occupation, it was handed over to civilian authorities and subsequently opened up to the public (Sharma 2009).

It can be said that within this politico-cultural complex, the motherhood of the Meira Paibis is symbolically associated with an autonomous, pro-people activism. Some local writers (for instance,

Arun and Arun 2009) commented that Meira Paibis as a group of mothers and elderly women could not bear to see the suffering of their wards and as a result they had come out to protect their sons and daughters from the clutches of the army. Meira Paibis have now emerged as a new political force that challenges the state and all its apparatus, struggling against curtailment of human freedoms and dignity and encroachment upon individual liberty (ibid.). The Meira Paibi gradually gained strength and started speaking out against repressive state atrocities and all forms of human rights abuse.

To the above commentators, the 12 Meitei women virtually disrobed the national judicial system, which had so long denied justice to the people of the state. It was felt that injustice was done all through the last half-century, affecting all the ethnic groups, genders, classes and regions of the state. Those nude women, with whatever courage at their command, evidently challenged not just the security forces of the nation then stationed in Kangla, but the entire nation state, perceivably overseeing the ongoing rape of Manipuri womanhood.

During my fieldwork, Ima Sakhi told me how the nude protest was organized. She said that the idea of the nude protest was the result of the helplessness among the women while resisting the state's repressive measures that violated human rights. The other forms of protest like sit-ins and relay hunger strikes seemed meaningless in the face of increasing state repression. Ima Sakhi said that she felt regret for not being able to be present at the nude protest due to personal reasons.

Another member of the same organization and close associate of Ima Sakhi told me that the theme of the dramatic protest was discussed only among a few selected members. There was a selection of women who would form part of the nude protest. The aged and weak women and young married women were asked not to be part of the protest. Women whose husbands and children would not be willing were also consciously dropped from participating in the protest. At the level of organizations, the leaders of PLMPAM expressed dissatisfaction with the attitude of other organizations that planned the nude protest. Apparently, the reason was that the PLMPAM was sidelined while planning for the protest. The nude protest was organized by AMKIL and Macha Leimai, both organizations associated with Nupi Samaj. However, despite this difference between the two organizations, both agreed that it was basically the ideology of motherhood that made the protest possible and which needs to be sustained.

The ideology of motherhood brings women activists together on the same page where they sometimes forget the divisions amongst them and the divergent views of various organizations. After all these divisions, the feeling of motherhood is the only feature and thread that brings them together towards their primary goal, to remove AFSPA and bring in a torture-less and equal society where people can live freely without fear and with the 'Right to life'. In this sense, motherhood plays a functional role of protecting the lives and interests of a struggling society.

The following section discusses how leading members of PLMPAM started to streamline the Meira Paibi identity and the movement after the nude protest, and how other related women's associations like Nupi Samaj responded to this effort.

THE MEIRA PAIBI IDENTITY

To the general observer and women's groups like Nupi Samaj and its partner AMKIL, Meira Paibi is a general and comprehensive term that represents a broader identity of women's presence in the public domain. According to one of my respondents, who had been part of the Meira Paibi movement in the 1980s, Meira Paibi is not an organized movement that needs to be led by a specific organization, and organizations like AMKIL and PLMPAM should not be categorized as Meira Paibis. To him, Meira Paibi is always a spontaneous movement, a people's movement, and a movement without support from any organization, neither is it similar to PLMPAM and AMKIL. Moreover, such institutionalization of the Meira Paibis may lead to ideological divides among the women, and they would become just like the women who have formed women's wings under a political party (for example, the women's wing of the Manipur People's Party).

Another respondent, an advisor to the All Manipur United Club Organisation (AMUCO) and PLMPAM, felt the Meira Paibis need to be organized or led by relatively defined organizations to develop beyond a mere spontaneous movement. He also argued that there should be a strict identification of who the Meira Paibis are. According to him, this is urgently needed because of the politics of the state government to engineer factionalism among the mothers (Meira Paibis) and depoliticize the movement. He further argued that there is increasing confusion within the movement as far as the basic goal is concerned. In his view, the movement should consolidate itself towards bringing an end to state repression and human rights violations. The latter argument is a response to the general image of Meira Paibis as associated with activities ranging from mediating in family matters, issues of elopement of women, investigating construction work in local areas, and auditing of distribution of essential items under the Public Distribution System (PDS). According to some, this broad range of activities does not suit the key goal of the Meira Paibi movement.

The PLMPAM president, Memchoubi, has defined the characteristics of the mother as Meira Paibi stating that Meira Paibi women are receiving respect and regard not only within Manipuri society but globally (Memchoubi 2010: 22–23). Her characterization of the Meira Paibi ima is also an ideal to be followed. First, the Meira Paibi should not only play a mother's role for her own children and grandchildren in the family, she should also be the mother of larger society. The ima should be impartial and unbiased, treating all the organizations of Meira Paibis equally. The ima should treat everybody's children equally as if they were her own. Secondly, women should have a good character (*lamchatsajat*): be well behaved at home as well as in public, fearless and always do what is right. Women should always keep in mind the fact that their future is yet to come. We are living in a colonized state of mind, she says, due to law and order conditions and the politics of lawmakers. Despite a 2,000-year plus history of respectable, independent living, people in contemporary Manipur are living in a colonized state. The Meira Paibi keeps in mind this context and understands the need to take the responsibility of a mother and work towards an equal, torture-less and independent society. With respect to the *meira* (torch) that mothers hold in their hand, it should always give light and protect the children and give directions to defend or counter the army and police repression. It was felt that women should always keep their torch ready.

From the above statements by Memchoubi, it can be seen that increasingly the role of the Meira Paibi is expected to cater to the protection of the larger society, and the fight against colonization. The state of being colonized is seen as a condition in which laws fail to protect the rights and life of the people. It is in this orientation of the Meira Paibi imas that many human rights organizations are looking to shape and define the movement today. However, this makes the role and identity of the Meira Paibi a field of contestation between the expectations of the high-level functioning body like PLMPAM and the local units. Many of the local units or branch organizations are located at the village level, functioning in accordance with local expectations, embedded in local community feelings. This situation has created a condition where Meira Paibi imas face the conflict between the expectations of society at large (the community, village and family) and the expectations of the larger organizations. Nevertheless, both sets of expectations are incorporated in the organizations and the roles performed by the imas. The key organizations thus take various initiatives to mobilize on the basis of the defined characteristics of Meira Paibi, discussed ahead.

HISTORY, MEMORY AND MOTHERHOOD

The narration and performance of history is an important aspect of the mobilization of mothers as Meira Paibis. History is given this role through the observation of historical events and commemorative days. One source of such history is the remembering of what is known as Nupi Lan in the history of Manipur. The first Nupi Lan occurred in 1904 as a protest against the colonial policy of using men as labourers at the order of then Political Agent Maxwell. The second Nupi Lan took place in 1939, after a famine caused by the profiteering activities of Marwari traders who were allowed to procure and export large quantities of rice. The picture of these women's movements during the colonial period has been perceived as the history of political activism among the women of Manipur and a frame of reference for contemporary women as they develop as progressive agents.

Recollecting these events, Nupi Samaj, together with their associate organizations, has been observing 12 December as Nupigi Numit (Women's Day).[6] Kh. Ibetombi, former president of Macha Leimai, emphasizes the significance of observing historical events such as the 'day of women's power' (Nupigi Numit). The significance of such observation is not merely to remember the bravery of the women of Nupi Lan who fought against the colonial authorities of their time. As expressed by leaders like Anandi (Managing Trustee of the Just Peace Foundation) and Ima Sakhi (of AMKIL) during my interaction, such observation was relevant to every woman in Manipur today. To accentuate this, they defined the current mobilization as the 'Third Nupi Lan' (frequently described as such in Meira Paibi movement's pamphlets), referring to the present Meira Paibi movement as the ongoing people's movement and large-scale women's agitation against AFSPA.

Several of my respondents claimed that the ongoing struggle against AFSPA became more forceful and vocal after the Manorama incident of 2004. It becomes clear that innovative strategies have been adopted for motivating and mobilizing the women. This is a kind of awareness-raising for illiterate women activists, exemplifying how the government violates the human rights of the people of Manipur. Like Nupi Samaj, PLMPAM also observes the Nupi Lan Memorial Day with a mass rally to remind contemporary women of the courage and strength of historical women and to positively impact the present movement. Representatives of several organizations and eminent social workers speaking on these occasions recall the effects of the women's uprisings of the past in awakening society to stay alert and strive for the preservation of social ethics, oppose imperialist designs, and protect society from all forms of evil. They often highlight the indispensability of a unified movement to achieve any cherished goal.

The observation of two historical moments that occurred in the 1980s is another source of strength and identity for the Meira Paibi. PLMPAM considers 28 May as Meira Paibi Numit (Day of the Meira Paibis). Nupi Samaj considers 29 December as Pari Kanba Numit (Day of Saving the Son). These refer to two different historical incidents. The PLMPAM relates to the incidents of the Patsoi Langjing case, explained ahead. On 26 April 1980, at around 9:15 a.m., unidentified gunmen fired upon the Central Reserve Police Force (CRPF) personnel stationed at Langjing Camp, Imphal West, killing two CRPF personnel. After the unidentified gunmen ran away, the CRPF personnel turned on local innocent people and started beating and torturing them. People were pulled out from their houses and a search was conducted to catch the soldiers of the People's Revolutionary Party of Kangleipak (PREPAK). Men from each family were made to stand with their hands up for the entire day. In the scuffle, a woman was killed and five others were injured by bullets.

Women of the area and others started an agitation against the atrocities of the security forces. A massive protest rally was held on 28 May 1980 in which more than 10,000 women participated, gathering at Mapal Kangjeibung, a big open ground near the 'women's market' of Imphal. However, the state security personnel picked up the women protesters in trucks and took them all to the army camp at Khurai in Imphal East. On the way, a pregnant woman, Piyari, fell down from the truck and lost her life. Her death was followed by mass mobilization of the women, protesting at numerous places. It is this mobilization that is regarded as the emergence of what we know today as the Meira Paibi movement. In remembrance of this event, the Meira Paibi Observation Committee constituted by the PLMPAM has been observing Meira Paibi Numit (Meira Paibi Day) on 28 May each year.

In another historical narrative by Nupi Samaj, the origin of the Meira Paibis is traced to an incident of 29 December 1980. On that day, three young boys were arrested by army personnel on allegations of having planted a bomb. Lourembam Ibomcha was dutifully cleaning his house in Maibam Leikai when the Jammu and Kashmir Army came and arrested him. Some local women activists of his home area immediately got together. They informed the leaders of popular Nishabandhi organizations like Nupi Samaj, including female activists Momon Devi, Chaobi Devi and Rani Devi. Together they went to the army camp at Canchipur, pleading for Ibomcha's innocence and demanding his immediate release. Ibomcha, who had been tortured in custody, was finally released. However, the army personnel then unleashed a reign of terror in Maibam Leikai, and men were harassed as soon as they ventured out of their homes. Consequently, women were compelled to take up the task of patrolling the locality at night with torches in their hands, and thus began the Meira Paibi movement.

Since the incident, 29 December has been regarded as the day women began to launch the movement to 'save innocent sons' from the hands of the brutal army. Every year, on 29 December, Nupi Samaj observes the day as the origin of the Meira Paibis, Meira Paibi Numit. In an interview, Ima Ramani, the present leader of Nupi Samaj, expressed to me that they struggled because the boy was innocent. The two incidents narrated above, though different in terms of their immediate cause, both support the view that Meira Paibis came into existence to stop atrocities of the security forces on innocent civilians.

FIGHTING STATE APPROPRIATION OF MOTHERHOOD

Celebration of historical events and memorization of the 'origins' of the movement are important opportunities for further defining and narrating the identity and values of the Meira Paibi. However, the leader of the Nupi Samaj, Ramani, stated that various local bodies, clubs, and women's associations have been swayed by corruption and selfish motives during elections.[7] It was also stated that no one has made any conscious effort to understand the true image of the Meira Paibi and the essence behind their movement. Instead, many people have started looking upon the Meira Paibis as some group of women who can be easily used by politicians as vote banks during elections. So, an effort has been made by these sorts of leaders that there is a need to discuss and understand state appropriation of Meira Paibi.

PLMPAM makes a distinction between Meira Paibi activities and government sponsored programmes. They even use pamphlets as a means to spread these messages, refining the boundary of activities and ideology of the Meira Paibis. These pamphlets explain that a Meira Paibi should only focus on issues like violation of human rights by the army, and repeal of the repressive law, AFSPA. Anything beyond these activities and frameworks are not a part of the duties of Meira Paibis. Observation days are a space to discuss the ups and downs of Meira Paibi activities, their successes and failures.[8]

A key strategy of the Meira Paibi organization was to understand what they called 'state sponsored Meira Paibis' and their increasing numbers in society. The PLMPAM assumed that the state sponsored Meira Paibis are the women's groups who organized and formed in relation to governmental policies and programmes such as the Civic Action Programme (CAP),

National Rural Employment Guarantee Act (NREGA) and Public Distribution System (PDS), and those who are also associated with or formed as the women's wing of any political party. These are considered an important means of depoliticization of the Meira Paibis, as well as increasing the numbers of women's groups in the name of Meira Paibi.

The leaders of PLMPAM have also raised the issue of state appropriation of mothers through the building of *Meira Sanghs*. The Meira Sangh is a small hut, traditionally used by women as a space for social and political activities. This space is also considered the local site of the Meira Paibi movement. It is treated by some as a holy temple for the Meira Paibis. It is said that there are about 2,000 Meira Sanghs in the valley. In recent years, around 800 Meira Sanghs and 100 community halls have been reportedly built under the CAP of the state army personnel. It is claimed that political parties, especially the ruling Congress party in Manipur, built these Meira Sanghs (Raicharan 2005: 44–46). These efforts and support of the political party and army personnel are being considered as among the sources of division in the collective Meira Paibi movement.

The perception of PLMPAM is that these government supported Meira Sanghs have stopped working for issues like human rights violations at the hands of state forces, but instead have begun to be the defenders of the lives and property of a class of people that includes bureaucrats and members of the Manipur state assembly. Hence, in my interview, Memchoubi, PLMPAM president, was especially concerned with the changing face of the Meira Sangh. She felt that these Sanghs have become more like credit associations, not relating with issues concerning common people. She also felt they have become sites of petty politics over local issues like electoral politics, competition for funds and loans through developing networks with the local politicians, competing for taking a big share of money in the distribution of essential items under the PDS. She is also concerned about the future of the local Meira Sanghs because of their increasing participation in the Self-Help Group (SHG) programme of the government.

The argument is that certain policies and programmes like the above programme are counterproductive to the Meira Paibi movement. This is the reason why new efforts are taken up by the PLMPAM to restrict and refine the sphere of activities and identity of the Meira Paibi. In doing so, the pamphlets circulated on the memorable days project the state and its apparatus anti-people; for instance, in one of the documents printed in the *Meira Paibi* journal, state is understood as an 'instrument of torture' and the politician as the 'nurturer of army and police rule'.[9]

CONCLUSION

To conclude, the following points can be made. The study of the Meira Paibi in Manipur has shown that all Meira Paibis are defined as 'mothers' (ima), but that not all the mothers of Manipur are Meira Paibis. This position has emerged only with an understanding that the movement needs to be relatively organized, and needs to be led by a defined body of women leaders. I have shown how PLMPAM defined the basic characteristics of the Meira Paibi. This exercise could be understood as a shift from the earlier understanding of Meira Paibi as that based on voluntary participation, a mass-based movement and identity, and as one that takes up social reformist works. This is where anti-alcoholism and anti-drugs as campaigned in the 1980s by the Nishabandhi and the Meira overlap. This earlier understanding has strong roots in the daily social life of the Meitei women, who are considered to play multiple social roles and organize informally as customary and economic associations.

Why is this changing? The study of the two organizations, the PLMPAM and Nupi Samaj, has shown that to be organized and led by these organizations gives the movement and the identity of Meira Paibi a sense of direction towards a defined set of goals. The goals are political only in the sense of engaging the state and the violence, and saving people from such violence. As discussed in the section on the nude protest, the acts of mothers were the defining moments of who the Meira Paibis (in the above sense) are.

I have also shown through various interviews with leading activists and stakeholders that the need for stronger organization emerged based on the perception among activists and stakeholders that there are state-guided developments (schemes for women, for example) that could depoliticize the Meira Paibis. Along with this, there is also a strong view that the Meira Paibi is not meant for all kinds of issues, rather only for political issues as noted above. There is an effort to distinguish the Meira Paibis from organizations like AMADA, which works on anti-drugs and anti-alcohol and emphasizes saving the lives of the youth. The key Meira Paibi organizations, PLMPAM and Nupi Samaj, feel that this generalized perception may dilute the core objective. In fact, the generalized perception of being relevant in many social issues was originally the strength of the movement and the basis for the Meira Paibis. But this has changed because of the nature of their encounter with the state. I have discussed how PLMPAM and Nupi Samaj confront and struggle against the appropriation of women's incorporation in electoral politics and development activities.

Though finely articulated by the leaders and stakeholders, this shift appears to be constantly negotiated with people's expectations of making Meira Paibis relevant in daily social life and in social reformist work. There is a continued effort to differentiate between the political goals and social reform activities (e.g anti-drugs and anti-alcohol movements). In the process of making a stricter definition of who the Meira Paibis are, PLMPAM and Nupi Samaj organize memorial days, meetings and awareness campaigns. These organizations select historical moments and events and organize meetings in public as pedagogical and performative events. During these they link the identity of the Meira Paibi with history and historical experiences. History is source of motivation, and it is also what these organizations think of as important to recollect and memorize. It is their relationship with the past, their sense of inspiration and motivation that makes their understandings of history distinct.

Lastly, this chapter has discussed the issue of organizational debates and varied interpretations among the PLMPAM and Nupi Samaj. On the identity of the Meira Paibi, the positions of these organizations are not necessarily divided on ideological grounds. Both agree to the position that motherhood (or the image of the mother as the strength of acts of protest) is the source of political activism. Their varied interpretations of history and the origins of the movement can be understood as a continuous negotiation of the future of the Meira Paibis.

NOTES

1. See, for a detailed ethnography, Chaki-Sircar (1984: 92–102).
2. Bhubon, a social activist and independent researcher in Manipur, gave this view when I interacted with him.
3. Quoted from Kh. Ibetombi Devi, 'Meira Paibi Amadi Miyamga Leinaba Mari', unpublished work.
4. Quoted in Sharma (2009).
5. Translated into English by the author.
6. See, for instance, 'State hails women spirit on Nupi Lan', *The Sangai Express*, 12 December 2004.
7. See *Imphal Free Press*, http://kanglaonline.com/2010/12/meira-paibi-founding-day-remembered; see also, 'Meira Paibi Martyrs' Day', *The Sangai Express*, 12 April 2009.
8. Pamphlet circulated by the Meira Paibi Observation Committee on 28 May 2007.
9. See for details, document printed in *Meira Paibi*, vol. 1(2), 2006, pp. 59–60.

REFERENCES

Arun, M.C. and Irengbam Arun. 2009. 'The Transcendental Role of Women in Manipur History', in H. Dwijasekhar Sharma (ed.), *New Insights into the Glorious Heritage of Manipur*, pp. 623–61. Delhi: Akansha.

Bagchi, Jasodha. 2010. 'Representing Nationalism: Ideology of Motherhood in Colonial Bengal', in Maithreyi Krishnaraj (ed.), *Motherhood in India: Glorification Without Empowerment*, pp. 158–85. Mumbai: Routledge.

Banerjee, Paula. 2008. 'The Space Between: Women's Negotiations with Democracy', in Paula Banerjee (ed.), *Women in Peace Politics*, pp. 201–17. New Delhi: Sage Publications.

Brara, N. Vijaylakshmi. 2002. 'Breaking the Myth: The Social Status of Meitei Women', in Walter Fernandes and Sanjay Barbora (eds), *Changing Women's Status in India: Focus on the Northeast*, pp. 193-201. Guwahati: North East Social Research Centre.

Chakravarti, Paromita. 2010. 'Reading Women's Protest in Manipur: A Different Voice?', *Journal of Peacebuilding and Development*, 5(3): 47–60.

Chaki-Sircar, Manjusri. 1984. *Feminism in a Traditional Society: Women of the Manipur Valley*. Delhi: Shakti Books.

Femenía, N.A. 1987. 'Argentina's Mothers of Plaza De Mayo: The Mourning Process from Junta to Democracy', *Feminist Studies*, 13(1): 9–18.

Fisher, J. 1995. *Mothers of the Disappeared*. Boston, MA: South End Press.

Haripriya, Soibam. 2012. 'Agitating Women, Disrobed Mothers', *Eastern Quarterly*, 8(1/2): 18–34.

Krishnaraj, Maithreyi. ed. 2010. *Motherhood in India: Glorification Without Empowerment*. New Delhi: Routledge.

Lakshmi, C.S. 2010. 'Mother, Mother-Community and Mother-Politics in Tamil Nadu', in Maithreyi Krishnaraj (ed.), *Motherhood in India: Glorification Without Empowerment*, pp. 186–227. Mumbai: Routledge.

Ma, Margaret E. 2004. 'Building Bridges of Memory: The Mothers of the Plaza De Mayo and the Cultural Politics of Maternal Memories', *History and Anthropology*, 15(2): 133–50.

Mehrotra, Deepti Priya. 2009. *Burning Bright: Irom Sharmila and the Struggle for Peace in Manipur*. New Delhi: Penguin.

Memchoubi, Longjam. 2010. 'Meira Paibi Eehou Mai Pakhanlashi', *Meira Paibi*, 5(1): 22–23.

Phuritsabam, Birmani. 2004. 'Chilhao Thiba Sa amasung Sayokshang', *Ichemma*, 7(3): 4–6.

Raicharan. 2005. 'Meira Sangh and Meiragi Maion', *Meira Paibi*, 1(2): 44–46.

Reger, Jo. 2002. 'Motherhood and the Construction of Feminist Identity: Variation in a Women's Movement Organization', *Sociological Enquiry*, 71(1): 85–110.

Schirmer, J.G. 1989. 'Those who Die for Life Cannot be Called Dead, Women in Human Rights Protest in Latin America', *Feminist Review*, 32: 3–29.

Sharma, Kalpana. 2009. 'Meira Paibi: Disturbed in Manipur', *India Together*, 23 March 2009. http://www.indiatogether.org/Manipur-op-ed (accessed on 12 July 2013).

Teresa, Rehman. 2009. 'Who is *Ima* Gyaneshwari?' *Infochange Agenda: Reporting Conflict*, 14: 32–33.

Umanski, Lauri. 1996. *Motherhood Reconceived: Feminism and Legacy of the 1960s*. New York: New York University Press.

Veda, Gunjan. 2005. *Tailoring Peace: The Citizens' Roundtable on Manipur and Beyond*. Guwahati: North East Network (NEN).

Yengkokpam, Bibi. 2012. 'Rebels, Victims and Heros: Representation of Manipuri Women's Bodies in Contemporary Documentary Films', *Eastern Quarterly*, 8(1/2): 35–43.

Walker, Cheryl. 1995. 'Conceptualizing Motherhood in Twentieth Century South Africa', *Journal of Southern African Studies*, 21(3): 417–37.

CHAPTER 8

Reimagining the Protesting Mother: Counter-narratives of Women as Citizens

Roma Dey

This chapter investigates the category of 'mothers' as citizens and political identities and their negotiations in the political sphere of the nation state. Mothers, carrying their breastfeeding children or holding the hands of their children, have been an iconic image in colonial and postcolonial protests (Kumar 2002; Thapar 1993). The last few years saw a global upsurge in protests by 'mothers' on different issues, from demands for the right to breastfeed in public spaces (perceived as indecent by proponents of the neo-liberal market) to concerns about gun violence in schools in the United States. As a category within the nation, 'motherhood' has a universal appeal in efforts to stop violence. History shows that Indian nationalists also promoted the participation of women in public protests and picketing, mainly within the frame of women as 'mothers' of the nation to maintain the traditional familial roles and sanctity of the home and distinguish 'women of the street' from 'women on the street' (Thapar 1993: 87).

The protest staged by the Meira Paibis (literally 'torchbearers'), a women's collective in the state of Manipur, against the rape of Manorama, alleged to be a member of the banned People's Liberation Front, marks a rupture in the political imagination of womanhood in the Indian context. Fraught with political upheavals and violence, the naked protest by the Meira Paibis brings to focus counter-narratives that destabilize hegemonic notions of womanhood and citizenship, creating spaces for women to negotiate their rights as citizens. This chapter argues that such counter-narratives have helped women negotiate their rights in the modern political space of the Indian nation state. There are four broad sections of the chapter, with each of these sections building the arguments towards the efficacy and need for reimagining protesting mothers as citizens, especially in conflict zones. Here the case of the Meira Paibis of Manipur is used to elucidate the same.

THE NATION STATE AND THE GENDERED CITIZEN

The concept of the modern nation state that developed historically in 19th-century Western Europe has been borrowed and moulded as per the requirements of diverse local contexts in different regions of the erstwhile colonized world. However, the basic conceptualization of the subject, statehood and the powers of the state have been retained. Keeping in mind the colonially mediated modernity, this chapter utilizes scholarship from both the Western and the non-Western world to develop the arguments.

In her essay 'The Disorder of Women', Carole Pateman (1994) unearths the processes and rationales that have gone into keeping women out of politics. She undertakes reading the works of Rousseau, Hegel and Freud to investigate their perspectives and finds that, even though considered revolutionary in their times, each of them thought women incapable of political and public life. Pateman finds that the clear separation and distinction between:

> [...] the private and the public, or particularistic and universal, spheres of association is a fundamental structural principle of the

> modern, liberal conception of social life. The natural, particularistic family nestles at the centre of the private sphere, and it throws into prominence and stands opposed to the impersonal, universal, 'conventional' bonds of public life. (ibid.)

Political institutions are based on conventions, in other words, contracts, consent and agreements that were against the basic nature of women who have 'disorder at their very centres—in their morality—which can bring about the destruction of the state'. The source of this disorder according to Rousseau and Freud is 'incompatibility of womankind with a fundamental bond of civil (public) society, that is, justice'. Also, for both of them anatomy is a destiny which influences women's moral character. Unlike men who can subdue and sublimate their sexual desires, women are slaves to their 'boundless sexual passion'. Around their natural capacity to reproduce, women's natural capacity to care was structured and the 'development of civilization was a work of men alone because it requires the instinctual sublimation of which women are little capable' (ibid.).

Political subjects under the modern nation state are individual men, who have sprung out, as in Hobbes' description, 'like mushrooms, come to full maturity, without all kind of engagement to each other' (Hobbes as quoted in Das 2007: 30) and are bonded through social contract to the state thus making up the political state. Political authority is grounded in the fatherly authority over the monogamous family, where the woman's duty as a citizen is confounded with duty to husband (ibid.: 42). The role of the women then is to produce legitimate offspring that perpetuates the rule of the state.

The image of the mother is juxtaposed with that of the woman as citizen in most nationalist and postcolonial discourses, where the mother image is used in a way to keep women out of political participation through reiteration of their 'natural' role as mothers and their duty to the nation to bring up legitimate citizens (Das 2007: 43; Najmabadi 1998: 92). At the same time, motherhood became a trope for female politicians to garner political mileage by provoking the image of the mother (Lakshmi 1990: 82). In a sense, the mother image is vital in the political arena because mobilization of women on the basis of motherhood does not challenge their conventional role in society (Strolovitch and Townsend-Bell 2013: 376).

As observed by Kumari Jayawardena (1986), in the erstwhile colonies, feminism and nationalism shared common goals, fighting for the political rights of both men and women, yet during state formation the assumed male-female differences were reinforced. In the Indian context, nationalists in the mid-19th century emphasized that women cannot transcend their naturalness and are incapable of public and political life. The role of the Indian woman was seen to be within the private realm of the home and hearth, leaving the public and political sphere to men. This separated the realms of the sexes on a dichotomous conception of the world into the spiritual and the material. The spiritual was invested with 'God like virtues' akin to the feminine and had to be 'protected and nurtured' by women, while the material was invested with 'animal' and 'masculine' characteristics to be borne by men alone (Chatterjee 1989).

According to Mrinalini Sinha, the relationship between early 20th-century Indian nationalism and the Indian women's movement was reworked and forged around American journalist Katherine Mayo's 1927 book *Mother India*. Mayo claimed in her book that India was unfit for self-rule owing to the condition of women, typified by the practices of child marriage and early maternity. Nationalists and women activists came together and voiced their views that this was part of a plan to deny India self-rule. Women activists such as Sarojini Naidu and Begum Shah Nawaz declared that the Indian women's movement was not a 'feminist' movement and aligned themselves with the national struggle (Kumar 2002: 88). However, this move also opened up avenues for the women's movement as leading nationalists such as Gandhi, Jawaharlal Nehru, Sarojini Naidu, and K.K. Natarajan acknowledged the need for social reform and amelioration in the condition of women. This led to the coming together of nationalists and women activists to pass the Child Marriage Restraint Act, 1929 (also known as the Sarda Act) in 1929 (Sinha 2006).

When the British withdrew their rule from the Indian subcontinent in 1947, two nation states, Pakistan and India, were created through the violent process of Partition based on religious nationalism. Women, culturally the repository of honour, were persecuted sexually and physically on both sides. During Partition, women were abducted on both sides of the border in the newly formed states of India and Pakistan. The governments on both sides, playing the role of protector, started operations of 'recovery' of abducted women, even forcefully returning them to their families. Many of these women were disowned by their families and communities as 'impure' and ineligible for marriage, in keeping with societal ways of attaching the honour of the family with the sexual purity of the women and the failure of the men of the family in their inability to protect them from sexual violations (Banerjee 2008: 203–4). Honour, for society, was derived from moral superiority in protecting and controlling female bodies.

The state played along with the accepted social views, trying to gain control over the bodies of the abducted women, denying agency to the abducted women and resting the power with their 'guardians' (male members of the family) to make decisions on their behalf. The abducted women had no legal identity or rights (ibid.: 205). It was their bodies and sexuality that threatened their security and the honour of the nation. Their bodies were marked vulnerable and they had to be protected and their sexualities controlled. This has been the perspective that the state has been using in the case of all women.

As argued by Paula Banerjee, the Citizenship Act of 1955 awards citizenship by registration to females who marry a male citizen of India, but not to males who marry a female citizen of India. This establishes the transfer of citizenship through patrilinearity (Banerjee 2008: 205). It is evident that women were not given equal status even in front of the law, and they had to carry the load of their bodily difference and their presumed 'uncontrollable' sexuality. It is, thus, not a surprise that the presence of women in legislative positions has remained miniscule and mainly involves women from families of political leaders. Even when there have been women holding important political positions, many have been family members or protégés of male political leaders, as has been the trend in some Asian nations (Fleschenberg 2008; Omvedt 2005: 4751).

THE MATERNAL FRAME, COLLECTIVE ACTION AND EMPOWERMENT

'Feminists have long recognized that it is when women recognize their "power within" and act together with other women to exercise "power with", that they gain "power to" act as agents' (Andrea Cornwall as quoted in Harcourt 2009: 35).

According to Wendy Harcourt, feminists over the years have challenged the notion that the lived experience of the female body is an obstacle to knowledge; rather they claim it to be 'a vehicle for making and remaking the world'. We can strategically reconceptualize bodies as cultural products on which the play of powers, knowledge and resistances are worked out (ibid.: 22). Harcourt quotes Liz Grosz saying the 'female body is both a source of oppression and power, both a site of normalization and resistance where social norms are being inscribed on the body' (ibid.: 17). Bodies, then, are not mere biological entities, but sites of social experiences and political resistances. Ahead, I look into protests as a form of negotiation in democratic politics and how women have been participating in this. I investigate the framing of women as mothers, or the maternal frame, and how it has been used in movements and protests worldwide to legitimize popular demands. How does this effect women at large and mothers in particular? Does it empower or disempower women, and how?

Through the oppressive experiences of the lived body of confinement, violation and invisibility and the resistance played through political struggles, the body is made the subject of politics (ibid.: 23). It is through various political processes such as awareness, resistance, collective action, and sit-ins that women and the other genders, left outside the bastion of power, can make themselves be heard and counted as political players. Often the political action of women and other genders is marginalized and seen as peripheral to politics. While this could be read as the patriarchal bias of the media and the state, another reading of it could be the perpetual drive to keep them out of political processes. It is important to note that it is this very portrayal of women's experiences in menstruation, pregnancy and childbirth as obstacles that keep them out of power and political action that had a generation of women in the West view motherhood as disempowering and mothers as disempowered. And, unfortunately, mothers were left out of feminism and the feminist movement (Freely 1995: 208).

Motherhood is a mode of women's politics traditionally available to them to organize democratic resistance (Das 2008). Women have used the maternal frame to organize themselves around their demands for information from the state regarding their family members, as in the case of the Co-Madres in El Salvador, Madres de la Plaza de Mayo in Argentina and the Grupo Apoyo Mutuo in Guatemala. Their position as mothers saves them from repression by governments as well as from the rebels. But does women's activism within the framework of motherhood lead to empowerment? Or, in Åshild Kolås's words, 'Is "motherhood" a vehicle for women's empowerment?' (Kolås 2014: 41).

According to Kelsy Kretschmer and David S. Meyer the political environment of a nation influences the choice of framing of a movement. In open political environments it is possible for women to organize and engage as political activists donning their identities as regular citizens, but in repressive regimes women deploy a maternal frame to justify their activism. They draw on existing gendered ideas of motherhood and domesticity to negotiate their demands with the state. This frame helps them to translate their demands into easily recognizable cultural terms and find support amongst the public. Using the maternal frame they can harness the gendered political structure that is open to women in ways and situations (as mothers, in conflict or repressive environments) that are not open to men (2013: 403). Through their study of movements, Kretschmer and Meyer come to the conclusion that women in movements using their traditional identities as mothers or wives do not experience transformation as they do not question their secondary status, unlike movements where there is an element of reform or restructuring of gender relations. According to Einwohner, Hollander and Olson (2000), gendered frames such as the 'maternal' is a double bind for women. Even if they apparently make their work easier, they simultaneously reinforce the gender stereotypes.

Dara Strolovitch and Erica Townsend-Bell (2013), on the other hand, come to a different conclusion, arguing that motherhood could be a starting point, while over time women participate in multiple political processes that offer transformative opportunities. She uses the example of the Madres de la Plaza de Mayo in Argentina who started by looking for their missing children and emerged as a leading group advocating for human rights. Motherhood also provides a common identity to the activists across differences in race, ethnicity and nationality.

This chapter is concerned with the issue of agency and collective action of women in conflict zones. However, it does not aim to only look at the ways in which collective action by mothers have imbibed them with citizenship and brought them recognition in the political arena; it also seeks to open up and address how the militarization of northeast India has disempowered people, especially women, in the region.

As evident from the existing literature, women in conflict zones have to constantly face social suffering and structural violence. On the other hand, conflict conditions compel women to take up new roles and make decisions in the absence of male members or in matters of survival. Rita Manchanda terms this as 'ambivalent empowerment' (Manchanda 2005: 4738), as these roles are often extensions of women's roles as mothers and nurturers and are directed towards saving their family and community members.

Women move out of their cultural framework and step into the public and political realm, but these transformations often do not sustain once peace is retained. However, women do use their agency as political subjects in the way they negotiate with institutional structures, even if this is an extension of their role as mothers and nurturers for the survival of their family and community members. They undertake collective action, organize and protest as political subjects of the state and learn to speak the political lingua that the state uses. Yes, the subaltern can speak and makes it a point to speak in the language of the mainstream.

Manchanda upholds the view that the suffering that women undergo in conflict conditions is related to the violence (physical, structural and cultural) that exists in women's everyday life in peacetime and it is just a different shade and of greater intensity in the continuum of violence experienced in 'normal' conditions (Manchanda 2005: 4738). This is a gross simplification of the situation. Since the violence perpetuated by the state in order to sustain its rule or 'law preserving violence' in the Benjaminian sense has legitimacy within the judicial and political boundaries of the state, when challenged this can be (and is often) coloured as anti-national and illegitimate. Everyday violence, even structural violence in peacetime, may be of the same quality but it is not dealt with using the same precision and exactness as the suspected anti-national. The notion of the nation state is so precariously balanced that even suspected anti-nationals become subjects to be absolutely crushed to deal with the crisis the nation state is born with.

Secondly, the viewpoint overlooks cultural differences and the presence of differences in societies in the ways in which women and their bodies and sexualities are constructed. The presence of matrilinearity and various shades of matriarchy in some of the states of the Northeast, and the completely different value systems and cultural ethos in the region, point towards a better social standing of women when compared to the north Indian hegemonic class. Thus, the nature and kind of violence that women face in the Northeast in peacetime is very different from the type of violence they have undergone under the masculine military regime of the Indian state. The deployment of military as the primary law and governing body along with constant surveillance and normalization of military atrocities has militarized everyday life. The burden of this is in itself a violence and usurpation of the rights of the people.

CONTEXTUALIZING THE NUDE PROTEST OF THE MEIRA PAIBIS

The northeast of India has always existed on the periphery of the nation's consciousness, and in the footnotes of the narrative of growth, progress and development. In a region where lawlessness, rape, murder, army excesses, arbitrary detentions, torture and repression are the order of the day, the man in uniform is a formidable and fearsome figure (Dhobal 2009: x).

The area termed as northeast India or the Northeast is not only geographically located in one corner of the nation, but it also remains at the periphery when it comes to the idea or imagination of India. One can sense this discrimination in the way the area has lagged behind in terms of infrastructural growth and development and the suspension of civil rights under the Armed Forces (Special Powers) Act, 1958 (AFSPA). According to Harsh Dhobal AFSPA is a replica of the 1942 Ordinance framed by the British to control the rising tide of Indian nationalism. The Act has been used by the Indian state to create a state of exception where the justice system is bypassed, and the armed forces can take decisions and act with impunity from investigation by the police and trial by courts of law (ibid.: xi).

AFSPA has been in effect in the Northeast (except for Sikkim) since 1958, in Jammu and Kashmir since 1990, and from 1983 to 1997 in Punjab. It applies to any area that is declared 'disturbed' by the central government. This declaration is done by the Ministry of Home Affairs or the governor of the state and until 1997 it had no time limit. It was the Naga People's Movement for Human

Rights that challenged the lack of time limit of the declaration and it was implied that the declaration had to be reviewed every six months. The declaration of a disturbed area is not open to judicial review, nor can the state government contest it (Deo and Mc-Duie Ra 2011: 51).

According to the Indian Army website,[1] AFSPA gives special powers to not just a commissioned officer but even to a warrant officer and non-commissioned officer in the armed forces to fire upon or use force, even to the effect of causing death, against any person suspected of acting in contravention of any law or order that prohibits the assembly of five or more persons as effective in a disturbed area, or if the person is carrying weapons, firearms, ammunition or explosive substances. It also gives them the power to arrest without warrant any person who has committed a cognizable offence or against whom a reasonable suspicion exists that he has committed or is about to commit a cognizable offence. While giving no time limit for the arrested person to be taken to the police station, the Act only mentions that this should be done at the earliest. It also gives the armed forces the power to forcefully enter and search without a warrant any premises to make an arrest as aforesaid, or to recover any person believed to be wrongfully restrained and confined, or any property reasonably suspected to be stolen property, or any arms, ammunition or explosive substances believed to be unlawfully kept in such premises. It also gives them the right to destroy such premises. The Act also protects the officer from any prosecution, suit or other legal proceeding except with the previous sanction of the central government.

AFSPA allows a non-commissioned officer to bypass the court of law and to decide on his own what to do with a person suspected of breaking the law, which in other regions of the nation would be a violation of the rights of the citizen. What the law does is create a state where the ordinary laws of the nation state are suspended and everyday life is militarized through special powers to the armed forces, otherwise posted to protect the country from external attacks. Here, the armed forces have been posted since the moment the nation state claimed the region to be part of India, and have power akin to the powers at the border where they do not have to go through the court of law and the Constitution stands suspended. People from AFSPA-affected states have been fighting against the Act on different fronts. One such fight was Irom Sharmila's fast unto death against AFSPA, which she started on 4 November 2000 and ended 16 years later in 2016 to start her own political party to fight elections with the aim of being part of the government and removing AFSPA (Laithangbam 2015).

Meira Paibis or 'Torchbearers'

In the 1970s, groups of Meitei women started working as *Nishabandhis*, groups of women to combat rising alcoholism and drug abuse amongst men in their villages (Mehrotra 2010: 7). Their call for deterrence of consumption of alcohol found support from the People's Liberation Army as well as the government, which declared the state an alcohol-free state in 1991. In the 1980s, after Manipur was declared a disturbed area, the women also took up campaigning against the atrocities of the armed forces, keeping night vigils to save villagers from the nocturnal combing operations of the army that camouflage atrocities such as detention of innocent civilians (Chakravarti 2010: 53). They would carry bamboo torches or *meiras* during their night vigils and hence came to be known as Meira Paibis or torchbearers.

In the early hours of 11 July 2004, three Assam Rifles (paramilitary) personnel stormed Manorama's house, beat her, her mother and her relatives before arresting her on suspicion of being an explosives expert of the People's Liberation Army (PLA), an insurgent group, although they did not find anything to support their suspicion.

> Less than three hours later, Manorama's lifeless body was discovered four kilometres from her house with torn clothes and bearing scratch marks all over, a wound on her thigh, probably inflicted by a knife, and bullet wounds on her back, upper buttock and vagina. One of her nipples had been plucked off. (Human Rights Watch as quoted in Chakravarti 2010: 48)

The Indian Army claimed that Manorama was shot dead as she tried to flee. Her body was eventually cremated by them as unclaimed.

This incident was followed by public protests and strikes. On 15 July 2004, 50 women came together to protest at the western gate of Kangla fort, then housing the Assam Rifles headquarters in Manipur. The women were carrying a banner that read 'Indian Army rape us, Indian Army take our flesh'. Twelve of them stripped themselves naked as they shouted: 'You dogs of Assam Rifles! Come rape us like you raped Manorama!'; 'We are mothers of Manorama. Come satisfy your lust. Play on our bodies. Eat our flesh. Come, Indian Army' (Human Rights Watch as quoted in Chakravarti 2010: 49). As stated by Paromita Chakravarti, the police was stunned, observers shocked and many of the protestors fainted and had to be hospitalized. The middle-aged protestors had 'found a language of protest that had disturbed both the complacent Indian Army, accustomed to complete impunity for its actions, and a jaded citizenry numbed by regular army excesses' (ibid.: 50). In their 45-minute agitation, the women demanded action against the culprits and a repeal of AFSPA.

From this case I unpack the gendered notions of politics, nation statehood and how the protest by the Meira Paibis questions these notions by defying the cultural ethos and morality imposed on women. What does the protest achieve? What are the linkages of masculinity, the nation state and its army, and its ideology that this protest tries to hint at? What necessitated this protest? Arguably, it is a moment of transgression as this act thrust the women and their demands on the national and world stage. It was not just an act of defiance against the political and armed powers, but also against patriarchal control and the male gaze over women's bodies.

The work of Imogen Tyler (2013) on the naked protest by 'illegal immigrant' mothers in Crane Wing, Yarl's Wood Immigration Removal Centre, the United Kingdom in 2008 shows how for them the act of protest identifies them as political actors despite the fact that they are severed from public life. Their protest transformed a non-place into a politically charged space of resistance and their non-animate positions are rendered animate with their capacity to act as political subjects. In that moment of protest they are naked but alive (ibid.). Tyler also gives us reference to an ancient powerful African symbolism of the mother's naked body: 'We all come through the vagina. By exposing the vagina, the women are saying: "We are hereby taking the life we gave you". Men who are exposed are viewed dead' (Teresa Turner as quoted in ibid.). Thus, in the Western gaze, the naked protest is a sensational sexualized act, but in the African context it invokes maternal power that threatens to render the objectifying male gaze impotent (Van Allan as quoted in ibid.).

The ageing bodies of the Meira Paibis were not meant to create the spectacle of sexualized female bodies one is accustomed to in the neo-liberal marketplace, rather they were meant to shock and make the army personnel victims in the face of maternal nudity, a cultural taboo. It was a public act of transgression and defiance of social norms, publically challenging the so-called protectors (masculine) to show their true colours and rape them (trying to hit at the protection-rape binary). The women managed to garner national and international media attention (of a region the media generally marginalizes) and take note of the incidents. They also sent out a message of non-tolerance of such atrocities. The women were bare but alive, positioning themselves in the political realm.

The marks of brutality on Manorama's body bore witness to the brutal naked force she was subjected to. In a show of the power that the state (in this case the army personnel under the protection of AFSPA) has over the bodies of the people, they made a point of it by letting her body lie half-naked and mutilated with a bullet wound through her vagina and one of her nipples torn off in public view. It was a show of the power that the army had, power to humiliate, torture, rape, mutilate and kill with state permission. It was a challenge to the rebels and their supporters. And it was legitimized under the pretext that she was a member of an insurgent group. The whole act was a sheer mockery of the law, in a way a show of power above the law.

The protest by the Meira Paibis exposed this truth to the world or, as a report in *The Telegraph* stated, it drew attention to the 'excesses committed by security forces in the state'.[2] It did not let the incident and the mutilated body of Manorama be hidden or made invisible. The protest was not a mere spectacle to get attention through nudity, as one often sees in other nude protests. It was rather an act of not letting Manorama be another rape victim of the army, of not allowing her custodial murder and torture be normalized and accepted. The women did not allow Manorama to be like another victim of rape, hiding in shame. The protest was an outpouring of anger and frustration over the inability to do justice to Manorama and others like her that triggered the women to transgress their roles as mothers. As explained by Thokchom Ramani, one of the 12 nude protestors, their anger shed their inhibitions that day.[3] A violent protest would have meant using the same tools as the perpetrators; a non-violent regular protest would not even have created a dent on the armours of the army and the state. The women thus needed tools that would not just shock the media and the state, but also humiliate them the same way they had Manorama. Humiliation was what they intended (Butalia 2004).

Rape is an act of power over another's body, so when the women asked the army to rape them they were no longer passive victims but protagonists, robbing the rapist of the power over their bodies. The masculine act of rape is re-read, its meaning negotiated in the act of denying the rapist the active role. The act also meant they were not being passive victims and could not be humiliated. They challenged the army and its power to use brutal force on them. They also challenged the legitimacy of the army's act of rape and mutilation by daring them to do the same publicly and in the presence of the media.

It is the traditional respect and place of women as mothers in the society that enabled the protestors to take such a step to shame the army and it was due to the cultural and social capital of the Meira Paibis. It also brought out the Meira Paibis as a group that can openly challenge and bring to task the army and render it speechless. This is possible not because of the protest but because of the attitude of the army personnel of objectifying and sexualizing women's bodies and sadistically raping and mutilating the genitalia of an unarmed woman in their custody. The protest is in that sense the holding up of a mirror to them, where women are coming up naked, unarmed and challenging the army to rape them in broad public view. The shaming is not in emasculating them, using the patriarchal rationale, but in asking them to acknowledge their misdeeds and challenging the very premises of the act of rape. Deepti Misri read the naked protest with Mahasweta Devi's story *Draupadi* (1988). In the story, the protagonist Draupadi, a tribal woman in Bengal, is subjected to custodial rape and she challenges the head of police to clothe her naked body as she stands unashamed. Draupadi, Misri says, 'hijacks the hermeneutics of rape' and strips the act of rape of its power making it an act of cowardice (Misri 2011: 621).

Within the patriarchal heteronormative framework, women's bodies are repositories of honour and women have to be protected. The notion of masculinity is based on men protecting women, and the state and its machinery protecting the citizen. On both these counts, the protestors challenge this notion as they ask the army to rape them in retaliation of a daughter's rape. They do not require the protection of the army men and the state; in fact, they question the role of both. The state and its armed forces derive their very existence from the patriarchal notion of protection of the people. The Meira Paibis reversed the gaze and challenged the very premise of the protector and the protected.

On a larger platform, the Meira Paibis have been able to challenge the notions attached to shame, rape and honour by reversing the patriarchal male gaze and putting the burden of shame with the rapists and not the raped (ibid.: 607). They have disturbed the very premise on which the act of rape is based—the violation of a woman's body that is the repository of honour and rape as a tool to shame and humiliate her and the men of her community. The 'mothers' (*ima*) of Manipur show their resilience and their ability to challenge these patriarchal notions. It is only through such resilience and constant negotiations of meanings that a decade after their protest and many such protests afterwards, at least in some sections of society, rape is being debated as shameful for the rapist rather than the raped. For example, following the protests and debates around the 16 December 2012 Delhi rape, the label of victim and victimhood is being debated in the media (Nair 2014).

At the same time, the 'mothers' have problematized the private-public divide. Not only have they donned the identities of the private sphere for their political claims, they have brought the bodies of mothers with their claims of being Manorama's mothers to public view, blurring the public-private dichotomy. Even as their protest received support from women's organizations in the state and across the nation, the Meira Paibis presented what Paromita Chakravarti calls a new 'language of protest' (2010: 53), an 'intimate and personal language of their bare bodies rather than the impersonal discourse of justice and law' (ibid.: 57). They brought the female body, with its lived experience of pregnancy, childbirth, menstruation, ageing, and violations such as rape, torture and mutilation, into the discourse of protest, strategy and political action.

That women undergo maternity, that women are mothers, that women's bodies are rape-able is not disempowering in itself, it is rendered disempowering when read socially within the existing gendered meanings and language. What the nude protest of the Meira Paibis has done is it has turned the tables on the perpetrators of violence. It has given new meanings to women's embodied experiences and has used women's bodies as the vehicle for transformation. The Meira Paibis have changed the equations and meanings of motherhood, adding nuances to the idea and concept of maternal citizenship and the maternal framework in collective action in the Indian political scene. Finally, the 'mothers' have given an edge to the maternal frame, that of a challenger and active agent rather than a passive victim. The 'mothers' have shown that they have agency over their own bodies and political identities.

NOTES

1. http://indianarmy.nic.in/Site/RTI/rti/MML/MML_VOLUME_3/CHAPTER__03/457.htm
2. 'She Stoops to Conquer'. 2004. *The Telegraph*, 25 July. http://www.telegraphindia.com/1040725/asp/look/story_3533201.asp.
3. http://www.theweekendleader.com/Causes/2050/mothers-diary.html

REFERENCES

Banerjee, P. 2008. 'The Space Between: Women's Negotiations with Democracy', in Paula Banerjee (ed.), *Women in Peace Politics*, pp. 201–17. New Delhi: Sage Publications.

Butalia, U. 2004. 'The Body as Weapon', *New Internationalist Magazine: People, Ideas and Action for Global Justice*, 1 September. http://newint.org/columns/viewfrom/2004/09/01/body-as-weapon/ (accessed on 28 November 2016).

Chakravarti, P. 2010. 'Reading Women's Protest in Manipur: A Different Voice?' *Journal of Peacebuilding & Development*, 5(3): 47–60.

Chatterjee, P.1989. 'The Nationalist Resolution of the Women's Question', in K. Sangari and S.Vaid (eds), *Recasting Women: Essays in Indian Colonial History*, pp. 233–53. New Delhi: Kali for Women.

Das, S.K. 2008. 'Ethnicity and Democracy Meet when Mother's Protest', in P. Banerjee (ed.), *Women in Peace Politics*, pp. 57–77. New Delhi: Sage Publications.

Das, V. 2007. 'The Citizen as Sexed: Women, Violence, and Reproduction', in M. Skidmore and P. Lawrence (eds), *Women and the Contested State: Religion, Violence and Agency in South and Southeast Asia*, pp. 29–49. Notre Dame, Indiana: University of Notre Dame Press.

Deo, N. and D. Mc-Duie Ra. 2011. 'Transnational Human Rights Advocacy and the Might of Local Action', in N. Deo and D. Mc-Duie Ra (eds), *The Politics of Collective Advocacy in India: Tools and Traps*, pp. 51–78. Sterling, VA: Kumarian Press.

Dhobal, H. 2009. 'Introduction', in *Manipur in the Shadow of AFSPA: Independent People's Tribunal Report on Human Rights Violation in Manipur*, pp. ix–xv. New Delhi: IPT and Human Rights Law Network.

Einwohner, R.L., J.A. Hollander and T. Olson. 2000. 'Engendering Social Movements: Cultural Images and Movement Dynamics', *Gender and Society*, 14(5): 679–99.

Freely, M. 1995. *What About Us? An Open Letter to the Mothers Feminism Forgot.* London: Bloomsbury.

Fleschenberg, A. 2008. 'Asia's Women Politicians at the Top: Roaring Tigresses or Tame Kittens?' in K. Iwanaga (ed.), *Women's Political Participation and Representation in Asia: Obstacles and Challenges*. Copenhagen: NIAS Press.

Harcourt, W. 2009. *Body Politics in Development: Critical Debates in Gender and Development*. London: Zed Books.

Jayawardena, K. 1986. *Feminism and Nationalism in the Third World*. London: Zed Books.

Kolås, Å. 2014. 'Mothers and Activists in the Hills of Assam', *Economic and Political Weekly*, 49(43): 41–48.

Kretschmer, K. and David S. Meyer. 2013. 'Organizing around Gender Identities', in G. Waylen, K. Celis, J. Kantola and S.L. Weldon (eds), *The Oxford Handbook of Gender and Politics*, pp. 390–410. Oxford: Oxford University Press.

Kumar, R. 2002. *The History of Doing: An Illustrated Account of Movements for Women's Rights and Feminism in India, 1800–1990*, 5th edition. New Delhi: Kali for Women.

Laithangbam, I. 2015. 'Irom Sharmila Resumes Fast After Release', *The Hindu*, 23 January. http://www.thehindu.com/news/national/civil-rights-activist-irom-sharmila-rearrested/article6814652.ece (accessed on 6 May 2015).

Lakshmi, C.S. 1990. 'Mother, Mother-Community and Mother-Politics in Tamil Nadu', *Economic and Political Weekly*, 25(42/43): 72–83.

Manchanda, R. 2005. 'Women's Agency in Peace Building: Gender Relations in Post-Conflict Reconstruction', *Economic and Political Weekly*, 40(44/45): 4737–45.

Mehrotra, D.P. 2010. 'Irom Sharmila's Protest Fast: "Women's Wars", Gandhian Non-Violence and Anti-Militarisation Struggles', *Peace Prints: South Asian Journal of Peacebuilding*, 3(1). http://www.wiscomp.org/pp-v3/pdfs/deepti.pdf (accessed on 6 May 2015).

Misri, D. 2011. '"Are you a man?" Performing Naked Protest in India', *Signs*, 36(3): 603–25.

Nair, M. 2014. 'From Victim to Survivor', *The Times of India*, 14 December. http://timesofindia.indiatimes.com/home/sunday-times/deep-focus/From-victim-to-survivor/articleshow/45509385.cms (accessed on 28 November 2016).

Najmabadi, A.1998. 'Crafting an Educaed Housewife in Iran', in L. Abu-Lughod (ed.), *Remaking Women: Feminism and Modernity in the Middle East*, pp. 91–125. Princeton, New Jersey: Princeton University Press.

Omvedt, G. 2005. 'Women in Governance in South Asia Author', *Economic and Political Weekly*, 40(44/45): 4746–52.

Pateman, C. 1994. 'The Disorder of Women', in *The Polity Reader in Gender Studies*, pp. 108–19. Cambridge: Polity Press.

Sinha, M. 2006. *Specters of Mother India*. New Delhi: Zubaan.

Strolovitch, D.Z. and E. Townsend-Bell. 2013. 'Sex, Gender, and Civil Society', in G. Waylen, K. Celis, J. Kantola and S.L. Weldon (eds), *The Oxford Handbook of Gender and Politics*, pp. 367–87. Oxford: Oxford University Press.

Thapar, S. 1993. 'Women as Activists; Women as Symbols: A Study of the Indian Nationalist Movement', *Feminist Review*, 44: 81–96.

Tyler, I. 2013. 'Naked Protest: The Maternal Politics of Citizenship and Revolt', *Citizenship Studies*, 17(2): 211–26.

About the Editor and Contributors

THE EDITOR

Åshild Kolås is Research Professor at the Peace Research Institute Oslo (PRIO). She holds a PhD in Social Anthropology from the University of Oslo. Her core fields of interest include ethnicity, identity politics and representation. She has carried out fieldwork in Tibet, Nepal, Inner Mongolia and Northeast India, and has written extensively on governmentality, cultural politics, and identity. She is the author of *Tourism and Tibetan Culture in Transition: A Place Called Shangrila* (2008) and co-author (with Monika P. Thowsen) of *On the Margins of Tibet: Cultural Survival on the Sino-Tibetan Frontier* (2015).

THE CONTRIBUTORS

Anungla Aier is Principal of Kohima Science College Jotsoma, an autonomous postgraduate college, under the Government of Nagaland. She also teaches in the department of anthropology of the same institution. As a Naga woman born and brought up in Nagaland, Aier has first-hand knowledge of women's lives in Naga society. She has been published in several journals and edited volumes and has contributed to the Nagaland State Human Development Reports. She has also been the lead author in the District Human Development Report of the state. Aier has authored *Pottery Tradition among the Chakhesang and Pochury Nagas*. Her latest book is titled *Oral Tradition of the Nagas: Memories and Telling of Origin Myth and Migration*.

L. Basanti Devi completed her PhD from the Centre for the Study of Social Systems, Jawaharlal Nehru University, New Delhi. She had been associated with the Omeo Kumar Das Institute of Social Change and Development, Guwahati, for a project on the Meira Paibis of Manipur under the project 'Making Women Count for Peace: Gender, Empowerment and Conflict in South Asia', funded by the Research Council of Norway. Her research interests include women and conflict studies, human rights and labour studies.

Arunima Deka is Assistant Professor (Peace Studies) at OKD Institute of Social Change and Development, Guwahati. Her research interests include gender, identity politics, state and development issues in Northeast India. She has been associated with a number of studies relating to peace and conflict, gender and identity politics in Northeast India and has presented several papers in national and international seminars. She is currently working on a project on ethnic identity and regional politics in Northeast India.

Roma Dey is a trained social worker and sociologist. She has a PhD from the Centre for the Study of Social Systems, Jawaharlal Nehru University, New Delhi. Her paper in this volume is from her dissertation *Engaging Exclusions: A Socio-Political Study of Body, Sexuality and Selfhood of Dalit Women* based on Dalit women's autobiographies. Her PhD on 'Interpreting Motherhood: A Study on the Meanings and Practices' is a multi-method study to understand how women make meaning of motherhood through their own experiences and cultural representations in myths, films, policy discourse and political activism of mothers.

Seema Kakran is Deputy Director with Women in Security, Conflict Management and Peace (WISCOMP), an initiative of the Foundation for Universal Responsibility of His Holiness the Dalai Lama. She has over a decade of experience in project management and research. Her research work focuses on conflict and peace issues in India and analysis of violence using the gender lens.

Rita Manchanda is Director-Research at the South Asia Forum for Human Rights, focusing on rights based approaches to conflicts and peacebuilding, media reporting conflicts and minority rights, with particular attention to gender perspectives. She is a scholar-researcher, journalist and human rights activist who has shaped the South Asia women peace and security discourse through her research and advocacy work. Among her many publications are: *Sage Series in Human Rights Audits of Peace Processes* (five volumes, 2015), *No Nonsense Guide to Minority Rights in South Asia* (2009), *Women, War and Peace in South Asia: Beyond Victimhood to Agency (2001)*, and *Women and Politics of Peace: South Asia Narratives on Militarisation, Power and Justice* (forthcoming). She is a core member of the Women's Regional Network (Afghanistan, India, Pakistan) and team leader of the research advocacy initiative for a South Asia Tribunal on Women's Human Rights.

Rakhee Kalita Moral is Associate Professor of English at Cotton College (State University), Guwahati, and a former Fellow of Nehru Memorial Museum and Library, New Delhi. Most recently a Visiting Faculty at the Centre for the Study of Social Systems, Jawaharlal Nehru University, New Delhi, she also coordinates the South Asia Platform of the Andrew Mellon programme on Humanities across Borders: Engaging Asia and Africa (hosted by IIAS, Leiden). Moral has been actively involved in research as well as peace activism on gender and conflict in Northeast India, and has presented at universities and forums worldwide. Her forthcoming works include a volume on insurgency, which is an introduction to the ULFA, and *Arms and the Woman: Female Warriors of ULFA and the Myth of Power*. She has edited *At the Frontier and Beyond* (2005) and *Gender and Society in Northeast India* (2010), and has published widely in international journals and books.

Dolly Phukon is Associate Professor and Head of the Department of Political Science, Dibrugarh University, Assam. She has authored *Women, Democracy and the Media: An Analysis of Current Trends in Assam* (2014). Her articles on gender issues have been published in several books and journals of national and international repute. She has participated in a number of national and international seminars and conferences. Her areas of interest include political theory, modern Indian political thought and gender studies.

Priyankar Upadhyaya holds the UNESCO Chair for Peace and Intercultural Understanding and serves as Professor of Peace Studies and Director of Malaviya Centre for Peace Research at Banaras Hindu University. He is a Global Fellow of the Peace Research Institute Oslo (PRIO) and has been honoured with the Guest Scholar Award of the Woodrow Wilson Centre of International Scholars at Washington DC, the Faculty Research Award of the Canadian Government, a Senior Fulbright Award and an Australia-India Council Senior Fellowship. He has also served as an adjunct/visiting professor at various universities in Europe and North America, and is currently leading a major UNESCO initiative to redefine peace after seven decades of UN practices.

The Zubaan Series on Sexual Violence and Impunity in South Asia

The Sexual Violence and Impunity in South Asia research project (coordinated by Zubaan and supported by the International Development Research Centre) brings together, for the first time in the region, a vast body of knowledge on this important – yet silenced – subject. Six country volumes (one each on Bangladesh, Nepal, Pakistan, Sri Lanka, and two on India) comprising over fifty research papers and two book-length studies detail the histories of sexual violence and look at the systemic, institutional, societal, individual and community structures that work together to perpetuate impunity for perpetrators.

A Difficult Transition: The Nepal Papers. Edited by Mandira Sharma. 2016. Demy; 366pp; Hardback; 9789385932052; Rs 695.

Breaching the Citadel: The India Papers I. Edited by Urvashi Butalia and Laxmi Murthy. Forthcoming. Demy. Hardback.

Disputed Legacies: The Pakistan Papers. Edited by Neelam Hussain. Forthcoming. Demy. Hardback.

Do You Remember Kunan Poshpora? Essar, Ifrah, Samreena, Munaza and Natasha. 2016. B'format. 224pp. Paperback; 9789384757663. Rs 395.

Fault Lines of History: The India Papers II. Edited by Uma Chakravarti. 2016. Demy. 362pp, Hardback; 9789385932083. Rs 795.

Of the Nation Born: The Bangladesh Papers. Edited by Hameeda Hossain and Amena Mohsin. 2016. Demy. 369pp, Hardback; 9789384757793. Rs 795.

The Search for Justice: The Sri Lanka Papers. Edited by Kumari Jayawardena and Kishali Pinto-Jayawardena. 2016. Demy. 464pp, Hardback, 9789385932069. Rs 850

Undoing Impunity: Speech after Sexual Violence. V. Geetha. 2016. Demy. 340pp. Hardback, 9789384757779. Rs 695.